BAKHTINIAN THOUGHT

Mikhail Bakhtin, and the writers associated with him, have come to be recognised as writers of trail-blazing importance. Working in the extraordinarily difficult conditions of Stalinist Russia, they nevertheless produced a body of writing in literary theory, linguistics, the history of the novel, philosophy, and what Bakhtin called 'philosophical anthropology', which continues to inspire and challenge people working in a number of different areas. Above all, Bakhtin insists on locating all utterances, whether spoken or literary, between the participants in a dialogue and thus involves them in considerations of power and authority.

This introduction and reader serves a double function. In the first place, Simon Dentith provides a lucid and approachable introduction of the work of Bakhtin and his circle, taking the reader helpfully through the many areas of their thought, and indicating the points of controversy, difficulty and excitement. This introductory section culminates in a discussion of the particular emphases lent by Bakhtin to current debates in literary theory. The other feature of the book is the anthology of writing by Bakhtin, Voloshinov and Medvedev, drawn from all the major areas of their work. This provides an especially helpful reader for a body of work otherwise published in disparate and relatively inaccessible forms. Special emphasis has been given to the still unsurpassed linguistic thought of Voloshinov, and the practical analyses of the novel found in Bakhtin's writing on Dostoevsky and Dickens.

This book will be especially interesting to readers new to the work of Bakhtin and his circle. The combination of an introduction and an anthology will allow such readers a context for their reading of Bakhtin, an indication of his importance for contemporary debates in literature, language and social history, and the opportunity to engage directly with the writings of this important and indeed, for the student of literary theory, essential writer.

Simon Dentith is Reader in English at Cheltenham and Gloucester College of Higher Education. He has previously published books on George Eliot and rhetoric, and has written extensively on nineteenth- and twentieth-century literature.

Critical Readers in Theory and Practice

GENERAL EDITOR: Rick Rylance, *Anglia Polytechnic University*

The gap between theory and practice can often seem far too wide for the student of literary theory. *Critical Readers in Theory and Practice* is a new series which bridges that gap: it not only offers an introduction to a range of literary and theoretical topics, but also *applies* the theories to relevant texts.

Each volume is split into two parts: the first consists of an in-depth and clear introduction, setting out the theoretical bases, historical developments and contemporary critical situation of the topic. The theory is then applied to practice in the second part in an anthology of classic texts and essays.

Designed specifically with the student in mind, *Critical Readers in Theory and Practice* provides an essential introduction to contemporary theories and how they relate to textual material.

Bakhtinian Thought: An introductory reader *Simon Dentith*

War Poetry: An introductory reader *Simon Featherstone*

BAKHTINIAN THOUGHT

An introductory reader

SIMON DENTITH

LONDON AND NEW YORK

First published 1995
by Routledge
11 New Fetter Lane, London EC4P 4EE

Simultaneously published in the USA and Canada
by Routledge
29 West 35th Street, New York, NY 10001

© 1995 Simon Dentith

Typeset in Janson by
Ponting–Green Publishing Services, Chesham, Bucks

Printed and bound in Great Britain by
Clays Ltd, St Ives PLC

British Library Cataloguing in Publication Data
A catalogue record for this book is available from
the British Library

Library of Congress Cataloging in Publication Data
Dentith, Simon.
Bakhtinian Thought: An introductory reader/Simon Dentith.
p.   cm. – (Critical readers in theory and practice)
Includes bibliographical references and index.
1. Bakhtin, M. M. (Mikhail Mikhaĭlovich), 1895–1975.
2. Philology.   3. Criticism–Soviet Union.   4. Philosophy,
Russian–20th century.   I. Title.   II. Series.
P85.B22D46   1995
801'.95'092–dc20   94–16524

ISBN 0–415–07751–6 (hbk)
ISBN 0–415–11899–9 (pbk)

For my parents, Edward Dentith and Ann Dentith

Contents

General editor's preface

The interpretation of culture never stands still. Modern approaches to familiar problems adjust our sense of their importance, and new ideas focus on fresh details or remake accepted concepts. This has been especially true over recent years when developments across the humanities have altered so many ideas.

For many this revolution in understanding has been exciting but difficult, involving the need to integrate advanced theoretical work with attention to specific texts and issues. This series attempts to approach this difficulty in a new way by putting together a new balance of basic texts and detailed, introductory exposition.

Each volume in the series will be organized in two parts. Part One provides a thorough account of the topic under discussion. It details important concepts, historical developments and the contemporary context of interpretation and debate. Part Two provides an anthology of classic texts or – in the case of very recent work – essays by leading writers which offer focused discussions of particular issues. Commentary and editorial material provided by the author connect the explanations in Part One to the materials in Part Two, and in this way the reader moves comfortably between original work and enabling introduction.

The series will include volumes on topics which have been of particular importance recently. Some books will introduce specific theoretical ideas; others will re-examine bodies of literary or other material in the light of current thinking. But as a whole the series aims to reflect, in a clear-minded and approachable way, the changing ways in which we understand the expanding field of modern literary and cultural studies.

Rick Rylance

Preface

It is now some twenty-five years since the writings of Mikhail Bakhtin (1895–1975) began to make an impact in the West – since, that is, the publication of *Rabelais and his World* in 1968. During that time his influence has grown enormously, not only in literary criticism but also in history, anthropology, linguistics and philosophy. But during that time also, the nature of his influence has been constantly changing, both as the range and variety of Bakhtin's own writing has gradually emerged and been translated, and as the intellectual, social and political climate in Europe and America has altered. In the heady days of the late 1960s and early 1970s, Bakhtin, in France at any rate, was the celebrator of carnival, of the force that subverts and upturns everything official, authoritarian and one-sidedly serious. As the work on Dostoevsky and the novel became known, Bakhtin came to be seen more as the supreme theorist of the novel, speaking directly to the openness of the novel form and praising Dostoevsky above all as the novelist of polyphony. When the connection became established between Bakhtin and two other Russian writers from the 1920s, P. N. Medvedev and V. N. Voloshinov, they jointly appeared as critics of Saussurean linguistics and Russian Formalism, and thus, to their readers in the West in the 1970s and 1980s, as pointing beyond the structuralism and formalism then prevalent. But during those decades also, different Bakhtins have appeared, first in Russian and then in English. He can now be seen as providing a profound, socially and linguistically grounded history of the novel; and also as a philosopher who emerges from early twentieth-century neo-Kantianism and in whose thinking ethics and the I–Thou relationship are central.

Moreover, this real diversity within the writings of Bakhtin and those connected with – what has been called the Bakhtin circle – has meant that he has been appropriated by writers and critics of widely different intellectual and political persuasions. In Russia, indeed, his apparent commitment to some kind of Christianity – though *what* kind exactly remains unclear – has meant that he has appealed, though not exclusively, to intellectuals of a conservative, Orthadox cast. In the West, by contrast, he is appealed to by writers whose allegiances are as various as liberal humanism, deconstruction, and Marxism – though Bakhtin's relationship to Marxism is as controversial as his relationship to Christianity. There are many now, doubtless, who would disclaim allegiance to any of these 'isms' and simply describe themselves as Bakhtinians. But at all events, there is now a struggle going on over the legacy of Bakhtin, Voloshinov and Medvedev, as indeed one would expect over the meanings and direction of any large, attractive and fruitful body of writing, especially when it is complicated, as it is in this case, by difficult questions of attribution, censorship, and a thirty-five-year interruption in publication history.

This book is an introduction to the work of Bakhtin and his circle, and therefore aims to give its readers some of the materials for judging amongst these various positions. I am suspicious of any attempt to find a real or definitive Bakhtin that will explain or explain away the evident diversity that marks his writing, especially if you include in that the writing of Voloshinov and Medvedev. In my account of the writings I shall seek to give as full weight as possible to the arguments as they actually appear – and not seek to find elaborate counter-interpretations of them, a practice often resorted to in the sometimes justified belief that conditions of publication in the Soviet Union demanded elaborate ruses and, especially, bows in the direction of the official version of Marxism. I am an agnostic on the question of the disputed authorship, for it has been strongly suggested, and widely believed, that the books attributed to Voloshinov and Medvedev were actually written by Bakhtin himself. However, in the first chapter I will set out what is at stake in the controversy that surrounds this question. None of which is to say that I am indifferent to the various claims that have been made about Bakhtin and his circle, or that I do not find some aspects of their writing more appealing than others, for I am especially attracted by the socially and historically grounded account of language and writing that emerges in the writings of the 1930s and in Voloshinov's book on language. You will see these preferences reflected in the anthology, and you may, if you choose, discount them as you read the text that follows.

The book falls into two parts. The first part consists of an introduction, which aims to give an overview of the writings of Bakhtin, and of the relevant works by Voloshinov and Medvedev. The second part consists of an anthology of these writings, and a brief word is required in explanation of my selection here. Bakhtin, notoriously, is not a succinct writer, his expansiveness and repetitions reflecting a philosophical and critical attitude in favour of argument by accumulation and averse to theoretical synopsis. This makes his writing difficult to anthologize, expecially if one has a preference, as I do, for complete sections of argument rather than excerpted paragraphs. As a result I have chosen, in the case of Bakhtin, a small number of lengthy extracts rather than a large number of short ones, and I have chosen extracts that demonstrate Bakhtin's actual analytical practice. As to Voloshinov and Medvedev, in each case I have chosen an extract which is sufficient to give you a sense of their distinctive manner of argument, and which equally gives some sense of their wider intellectual position. It need hardly be added that the book only aims to orient you with respect to a considerable body of writing, and that it is hoped that it will both encourage and equip you to embark on a much fuller engagement with the writings of Bakhtin and his circle.

Acknowledgements

My primary thanks are due to the many translators and editors of Bakhtin and his circle who have made an introductory work of this kind possible. Thanks are also due to Rick Rylance, Kay Richardson and John O'Brien who read all or part of the manuscript, who made many helpful suggestions, and who saved me from many embarrassing errors. Any that remain are of course solely my own responsibility.

For permission to reprint copyright material I gratefully acknowledge the following:

Academic Press, Inc., for 'Language, speech, and utterance' and 'Verbal interaction', in *Marxism and the Philosophy of Language* by V. N. Vološinov, translated by Ladislav Matejka and I. R. Titunik, copyright © 1973 by Seminar Press; the Johns Hopkins University Press for 'The proper formulation of the problem of the poetic construction', 'Social evaluation and its role', and 'Social evaluation and the concrete utterance', in *The Formal Method in Literary Scholarship: A Critical Introduction to Sociological Poetics* by M. M. Bakhtin and P. N. Medvedev, translated by Albert J. Wehrle, copyright © 1978 by the Johns Hopkins University Press; the University of Minnesota Press and Manchester University Press for 'The hero's monologic discourse and narrational discourse in Dostoevsky's short novels', in *Problems of Dostoevsky's Poetics* by M. M. Bakhtin, edited and translated by Caryl Emerson, copyright © 1984 by the University of Minnesota Press; the University of Texas Press for 'Heteroglossia in the novel', reprinted from 'Discourse in the novel' in *The Dialogic Imagination: Four Essays* by M. M. Bakhtin, edited by Michael Holquist, translated by Caryl Emerson and Michael Holquist, copyright © 1981 by the University of Texas Press; the MIT Press for 'The grotesque image of the body and its sources', in *Rabelais and His World* by M. M. Bakhtin, translated by Helen Iswolsky, copyright © 1968 by the MIT Press.

Abbreviations

The following abbreviations have been used:

AA   M. M. Bakhtin, *Art and Answerability: Early Philosophical Essays by M. M. Bakhtin*, edited by Michael Holquist and Vadim Liapunov (University of Texas Press, 1990).

DI   M. M. Bakhtin, *The Dialogic Imagination: Four Essays*, edited by Michael Holquist; translated by Caryl Emerson and Michael Holquist (University of Texas Press, 1981).

FM   M. M. Bakhtin and P. N. Medvedev, *The Formal Method in Literary Scholarship: A Critical Introduction to Sociological Poetics*, translated by Albert J. Wehrle (Harvard University Press, 1985).

FMC   V. N. Vološinov, *Freudianism: A Marxist Critique*, translated by I. R. Titunik (Academic Press, New York, 1976).

MPL   V. N. Vološinov, *Marxism and the Philosophy of Language*, translated by Ladislav Matejka and I. R. Titunik (Academic Press, New York, 1986).

PDP   M. M. Bakhtin, *Problems of Dostoevsky's Poetics*, edited and translated by Caryl Emerson, with an introduction by Wayne C. Booth (Manchester University Press, 1984).

RW   M. M. Bakhtin, *Rabelais and His World*, translated by Helene Iswolsky (Indiana University Press, 1984).

SG   M. M. Bakhtin, *Speech Genres and Other Late Essays*, translated by Vern W. McGee (University of Texas Press, 1986).

In general I have followed standard transliterations in writing Bakhtin and Voloshinov; however, where authors or translators have used Baxtin or Vološinov I have retained these spellings when providing references.

PART I

*An overview of the writings of
Bakhtin and his circle*

Introduction

One of Mikhail Bakhtin's basic principles is that communicative acts only have meaning, only take on their specific force and weight, in particular situations or contexts; his is an account of the *utterance*, of the actual communicative interaction in its real situation. Nothing demonstrates this principle more clearly than the fate of Bakhtin's own utterances, many of which could have no life, no specific force and weight, in his own lifetime, because they could not be published in the Soviet Union; and when they were published and translated in the West, they issued into specific situations which lent them the force of other expectations and agendas. There is no betrayal here, no departure from a fixed original meaning, for the life of any word is as a succession of utterances, in each of which its meanings are enriched, contested, or annexed. The words of Bakhtin himself are no exception. Yet there is an interesting corrolary to this emphasis on the 'situatedness' of all utterances, which is that they must issue forth from one historically unique and particular place to another, indeed from one person to another, necessarily caught up in the complexities and inequities of social life. In this first chapter I aim to give you a sense of the situation out of which Bakhtin, and Voloshinov and Medvedev, speak. These are extraordinary and courageous voices that speak out of the aftermath of the Russian Revolution about language and literature, and about ethics and history; and they speak to us in the West, now spectators of another Russian Revolution which might yet, among its more minor consequences, upset our notions of some key Bakhtinian themes. In short, dialogue with another – at the heart of Bakhtin's thinking – does not invite us to cancel what historically separates us but rather to understand that other's historical specificity as fully as possible.

I

The only biography of Mikhail Bakhtin was published in 1984, written by two American scholars, Katerina Clark and Michael Holquist.[1] What

[3]

follows is of course deeply dependent on this pioneering work. It is a considerable achievement, not only for what it managed to discover, in inauspicious circumstances, about the actual life histories of Bakhtin and the members of his circle, but also because of the way it weaves together these biographical facts with the intellectual history which makes them important. For although Mikhail Bakhtin led a scholarly life, and was profoundly committed to such a life in the great tradition of the Russian intelligentsia, his life was not without its dramatic vicissitudes, thrust upon him by the times he lived in. There is reputed to be a Chinese proverbial blessing: 'May you not live in interesting times.' If anyone lived in interesting times, it was Mikhail Bakhtin, who was twenty-two at the time of the Russian Revolution in 1917, and thus lived through the Revolution, the Civil War that followed it, the excitements of the 1920s, the imposition of Stalinism, the purges of the 1930s, the German invasion of the Soviet Union, the cultural freeze of the Cold War, the Khruschev thaw, and the stagnation of the Brezhnev years. Bakhtin's writings were profoundly affected by this extraordinary history, not least because they could not be published between 1929 and the 1960s.

Mikhail Bakhtin was born in 1895 into a provincial banking family. He was the younger of two sons, and his elder brother Nikolai was to prove equally gifted. Mikhail grew up in Orel, and then in Vilnius and Odessa, both polyglot cities which gave him early experience of the linguistic heterogeneity which features so markedly in his later accounts of language. In addition, the two boys had a German governess who early made them fluent in German and introduced them to Classical literature. After studying for a year at Odessa University, Bakhtin followed his brother's footsteps to study classics in the University of Petrograd between 1914 and 1918. But the paths of the two men permanently diverged as a result of the Revolution and Civil War, for Nikolai joined the army during the First World War and was then persuaded that he should join the White Guards. As a result he followed them into exile. When he died in 1950 he assumed that his brother had perished in the purges in the 1930s.

But this was not the case, though Mikhail did indeed come in danger of dying from Stalinist repression. In 1918, along with many other Petrograd intellectuals, he moved to Nevel, and then in 1920 to Vitebsk, small towns in which many sought to escape the hardships of the Civil War period in the great cities. Here he formed the intellectual friendships that were to last in some cases for the remainder of his life, though most of the friends of the 1920s were to die within twenty years, killed either by purges, illness, or the German invasion. At all events, in Nevel, Vitebsk, and from 1924 in Leningrad, Bakhtin was part of small informal groups of young intellectuals who together discussed philosophical and perhaps religious questions. Some of these intellectuals, like V. N. Voloshinov, whom Bakhtin met in Nevel, and P. N. Medvedev, whom he met in Vitebsk, wrote in an avowedly Marxist way; others, like the Jewish philosopher and mathematician M. I. Kagan, wrote and thought in quite a different idiom. Clark and Holquist do well to capure the heady excitement of those early revolutionary years, when the young members of Bakhtin's circle could debate endlessly with themselves and with the equally young Marxists who governed in Nevel and Vitebsk; where the walls of the one-storey wooden buildings of this small provincial town were covered with avant-garde paintings; and where endless philosophical projects could be formed despite the acute poverty in which Bakhtin in particular lived. This was compounded by Bakhtin's poor state of health – throughout his adult life Bakhtin suffered from osteomyelitis (an inflammatory disease of the bones), which was so severe that in 1938 he had to have his right leg amputated. In 1921 he married, though he was not to have a secure and permanent source of income until after the Second World War.

A number of unpublished writings have survived from the 1920s, of which the longest has now been published in English as 'Author and hero in aesthetic activity' (in AA, pp. 4–256). Characteristically for Bakhtin's early concerns, it seeks to combine considerations of aesthetics with epistemology and ethics. Though there are undoubted continuities with the later work, and though Bakhtin was to return to some of the same questions at the end of his life, the extent to which this early writing is to be thought of as a 'key' to the whole of Bakhtin's career is in fact controversial. The only piece of writing he published before 1929 was a short but dense article on the philosophy of authorship in a miscellany published in Nevel in 1919 (also in AA, pp. 1–3).

The year 1929 marks the end of this first phase of Bakhtin's adult life, for it saw two important events: the publication of his book on Dostoevsky, and his arrest as part of a purge of religious intellectuals in Leningrad. While in Leningrad Bakhtin had no regular job, and was supported by small pensions due to him for his illness. He was at the centre of a group of active scholars and thinkers, but had no institutional position, though he did give private lessons. He was also a member of, or on the fringes of, some unofficial religious groups, which in their various ways sought to reconcile theology with the intellectual and scientific currents of the day. It was because of his association with one of these groups that he was arrested; he was variously charged with being part of anti-Soviet conspiracies and of 'corrupting the young', for which he was at first sentenced to five years in the rigours of Solovetsky Islands. However, after numerous appeals on his behalf, on the grounds of his health, and perhaps thanks to a favourable review of the Dostoevsky book by the Bolshevik intellectual Lunacharvsky, the sentence was reduced to five years of internal exile in the Kazakh town of Kustanai. Bakhtin left Leningrad in early 1930.

Bakhtin was to see no more of his writing published – except for an article on book-keeping in collective farms – until the 1960s. Thanks to his arrest he was now politically suspect, and his fortunes wavered with the political climate. Yet, paradoxically, the 1930s were an especially productive period for him; in this time he wrote a full-length study of the novel of education, several book-length articles on the history of the novel, and a doctoral dissertation on Rabelais. He did not spend the whole of this period in Kustanai. After he had served out the time of his sentence, he got a job at a teacher training institute in Saransk, in Mordovia, about four hundred miles east of Moscow. However, he was forced to resign from this post after a year at the height of the Stalinist repression in 1937, and in August of that year moved to a small town north of Moscow called Savelovo, where he remained until the end of the War. This was the nearest that one-time political exiles were permitted to live near Moscow. The mild political thaw at the end of the 1930s meant that his book on the *bildungsroman* or novel of education was accepted for publication and that he was permitted to submit his thesis on Rabelais for examination.

However, the German invasion of Russia prevented both of these projects from coming to fruition. Although the dissertation was submitted, the onset of war meant that it was not be examined until the late 1940s when the political climate had again changed and it became politically controversial. But a still more extraordinary fate overtook the book on the novel of education. The only complete manuscript was destroyed by a German bomb on the publishing house where it was stored. Two of Bakhtin's own vices combined to destroy the partial manuscript that remained. Throughout his life he was cavalier with respect to his writing and his manuscripts; in addition he was a lifelong and incessant cigarette smoker. He solved the acute shortage of cigarette papers during the war by smoking the manuscript. Only a portion of it remains.

[6]

After the war he was reinstated in his job in Saransk, and played the role of an active teacher and academic administrator until his retirement in 1961. He was eventually awarded the candidate's degree – not a full doctoral degree – for the dissertation on Rabelais in 1952 after political controversy had dogged the examination process. In brief, Bakhtin fell foul of the 'anti-cosmopolitanism' campaign of the late 1940s, which was not just a code for anti-Semitism but which made all intellectual students of non-Russian literature suspect. In addition, the celebration of the 'lower bodily stratum', which characterizes the thesis, offended the puritanism of the Soviet literary establishment. But in general Bakhtin was not productive during the years of his full-time employment. It was not until his rediscovery by a group of younger intellectuals in the early 1960s that he began to be published. One striking essay on 'Speech genres', written in the early 1950s, contrasts markedly with the prolific creativity of the 1930s.

The story of Bakhtin's rediscovery in the 1960s is itself an interesting one. In 1960 some postgraduate students at the Gorky Institute in Moscow came across Bakhtin's book on Dostoevsky and then his dissertation in the archives. At first they believed him to be dead. When they discovered he was still alive they undertook to get his work published. Even in the relatively liberal climate of the 1960s this was not easy, and the Dostoevsky book was successfully brought out, with substantial revisions by Bakhtin himself, before the more controversial Rabelais dissertation was finally published in 1965. Bakhtin became a cult intellectual figure in the Soviet Union before and after his death; in 1969 his state of health was such that he was brought from retirement in Saransk to a clinic in Moscow, and eventually, after his wife's death, he was found a large flat with constant nursing attendance. He produced a series of notes and interviews in his final years, returning especially to the philosophical themes of his young adulthood. He died in 1975, and in the same year a collection of his writings from the 1930s and early 1940s was published. Since then practically all his unpublished writing has been brought out in Russian and translated into English.

In the most substantial of the early unpublished writings, 'Author and hero in aesthetic activity', Bakhtin insists that a life never appears completed from within; that since, strictly speaking, we do not experience our own birth and our own death, only the life of another can be complete for us. Thus we can never be the hero of our own lives; a condition of heroic completedness is that it should be perceived by another, situated outside the hero's life. Bakhtin's life is now certainly completed, and others, rightly and necessarily, have been busy constructing a completed meaning for it. But all such constructions are two-way affairs – dialogues – in which one historically specific moment comes into contact with another. Like many of Bakhtin's ideas, this has at once the status of a description, apparently of the absolute conditions of human knowledge, and simultaneously appears as an ethical imperative, a profound urging to respect the otherness of the other person. In his early writing Bakhtin certainly felt the two to be inseparable. Part of the disagreements about the subsequent course of his writings involve precisely this issue, the extent to which these early, ethically-based concerns persist in the later, more explicitly social writing. Above all, the question is important with respect to the Marxist writings of V. N. Voloshinov and P. N. Medvedev, which have been confidently attributed to Bakhtin. This celebrated 'authorship question' is the topic of the next section.

II

In 1970 the Russian linguist Vyacheslav Ivanov attributed to Bakhtin books previously thought to be by Voloshinov and Medvedev. These books are the former's *Freudianism: A Marxist Critique* (1927), and *Marxism and the Philosophy of Language* (1929), together with some articles also written in the 1920s; and the latter's *The Formal Method in Literary Scholarship* (1928). The actual documentary basis of the attribution remains unclear, and when Bakhtin himself was asked directly on the matter he was silent or evasive. However, Clark and Holquist have accepted the attribution, though other scholars have challenged it. In the absence of any conclusive evidence either way, much of the argument on both sides of the question has been frankly speculative. But this much is clear. There really were two people called Voloshinov and Medvedev, who were members of the same intellectual circle as Bakhtin throughout the 1920s. So we are not dealing with a simple case of writing being published under pseudonyms. These two writers also published, under their own names, writing that is undoubtedly their own – indeed, Medvedev was a considerable journalist and publishing functionary in Leningrad in the late 1920s and 1930s. It is also clear that there is a very substantial coincidence between the arguments of the books appearing under their names, and, in particular, the arguments produced by Bakhtin in his unpublished writings of the 1930s. It is also clear that the books by Voloshinov and Medvedev are explicitly Marxist in idiom, while those of Bakhtin are less so, though at the very least Bakhtin, in his own writing, both published and unpublished, makes obeisance towards Marxism, and, more strongly, appears to be influenced by it in some fundamental respects.

So what is at stake in the dispute about the authorship of these books by Voloshinov and Medvedev? First and most evidently, of course, is the highly charged question of Bakhtin's relationship to Marxism. If it can be shown that Bakhtin was the author of the disputed texts, it would follow, would it not, that he was therefore 'really' a Marxist; if it could be shown that he was not the author, then the attempt to claim him for Marxism and the left more generally would be that much weaker. But things are not quite as simple as that, so I will attempt to lay out what seem to me to be the fundamental argumentative moves in this remarkable controversy.

There are certainly those who have gratefully accepted the attribution of explicitly Marxist writing to Bakhtin as a way of claiming Bakhtin for a sophisticated and non-reductive Marxist account of literature and language. They are not altogether helped by the fact that there is some writing, indisputably by Bakhtin, which is written in the rather reductive idiom of Soviet Marxism of the late 1920s – two prefaces to Tolstoy which Bakhtin wrote in 1929, and which form part of a collected edition. At all events, the substantial coincidence between the writings of Voloshinov, Medvedev and Bakhtin has formed the ground for some intelligent appropriations of the whole Bakhtinian canon by writers on the left.

But in fact this has not been the dominant strategy adopted by those who have insisted on Bakhtin's authorship of the disputed texts. In the West this position has most prominently been occupied by Clark and Holquist. In their biography they argue that the Marxism of the books by Voloshinov and Medvedev is more a matter of idiom – even, in one extreme formulation, a matter of 'window-dressing' – which permitted otherwise controversial arguments to be published. This permits them to preserve the essentially non-Marxist character of Bakhtin's writing intact. The philosophical key to unlock the whole body of writing, in this account, is to be found in Bakhtin's neo-Kantian inheritance, and is grounded in the I–Thou relationship. Hence Holquist's insistence, especially, on 'dialogism' as an overarching concept for encompassing the range of the writing. In this account, therefore, the Marxism of the disputed texts has almost to be argued away.

On the other hand those who have resisted the attribution have equally done so for different reasons. There have always been those who have done so on scholarly grounds – that the documentary evidence for changing the traditional attributions of the books to Voloshinov and Medvedev is simply too slight to warrant such a major change. But these scholarly reasons are inevitably caught up in ideological ones also. Thus there are those who wish to drive a wedge between Voloshinov and Medvedev on the one side, and Bakhtin on the other, because they are impressed by the sophisticated Marxism of the former two and are suspicious of what appears the softer, even liberal–humanist accents of the latter. In this they may have been excessively influenced by some of the ways in which Bakhtin has been assimilated in the West. Finally, there are those who wish to separate Bakhtin from the others because they do not see Bakhtin as an essentially Marxist writer. They see the Marxist gloss given to what are undoubtedly shared ideas as simplifications, distortions or 'monologizations' of Bakhtin. Sometimes this is driven by straightforward anti-Marxism, sometimes by a more productive recognition of the genuine differences that separate the various writings of the three.

So it can be seen that the stakes in this dispute are high – no less than the overall direction and emphasis to be given to the writings of Bakhtin and his circle. It has, moreover, generated some not always productive reading practices, in which the overt and primary meanings of the writing have been overlooked in order to decode those writings or to make them fit some constricting model of coherence. Nevertheless, whatever the extent of Bakhtin's responsibility for the disputed texts, there is a substantial convergence between the ideas expressed in them and in those which are indisputably by Bakhtin alone. And finally this is what matters: the content of the arguments far outweighs the interest of the authorship question. So while the resolution of the attribution remains unsettled, and is likely to remain so, the sensible course seems to be to continue to refer to the authors of the various writings by the names which originally appeared over their writing. I shall be content to note both differences and similaritites between the three authors as appropriate. And finally it is important to recognize that there is as much variety of argument and idiom within the indisputably Bakhtinian texts as there is within the whole body of writing from the circle.

III

Whatever the status of the disputed texts, we need to get a better sense of the intellectual milieu out of which Bakhtin, Voloshinov and

Medvedev emerged in the second and third decades of the twentieth century in Russia. If the most remarkable event of that period was the Russian Revolution, this by no means meant that the dominant intellectual force of the time was Marxism, or that Marxism was immediately imposed as the deadening intellectual orthodoxy one version of it was later to become. Both before and after 1917, Russia was a place of lively intellectual excitement, in which different currents of thought emerged and contested each other. Indeed, it is out of the contestation of several such currents that the distinctive emphases of Bakhtin and his circle emerge. It is by vitue of the extraordinary mutations of twentieth-century intellectual history that these emphases now appear, some sixty years later, to speak with the force and resonance that they do.

Bakhtin's own intellectual formation, both before and during his time at university, was above all in classical German philosophy, especially in its then dominant form of neo-Kantianism. This influence largely reflects the prestige of German academic culture throughout Europe before the First World War, but this prestige was particularly important in Russian universities. At all events, Bakhtin's starting-points for his intellectual development were in neo-Kantianism, though that certainly does not mean that his whole development is to be explained by the surviving writing in that tradition.

Neo-Kantianism is a philosophical position (or rather, the general name for a range of particular positions) which was especially important in German academic thought at the end of the nineteenth century and in the early twentieth century. It is a general philosophical orientation which sought to go back to Kant, in part as a reaction against what was felt to be the excesses of nineteenth-century positivism and empiricism. Perhaps its particular attraction to intellectuals is that it grants especial importance to the activity of consciousness; in this way of thinking, consciousness cannot be explained as a mere reflection of the external world, for the mind is not a blank sheet on which the objects of the external world are impressed. On the contrary, consciousness brings its own independent forms to apprehending and explaining the world outside itself, especially conceptions of time and space which cannot be deduced from the world itself. But Bakhtin's interest springs not from these general questions in the theory of knowledge (indeed he is consistently hostile to arguments conducted solely in this dimension) but in the particular way that he can modulate this neo-Kantian way of thinking into a way of talking about the relationship between self and other.

Bakhtin's longest essay in this manner is the extensive philosophical fragment, unpublished in his lifetime, called 'Author and hero in aesthetic activity'. Bakhtin's starting-point in this essay is the relationship between self and other, between I and Thou. Our sense of self, and our sense of the otherness of the other person, are grounded in and indeed constituted by this relationship. Bakhtin goes on from there to describe the aesthetic act as only a more developed version of this founding and constitutive relationship. So in one way the essay can be thought of as an attempt by the young Bakhtin to provide a phenomenology of aesthetic activity in the immediacy of the relationship between the self and the other, between I and Thou – that is, in the essay Bakhtin seeks to ground the aesthetic in the inescapable relationship with others in which our sense of self is constituted and in which our sense of the other is constituted. In this account, the aesthetic act – the attempt to give form and meaning to another's life in art – is a supreme form of all genuine human interactions, in which our sense of another person emerges from the distance which divides my situation from yours, and from the various bridges which can be built across that distance, which can never, for all that, be abolished.

Bakhtin generates a formidably complex argument in this attempt to combine aesthetic questions with ethical concerns and with problems of knowledge. But the constant emphasis of the essay – it is scarcely an essay since it runs to 250 pages – is on aesthetic activity as the expression of a *relationship*, not as the product of an isolated consciousness. This can be seen, for example, in what he has to say about aesthetic form:

> Contrary to 'expressive' aesthetics, however, form is not *pure* expression of the hero and his life, but an expression which, in giving expression to the hero, also expresses the author's relationship to the hero, and it is this relationship that constitutes the specifically aesthetic moment of form. Aesthetic form cannot be founded and validated from within the hero, out of his own directedness to objects and meaning, i.e., on the basis of that which has validity only for his own lived life. Aesthetic form is founded and validated from within the *other* – the author, as the author's *creative* reaction to the hero and his life. As a reaction, that is, which produces values that are transgredient in principle to the hero and his life and yet are essentially related to the latter. (AA 89–90)

For those of us who are not familiar with the idiom of neo-Kantian philosophy, this manner of writing poses its own problems, though it is not the manner which will be characteristic of the mature Bakhtin. Moreover, when he wrote this he did not have the incentive of probable publication to lead him to a more popular style. Nevertheless, the main shape of the argument is I hope clear. Aesthetic form is neither the 'natural' shape into which a life falls, nor an arbitrary imposition of shape upon that life by an author, but emerges from the complexities of the relationship between the two, complexities which Bakhtin seeks to map but which can never transcend the particular situations of both.

This is undoubtedly a central emphasis throughout Bakhtin's writing life – that artistic form and meaning emerge *between people*. This has led some writers to see these *dialogic* relationships, given their first full expression here, as providing the fundamental context for all of Bakhtin's writing. Equally, others have found in the undoubted ethical element in this early writing a similar key to the whole Bakhtin canon. But there is a clear distinction to be drawn between the kind of argument to be found in this writing of the early 1920s, and that of Medvedev and Voloshinov later in the decade and of Bakhtin himself in the 1930s. There, the relationships between people are understood in a more profoundly sociological way than the abstractedly philosophical and ethical manner of 'Author and hero', and the forms of consciousness which an author brings to bear are understood as being themselves historically formed. The question is, whether this transformed emphasis is to be understood as only a superimposition of social and historical considerations on dialogical or ethical relationships which remain fundamentally un-altered, or whether there is indeed a real transformation of these personalistic categories into social ones. At the very least, the change in emphasis is in part produced by the engagement on Bakhtin's part with other powerful currents of thought, to which we must now turn.

Evidently, a major intellectual force in early twentieth-century Russia was Marxism; the success of the Bolsheviks in 1917 and after meant that it became increasingly difficult for any intellectual position to be developed without some engagement with Marxism. As we have seen, the exact nature of Bakhtin's engagement with the official philosophy of the Revolution is ambiguous and bound up with the complexities of the authorship question and the disputed texts. It is also important to recognize that Marxism was not only the monolithic orthodoxy that it was to become under Stalin; it was and indeed remains a complex political and social philosophy capable of very different emphases. Still more important, we have to recognize that Marxism did not 'cause' the

Russian Revolution; explosive social and political tensions, precipitated by the First World War, were the cause of the Revolution and were settled, in however unsatisfactory a manner, in the extraordinary times that followed it. So the most profound influence on Bakhtin was not Marxism so much as the profound social upheavals that occurred in Russia in the early twentieth century and which provided an over-whelming sense of the transfigurative power of collective life. The particular formulations of Marxism are surely secondary to this. Never-theless, we can see that certain different emphases within it were more or less attractive to Bakhtin.

In the first place, Marxism as the philosophy of historical materialism, which stresses the socio-historical ground of all action, is certainly at least cognate with Bakhtin's characteristic emphasis on the social and historical particularity of all actions, particularly linguistic and literary utterances. This is the connection that Medvedev and Voloshinov were keen to underline in their writing at the end of the 1920s. But there is an evident danger here, if the connection is established at this level of generality, of simple banality – obviously both Marxism and Bakhtin provide social accounts of the utterance, but so do many other philosophies and social theories. Two further points can be made. First, the historical materialism of Marxism is founded on the historical reality of social class; Bakhtin himself, and not only Voloshinov and Medvedev, also acknowledges the importance of class and makes it indeed the ground of his account of language through the notion of 'heteroglossia' (see chapter 1 for a fuller account of this key Bakhtinian term; and see Part II, extract 3, for Bakhtin's deployment of the term with relation to the novel). In addition, the account of carnival he provides in the book on Rabelais is dependent on a notion of the social division of society. But this statement needs immediate qualification; class is indeed the ground of these accounts but in a subtle and nuanced way in which the multiple contradictions of social life can be seen as operating in and through the utterance. Both the artistic utterance and the utterance of spoken language are formed in a social context and are carriers of social meanings, in such a way that the utterance remains a unique and particular occasion and not merely the reflection of the underlying base as in one widespread and reductive version of Marxism. The second point to make in relation to this general question of Bakhtin's relation to Marxism is that, perhaps because of the peculiar nature of Russia's path of historical development, Bakhtin shares a profound sentiment of anti-capitalism with Marxism. It is worth recalling that capitalism was a relatively novel social formation in Russia, certainly compared to the countries of Western Europe; one consequence of this was that individualism, and social relations premised on individualism, remained, in general terms, comparatively unattractive. At all events, Bakhtin's explicit hostility to the isolating and alienating nature of capitalist social relations is cognate with one version of Marxism though it clearly does not imply any commitment to a belief in the socialist transformation of society.

A further ambiguity surrounds Bakhtin's attitude to the Hegelian inheritance in Marxism, particularly the notion of the dialectic. Classically Marxism has appropriated this notion as a way of talking about social contradictions and their resolution or 'transcendence'. Towards the end of his life Bakhtin gave a very hostile account of this Hegelian way of thinking, and there are indeed many thinkers within the Marxist tradition itself who have seen it as a substantial remnant of mysticism within Marx's thought, because it implies some ultimate or final resolution to the struggle between classes. The notion of transcendence especially conflicts with Bakhtin's characteristic ways of thinking, for he is a thinker who always seeks to ground utterances in their particular situations, and the dialogic engagement that characterizes the utterance remains inextricable from the situations of the participants in the dialogue. Yet the dialectic certainly figures importantly in the writing of both Medvedev and Voloshinov, though usually without any anticipated transcendence, so that it becomes a means of discussing social process and interaction, the vastly complex ways in which words, voices, people and social groups act and react upon each other and are transformed in the process.

Bakhtin was not the only Russian thinker in the 1920s and later who was obliged to make an accommodation with Marxism, though as we have seen this way of putting things suggests that Bakhtin came from a position wholly outside Marxism and was forced to submit to a simply repressive official ideology. As we have seen, the situation was far more complicated than that. Yet something like this did indeed occur in the case of formalism, the subject of Medvedev's major contribution to the writing of the Bakhtin circle, *The Formal Method in Literary Scholarship: A Critical Introduction to Sociological Poetics*. Formalism enjoyed a remarkable flowering in Russia at the time of the Revolution and in the 1920s; it was the creation of a group of brilliant publicists and scholars who rapidly established themselves as perhaps the most influential voices in literary scholarship at the time that Bakhtin's own ideas were coming to maturity.

It was thus in part in contradistinction to formalism that Bakhtin's own distinctive emphases emerged.

Formalism's starting-point was the attempt to define what it is, precisely, that distinguishes literary art from other forms of language use. The answers that the formalists produced had the great merit of seeking to be specific and appropriate to the artistic material they discussed, though always tending to found their sense of the formal specificity of literature on its contrast with 'practical' or 'ordinary' language. Thus literature is characterized precisely by its difference from practical forms of expression, seeking to roughen or retard its own linguistic forms for their own sake, or to 'make strange' those forms as a way of drawing attention to their own artfulness. It is a point of view which inevitably elevates form over content, which indeed sees content as no more than the indifferent material on which art works. Thus some of the attractiveness of formalism, apart from the straightforward gain of direct attention to the literary object in itself, is the ebullient cheerfulness with which matters of 'content' – all those earnest questions of ethics, history, and values – are downgraded to provide material on which the real business of literature can operate.

Not surprisingly, such a position provoked some considerable opposition, from Marxists among others, though it is interesting that formalism continued to develop throughout the 1920s and it was not until the end of the decade that cultural orthodoxy began to be imposed. One of the critiques of formalism, offering itself as explicitly Marxist, came from Pavel Medvedev – though as we have seen, there are now those who believe it to have been substantially written by Bakhtin. Medvedev's polemical tone is sharp, though he does conclude the book with this concession to his formalist adversary: 'Every young science – and Marxist literary scholarship is very young – should value a good opponent much higher than a poor ally' (FM 174). The heart of Medvedev's critique of his 'good opponent' concerns precisely formalism's attempt to divorce literature from practical language, and thus to remove from criticism and scholarship all questions of content and values. Against this Medvedev insists upon the 'ideological environment' in which all writing occurs, so that every literary utterance necessarily draws upon and contests the values that are articulated around it, inside and outside literature itself. As he puts it in one striking formulation, 'the language of art is only a dialect of a single social language' (FM 36).

However, Medvedev's critique of formalism does not amount to a

[16]

simple restatement of the importance of content over form, though he certainly does wish to resituate literature back into the inescapably social world of values and meanings, of what he calls ideology. One way of understanding his critique – what makes formalism, in fact, a 'good opponent' – is that formalism is not formal enough, that is, it restricts the concept of form unduly to literature (or art), and does not recognize that the notion of formal specificity needs to be extended to *all* ideological forms, not only literary ones. Once this extension has been made the question of the relationship between literature and the surrounding ideological forms can be put intelligibly, and turns out to be a complex dialectical process (though Medvedev calls it a 'simple' dialectic (FM 29)) in which meanings ceaselessly pass from one area to another, taking on the specific forms of each area as they do so. The whole process is understood as taking place 'within the bounds of the unified sociological laws of development' (ibid.). Thus, in a way that is at least cognate with some fundamental Bakhtinian themes, Medvedev concedes to formalism the formal specificity of literature, but wishes to extend this insight to a recognition of the formal specificity of all utterances.

There is an extract from Medvedev's book in Part II, in which the role of 'social evaluation' in all utterances is used as a way of criticising the formalist elevation of the literary 'device' over 'material'. Here it is sufficient to note a remarkable historical irony, which continues to give force to these polemics from the Russia of the 1920s. Some key Russian formalist themes re-emerged in France and elsewhere in the 1950s and 1960s under the name of 'structuralism'; the characteristic formalist stress on 'estrangement' or 'defamiliarization' can even be thought of as a version of the deconstructive emphasis on literature as a system of differences in which there is no positive term, so that full and definitive meaning is constantly deferred. Medvedev's critique of these themes in formalism thus provides us now with some of the materials for a critique of formalist currents within contemporary literary criticism. In particular, his insistence on the emptiness of the notion of 'estrangement', when it is abstracted from the struggles over the social values which are actually being 'estranged', seems to me to apply forcefully to any critical position which understands 'difference' in purely negative or differential terms. Some of these themes will be pursued more fully in chapter 4, when I consider the relevance of Bakhtin and his circle to some of the debates within contemporary criticism.

Formalism provided the most powerful *literary* position with which the members of the Bakhtin circle had to settle accounts in the 1920s. As I have suggested, this was a period of intense intellectual experiment and adventure in the Soviet Union, in which positions which would later simply be a matter for condemnation and suppression could be discussed openly. One such position was that of the new psychology of Freud, which was widely debated. The Bakhtin circle contributed to this debate with a book by Voloshinov called *Freudianism: A Marxist Critique*, published in 1927 (The original title was 'Freudianism: A Critical Sketch'; the subtitle of the English translation was provided by the translator). In some ways it is the least satisfactory of these critical writings of the 1920s, being comparatively short and doing less than justice to its topic; but it is nevertheless a richly suggestive book, for it seeks to replace the whole Freudian conception of the *unconscious* with the multiplicity and contradictions of internalised social language.

Voloshinov begins his critique by seeing Freud as a representative of a wide intellectual trend which seeks to explain and ground human behaviour in fundamentally biological rather than social and historical terms. Voloshinov is thus making what is in effect the fundamental historical objection to Freudianism, that '*Only as a part of a social whole, only in and through a social class, does the human person become historically real and culturally productive*' (FMC 15; Voloshinov's emphasis, here and in all subsequent quotations). The whole discussion of Freud throws up some intractable questions on the nature of the relationship between biological and social life, which Voloshinov can hardly be expected to solve. However, he criticizes Freud for being at once too biologistic, and for not being biologistic enough; that is, that Freud gives the impression of locating human behaviour in biology, but that actually his notion of the unconscious is completely detached from its bodily roots. This is perhaps the least satisfactory aspect of the book, but Freud's detachment of the unconscious actually provides Voloshinov with the occasion for some of his most interesting suggestions concerning the relationship of the life of the psyche to its social milieu.

For in his most radical move, Voloshinov concedes a portion of psychic life directly to the physiological – he was, after all, a contemporary of Pavlov – but claims that for the rest the '"content of the psyche" is ideological through and through' (FMC 24). Working in effect from Freud's starting-point in his analyses – patients' language and the 'talking cure' – Voloshinov sees the contents of the psyche as made up of multiple and contradictory speech material, as being indeed made up of 'inner speech'. Since language is inescapably social and occurs only *between* people, the valuations of the social milieu reach right to the innermost depths of the psyche. In the light of this assertion, Freud's distinction between the 'conscious' and the 'unconscious' needs to be recast. What in Freud remains a distinction within the individual becomes, in this new perspective, a distinction between the 'official' and the 'unofficial' consciousness. The drama, the conflicts and the tensions of psychic life, as revealed by Freud, are not disputed by Voloshinov but recast as versions of the conflicts of the social milieu.

This is a suggestive but also a reductive account of Freud. It should be stressed that the book is a schematic and avowedly popular account of the topic, a large part of which is made up of straightforward exposition of the various phases of Freud's thought. Its suggestiveness lies in its insistence on the verbal content of both the 'official' and the 'unofficial' conscious – a suggestion which, in the best spirit of the Bakhtin circle, sees in the operation of 'inner speech' the inextricably social coming-to-consciousness of the historical subject. Its reductiveness lies in its essential negation of Freud's efforts to see the individual as at once a biological being and one formed within specific networks of relationships.

IV

What, then, are we to make of these efforts by Bakhtin and the members of his circle to orient themselves among the conflicting currents of thought in post-Revolutionary Russia? With respect to Bakhtin's lifelong and sometimes subterranean engagement with Marxism, I hope that the following pages, devoted to an exposition of his writing on language, the novel, and carnival, will shed further light on this topic, but two important things need to be said at this point. As we have seen, Bakhtin's philosophical starting-point is clearly not in Marxism, and his centre of gravity remains outside the classical concerns of Marxism throughout his life. Secondly, and more importantly, it is worth having disputes only about substantial issues – canonical questions or questions of orthodoxy are really only ever interesting if they serve substantial questions. What matters about Bakhtin is not the extent or otherwise of his Marxist orthodoxy, but his capacity to articulate a poetics, and an account of language, which sees all utterances as at once implicated in social and historical particularity and also, by virtue of that very fact, capable of being engaged by other social and historical particularities – that is, you and me in a later period.

A similar consideration applies to the writings of Voloshinov and Medvedev, who write as explicit Marxists, yet whose Marxism is certainly unlike that of most of their Soviet contemporaries. If there is a common theme in the two books I have discussed here – the next chapter is mostly devoted to Voloshinov's account of language – it concerns the immersion of literary and psychological life in what they respectively call the 'ideological environment' and the 'social milieu'. That is, both writers seek to find ways of describing how the apparent commonsensical givenness of the individual phenomena of artistic and psychological life turn out to be complex refractions of realities that are in fact social, and therefore value-laden and contested. The ideas and attitudes that spring from this assumption are the ones that require engagement; such engagement ought not to be side-tracked by the questions of their Marxist orthodoxy or the authorship dispute.

Before we move to a detailed account of language, two other issues need to be briefly mentioned. The first concerns Bakhtin's lifelong interest in science. In notes made at the very end of his life, now published under the title 'Towards a methodology for the human sciences', Bakhtin draws a fundamental distinction between the 'exact' and the human sciences (SG 159–72). Where the exact sciences are monologic because they are concerned with *objects* of knowledge, the human sciences are necessarily *dialogic* because they are concerned with other subjects. But this distinction does not mean that Bakhtin repudiated scientific knowledge, either for itself or as a source of knowledge and analogies about human behaviour. In the 1920s he showed a keen interest in the new Einsteinian physics and in biology – so much so that one of his crucial concepts, the 'chronotope', was taken from a lecture he attended on biology, though to be sure the notion has Kantian roots also (this notion is discussed more fully in chapter 2). Voloshinov and Medvedev too are keen to claim the authority of science for their arguments, though this is perhaps a rather different matter, to do with the idiom in which they argue.

The second theme that remains to be mentioned is altogether more elusive; it concerns the nature of Bakhtin's religious commitment. I have mentioned that the official reason for his arrest and exile in 1929 was his association with an unofficial religious discussion group. It seems likely that he retained some sort of commitment to Russian Orthodox Christianity throughout his life, a commitment which can appear in his writing in unexpected ways. Yet this could be combined with an anti-clericalism, and an apparent hostility to the authority of the 'sacred word', in ways which are difficult to understand to one who is inexpert in the history of Russian Orthodoxy. Yet there are several points at which Bakhtin's religious orientation is perhaps operating: in that undoubted ethical commitment which we saw as fundamental to his understanding of aesthetic activity in 'Author and hero', and, paradoxically, in his celebration of the body-based meanings affirmed in carnival against a modernity drained of emotional affect. At all events, we must now consider the substantial accounts of language and literature that Voloshinov and Bakhtin provide.

I
Voloshinov and Bakhtin on language

The major consideration of language produced by a member of the Bakhtin circle is to be found in Voloshinov's *Marxism and the Philosophy of Language*, published in 1929. This will form the main topic of this chapter, together with Bakhtin's own accounts of language at various moments in his writing. What Voloshinov and Bakhtin have to say about language, and the study of language, is remarkable, not only because what they wrote in the late 1920s appears to anticipate some of the directions of contemporary thought, but more importantly because it suggests some exciting and fruitful ways of thinking about language and the manner in which we act and interact with each other through language.

I

Voloshinov wrote as an explicit Marxist, and, for the reasons I suggested in the Introduction, I do not wish to discount this as mere protective camouflage. This commitment led him to two fundamental predispositions, which are at the heart both of his account of language and of the critique he provides of the main contending theories. These predispositions are, first, that he seeks a materialist theory – that is, a theory which is grounded upon material reality and which does not resort to ideal constructions to explain the origin or mode of existence of language. Second, Voloshinov is predisposed to give an account that locates the phenomenon of language in the life of society. Let us take each of these predispositions in turn.

His materialism produces a particular account of the relationship between language, ideology, and the basic medium of social and ideological life, namely the sign. In effect, Voloshinov grounds his account of language on the materiality of the sign, for as a provisional statement we can say that at one pole language is a system of signs. But signs are not confined to language; it is not only the articulate sounds the we make, or the graphic marks that we write, that carry meaning. Many of the material objects and artefacts that surround us can, in particular circumstances, carry meanings also (one example that Voloshinov provides is the meaning given to the material objects of bread and water in the Christian sacrament of communion). However, as soon as we are in the domain of meanings, we are also carried, willy-nilly, into the domain of ideology. That is to say, the meanings carried by signs, whether of language or not – though it is language we are interested in here – take us into the world of values and are therefore ideological, though to be sure this is to give a more extended meaning to the concept of ideology than is common in English. This is how Voloshinov summarizes these relationships in the book on language:

> Signs also are particular, material things; and, as we have seen, any item of nature, technology, or consumption can become a sign, acquiring in the process a meaning that goes beyond its given particularity. A sign does not simply exist as a given part of reality – it reflects and refracts another reality. Therefore, it may distort that reality or be true to it, or may perceive it from a special point of view, and so forth. Every sign is subject to the criteria of ideological evaluation (i.e., whether it is true, false, correct, fair, good, etc.). The domain of ideology coincides with the domain of signs. They equate with one another. Whenever a sign is present, ideology is present, too. *Everything ideological possesses semiotic value.* (MPL 10)

Voloshinov's materialist account of the sign, therefore, leads him to give a materialist account of language, and since all actual uses of language take us into the realm of value and ideology, we have here the potential for a materialist account of ideology also.

The second predisposition is still more important, for it is a crucial presumption not only for Voloshinov but for Bakhtin also, one which underlies their accounts not only of language but of aesthetics as well. This is the assumption that language is a social phenomenon, though this anodyne formulation scarcely captures the radical implications that follow from this starting-point in Voloshinov's hands. We shall see some more of these implications when we come on to his critique of the linguistics contemporary to him. For now we need to notice that this insistence on the sociality of language leads to a notion of what Voloshinov calls the 'multiaccentuality of the sign', the idea that the signs of language (words, above all) bear different accents, emphases and therefore meanings with different inflections and in different contexts. Meanings emerge in society and society is not a homogenous mass but is itself divided by such factors as social class; signs do not therefore have fixed meanings but are always inflected in different ways to carry different values and attitudes. This is most obvious in the realm of political debate and polemic; what a conservative means by 'socialism', the particular condemnatory and dismissive intonation she gives to the word, is evidently very different from the meaning attached to the word by a member of a socialist party. But Voloshinov's point is that all signs, all the words of a language, are charged with these multifarious and conflictual meanings. For this reason arguments and debates cannot be settled by reference to dictionaries; these provide at best only records of usage, records that can scarcely capture the continuous pulling to and fro that actually constitutes the meaning of any word in any living language. Dictionaries are the graveyards of language.

Voloshinov understands the sociality of language in a very particular way, then, a way which distinguishes him from the mainstream of linguistic thought in the twentieth century, which stems from the Swiss linguist Ferdinand de Saussure. Indeed, a substantial part of *Marxism and the Philosophy of Language* is devoted to a critique of Saussure and the style of linguistic thought that Voloshinov sees him as representing. In this account, Saussure's thought about language is an example of what Voloshinov calls 'abstract objectivism'. This critique is matched by an account of another tradition of linguistic thought, mostly springing from the early nineteenth-century linguist William von Humboldt, which Voloshinov characterizes as 'individualistic subjectivism'. These two parallel critiques, which Voloshinov will eventually try to synthesize in a more complete account of language, take us to the heart of what is radical and distinctive in his work.

Voloshinov begins with his account of individualistic subjectivism, whose basic presumption is that 'The source of language is the individual psyche' (MPL 48). Though this fundamentally asocial presumption is sufficient to invalidate this whole trend in linguistic thought from Voloshinov's point of view, there are nevertheless some attractive features in it. These stem from von Humboldt's famous dictum about language that it is not *ergon* (completed work) but *energeia* (creative process) – that is, that language is not an achieved thing, but a ceaselessly changing, evolving and producing process. So while Voloshinov will wish to repudiate this way of thinking about language insofar as it tends to locate the source of meaning in the individual, rather than in the evaluatively charged social interactions between people, he will nevertheless find sympathetic the attempt to retain the stress upon the productive capacities of individual speakers.

There is a similar balanced approach in his account of 'abstract objectivism', though here his critique is so fundamental that it is at times difficult to see what survives of this attitude to language, and of the whole Saussurean project, by the time that he has finished. To understand the full force of his critique, it is worth briefly outlining Saussure's account of language. Saussure starts, in effect, from a methodological question: what is the object of linguistic science? The answer he provides has had the most extraordinary and far-reaching implications, for he concludes that the vast number of actual uses of language cannot possibly form the object of a science; rather, linguistic science must concentrate on the underlying system which enables each and every use of language to be meaningful. He calls this underlying system *langue*, distinguishing it, in French, from *langage*, which alludes to the totality of language both in its underlying systematic aspect and in the actuality of its actual use. This domain of use, of the actual instances and occasions in which language manifests itself, Saussure relegates to the domain of *parole*, or speech; this falls out of the domain of objective science as an inappropriate or impossible object of study. If linguistics is to be a science, like say geology, it has to study the types of rock and not each and every pebble on the beach. This fundamental distinction between *langue* and *parole* has had wide effects on the intellectual history of the twentieth century, not only in linguistics but in a variety of areas of study which have been seduced by the apparent objectivity of the linguistic model conceived in the spirit of Saussure.[1]

For what begins as a methodological principle rapidly becomes a powerful account of the way language works, namely that it is based upon some underlying system or code which is actualized in each individual utterance. This in turn has implications for the way you conceive of the state of a language at any given moment, and its history. The system holds together as a system by virtue of the relations between all its elements; this Saussure describes as a synchrony, and he opposes it to the history of the individual elements of the system which can indeed be studied separately but which thereby form a different kind of study – diachronic linguistics. Once again an apparently methodological principle – a way of distinguishing between the study of a contemporary language, and the study of the history of language – becomes solidified in a way that tends to abstract the synchronic 'system' of a language from its constantly evolving historical actuality.

The nature of Voloshinov's objections to all this can in part be anticipated from the name he gives to this whole trend of thought, which he accuses of *abstracting* a false object of study, and indeed of treating the living actuality of language inappropriately as an object or thing. It is in this accusation of abstraction that he provides some of his most surprising and interesting suggestions. For though Voloshinov praises Saussure for the clarity and consistency with which he articulates his system, he by no means sees this way of thinking about language as originating with him. On the contrary, he sees in Saussure only the clearest exponent of a long tradition of linguistic reflection, in which the essence of language has been thought of as a system of rules. The historical ground of this tradition has been the remarkable necessity, in a whole variety of different societies in the course of history, of both teaching and enforcing the authority of a sacred or nationally authoritative language other than the vernacular. The most obvious example would be the centuries-long prestige of Latin after it ceased to be spoken as an actual language. Saussure becomes the inheritor of this tradition; in one of the few aphorisms that Voloshinov allows himself, he startlingly asserts that 'The first philologists and the first linguists were always and everywhere *priests*' (MPL 74).

Further difficulties arise for Saussure with the concept of *langue* in Voloshinov's account, which start as difficulties of conceiving its mode of existence, but point to profound differences between the ways the two thinkers conceive of society. Voloshinov contends that few thinkers in the tradition of abstract objectivism have really confronted the question of where and for whom *langue* exists. Rationally, such a system can only exist in the subjective individual consciousness; if this is not admitted this abstract object becomes hypostasized, given an unreal existence, perhaps as some kind of collective mind. But for the individual language user, language never exists only as such a set of norms; it is not the sameness or identity of language that matters to the speaker but its adaptability to the new situation in which language must take on meaning: '*What is important for the speaker about a linguistic form is not that it is a stable and always self-equivalent signal, but that it is an always changeable and adaptable sign*' (MPL 68). We will return to this distinction between a *sign* and a *signal*; but first we need to recognize that in this conception the quality of systematicity in language is subordinated to the multiple and non-systematic (or at least differently systematized) occasions of its use, for only in these occasions does it become meaningful. Under abstract objectivism, language and hence society has to be conceived as a set of abstract norms and rules that you carry around in your head; in Voloshinov's conception, by contrast, language and linguistic interaction are the very means by which society in all its conflicts and contradictoriness is realised.

What remains, then, of Saussure and the whole tradition of linguistic thought he represents after Voloshinov has finished with him? It is sometimes said that the latter provides a powerful critique, but fails to provide any adequate alternative conception. It is certainly true that a comparatively short book like *Marxism and the Philosophy of Language* is unlikely to provide more than suggestive pointers to these problems of general linguistics, especially since by its own account some of the modes of thought with which it is grappling have long histories in Western – and indeed Indian – thought. Moreover, when Voloshinov does provide a substantive and extended analysis of particular linguistic usage, he does so as an analysis of the various phenomena of reported speech, which might not be thought of as central to these more general problems we have been discussing. Nevertheless, he does attempt what he describes as a dialectical synthesis of the two traditions of thought about language (in some late notes, by contrast, Bakhtin will explicitly reject the dialectic as a mode of thought[2]) and this attempted synthesis seems to me to be extremely suggestive. If the abstraction of Saussure and others like him has to be rejected, then his account of language does at least retain, in however hypostasized a form, some notion of the sociality of language. If the individualism of the alternative tradition is likewise inadequate, it too retains a worthwhile sense of the productivity of language. The synthesis that Voloshinov proposes is to be found at the end of his chapter on verbal interaction, reproduced on p. 143; it would be helpful if you could refer to his conclusions.

These formulations are full of interest. The first conclusion, that 'Language as a stable system of normatively identical forms is merely a scientific abstraction', summarizes the critique of Saussure and the tradition of abstract objectivism. It is worth noting that Voloshinov allows this conception a partial validity but that he contends that such abstraction is inadequate for a complete account of language. The way in which such an account might be completed is intimated in the second formulation, that 'Language is a continuous generative process implemented in the social-verbal interaction of speakers.' This formulation retains the

Humboldtian emphasis on the productivity of language but resituates it in the interactions between speakers, which are necessarily social since we are all social beings. This dialectical assimilation of 'individual subjectivism' is continued in paragraph 3, where Voloshinov repudiates any individualist equivalence between the laws of language and the laws of psychology, but retains a strong emphasis on the activity of speakers in the production of language, always understood as occurring in a sociological context.

Paragraph 4 adds to the critique of German idealist positions on language – that the highest manifestation of language is in aesthetic activity and that linguistic creativity is essentially aesthetic – by repudiating any special status for the aesthetic. But this does not mean he repudiates the notion of linguistic creativity; on the contrary, he retains a strong stress upon it. But he understands the creative activity of speakers to manifest itself in the various ways they use and transform the ideological meanings and values that confront them in their uses of language. In this way speakers are not the passive victims of language – are not merely subject to 'blind necessity', but are also agents in the continuing production of language, are subject in this sense to 'free necessity'; people speak a language, make new meanings with it, as much as they are spoken by it.

Where these formulations point above all is to a sociological pragmatics, pragmatics being the name that contemporary linguistics has given to the study of language in context, though Voloshinov's insistence on sociology is one that is absent from much contemporary pragmatics. But his attempted synthesis ought to do more than point to a productive area of reflection and research; it ought also to solve some of the general problems that he has raised in ways that do not simply add together the attractive bits of the theories he criticizes while repudiating the unacceptable elements. It is fair to ask if the synthesis does so.

I believe that it does, though necessarily in a condensed and incomplete way. The key move is to take as your starting-point language in use rather than language as a code or underlying system. This is not to deny that language has a systematic character; rather this systematicity has to be completed, and is always completed in actual language situations, by the necessity to make language carry immediate meaning and by the hearer's necessarily active role. This completed utterance is just that – an utterance, and not a mere sentence; it uses signs, not signals. Moreover, the nature of the relationship between the set of linguistic norms and the occasions of the use of language is itself a dialectical one in which each acts and reacts back upon one another, so that each and every use of a word or an expression changes, extends or reinforces its meaning and thus alters or confirms the set of norms which is one of the conditions for its use. And all of these processes are sociological and ultimately historical ones; what govern the to and fro of linguistic interaction are the social positions of the speakers, while these social relationships are themselves realized, in part, through language.

This apparently takes us away from the more obvious concerns of Bakhtin himself, but actually this is not the case at all. By shifting the conception of language towards pragmatics understood in this way – that is, as the study of language as it takes on meaning in the socially-marked interactions between people – Voloshinov restores the study of language to typically Bakhtinian territory, namely dialogic relationships. But before we go on to look at Bakhtin's accounts of language under his own name, the specific intonation that Voloshinov gives to dialogic relations, as part of his account of language, deserves some fuller treatment.

Voloshinov first outlines his version of what we can now call pragmatics in an essay that predates his major book on language, an essay called 'Discourse in life and discourse in art' published in 1926. The kind of problem that he is dealing with can be assessed from the example that he discusses most fully: 'Two people are sitting in a room. They are both silent. Then one of them says, "Well!" The other does not respond' (FMC 99). Clearly we cannot know the meaning of such an utterance on the strength of an internal analysis of the word 'well'. To understand it, and the particular force of the intonation with which it was pronounced (Voloshinov describes it as 'indignation and reproach moderated by a certain amount of humour' (ibid.)), we have to know about the extra-verbal situation, and we are provided with a little narrative: it is May, winter has been especially persistent, both interlocutors are sick and tired of winter, they both look up and see that outside it has begun to snow. Only if we know all this can we understand the full force of the utterance, understood not just as the word, but as this word with its particular intonation in this particular situation. And this becomes the model of the actual working of language for Voloshinov. Language always occurs in situations, so the force of an utterance can never be decided by a mere account of its formal meaning.

But there are some distinctive features to this pragmatics which make it more than an account of the conditions by which utterances have force.

For Voloshinov, intonation is the link between an utterance and its extraverbal context, and an intonation always carries some active evaluative charge. So it is not simply that formally or logically you have to build in to your model of language a recognition of extraverbal context in order even to understand how language works – though this is certainly the case. Language users simultaneously take an active relation to that context, of approval or disapproval, of fear or mastery, of wonder or contemptuous indifference or of any of a hundred other such attitudes indicated by the intonation they lend to their speech. This active evaluative attitude takes you towards sociology; but so does the other element in any utterance, the interlocutor. Voloshinov thus has three active forces between which the utterance occurs: the speaker, the topic of the utterance, and the interlocutor. This is a powerful and distinctive position. It sees the process of language production as dynamic and value-charged; it situates it in the sociologically significant relationships between people; and it retains an epistemological dimension (that is, it retains a strong sense of the reference language makes to the world).

This pragmatic account of language in 'Discourse in life and discourse in art' is extended in *Marxism and the Philosophy of Language*. In particular, Voloshinov elaborates a distinction between *theme* and *meaning* which seeks to capture the fundamental distinction between, yet also inseparability of, language as system and language in use, or to put the same distinction another way, the normative and occasional – provided that you recognize that all uses of language are occasional. Thus,

> *Theme is a complex, dynamic system of signs that attempts to be adequate to a given instant of generative process. Theme is reaction by the consciousness in its generative process to the generative process of existence. Meaning is the technical apparatus for the implementation of theme.* (MPL 100)

This rather dense formulation attempts to capture the relationship between any particular whole utterance – by definition unrepeatable – and the repeatable linguistic elements on which the utterance depends. Voloshinov's example is the question 'What time is it?' (ibid.), which always has a different theme whenever it is asked, but always uses the same combination of meanings. In the light of this distinction you can see the unsatisfactoriness of related distinctions, such as those between usual and occasional meanings, or central and lateral meanings, or between denotation and connotation. Each utterance has a theme which relies upon meaning; meaning only ever exists *in potentia* (though this does not imply that the socially created multi-accentuality of the sign is fixed or diminished in use). Thus there is no denotative core to a word from which the connotations stray, for all uses are equally connotative; all uses are charged with an evaluative accent, that is, all uses take up an attitude of some kind in the act of utterance. But the double focus of this evaluation is crucial; it is not only towards the world 'in its generative process', but also towards the interlocutor; as Voloshinov remarks at a later moment in the book, 'Life begins only at the point where utterance crosses utterance, i.e., where verbal interaction begins, be it not even "face-to-face" verbal interaction, but the mediated, literary variety' (MPL 145).

The context of this remark, however, is the extensive discussion of the phenomena of direct and indirect discourse with which Voloshinov concludes the book. How does a language permit you to report on the speech of another? Have the conventions altered over time? What sort of relationships are implied by different conventions for reporting speech? The immediate relevance of these questions to the themes we have been discussing so far may not be immediately clear, but on further reflection they may perhaps become so. First, they permit a technical demonstration of the way sociological factors can influence and reach into the apparently most purely grammatical features of a language. Thus changes in the modes of reported speech, in such matters as the use or not of direct speech, the extent to which indirect speech retains the characteristics of the other's speech, and the extent to which the other's speech is analytically broken down, all reflect changes in the social environment. These are indeed matters of grammar, as anyone will tell you who has had to learn the rules for *oratio obliqua* (reported speech) in Latin – though this example reinforces Voloshinov's point that our notions of grammar are profoundly marked by the pedagogic environment in which we encounter them. But such questions of reported speech are also a matter of style, in which the relations between writer, topic and reader are managed (these questions are especially acute in writing, though they apply to speech also). Grammar, style and questions of sociology are therefore inseparable.

In addition, such phenomena are the most evident way in which the interlocutive character of language appears at the grammatical and stylistic level. Direct and indirect speech, and the different kinds of indirect speech, obviously dramatize the fact that language is something that exists between people. In this respect Voloshinov's attention to these phenomena is clear evidence of his closeness to some central Bakhtinian concerns. Moreover, the choice between different possible ways of reporting speech displays different possible attitudes to the other and her point of view; Voloshinov's analysis of 'Quasi-direct discourse' – variously known as free indirect style, *style indirect libre* and *erlebte rede* – is especially important in indicating how another's evaluations can infiltrate one's own. Such phenomena appear extensively in literature, of course, and indeed in their fullest complexity, in novels by say Flaubert or Dostoevsky or James Kelman, defy the capacity of the speaking voice to reproduce the multiple voices and perspectives that can be heard in them. This analysis too is directly cognate with Bakhtin's interest in 'double-voiced' writing in its various forms. So this is a convenient place to turn to Bakhtin's various explicit accounts of language.

II

To move directly from Voloshinov to Bakhtin invites, of course, some interesting questions about the 'authorship question'. The situation is full of ironies, some of them ferocious ones. Voloshinov wrote *Marxism and the Philosophy of Language* as an explicit Marxist, indeed as a member of the Communist Party, in the full expectation of publication and of contributing to a public debate. Bakhtin wrote 'Discourse in the novel', which contains some of his most interesting ideas about language, while in internal exile after having been imprisoned; he could have had no expectation of the study ever being published, as indeed it was not for over thirty years. Yet it is Voloshinov who was 'illegally repressed' under Stalinism, while Bakhtin, politically much more ambivalent it would seem, survived and produced, in the most unpropitious circumstances, a substantial body of work. It pays to bring a Bakhtinian perspective to bear on the question of whether their arguments are identical or not. Clearly some of the fundamental ideas of both writers are the same. But just as meaning only exists *in potentia* and requires theme for its potential to be realized, can a 'fundamental idea' exist independently of its particular expression? An answer in the spirit of Bakhtin would surely be that it cannot, so that the explicit Marxism of Voloshinov's writing means that it positions itself differently in debate, assumes a different relationship to authority, anticipates a different response. Its *theme*, in short, is quite different from Bakhtin's even apart from the conceptual differences.

There are three discussions of language by Bakhtin which form significant comparisons and contrasts with the linguistics provided by

Voloshinov. The first occurs in *Problems of Dostoevsky's Poetics* (1929 and 1963), and forms the prelude to the chapter on 'Discourse in Dostoevsky', an extract from which is reproduced in Part II. The second comes in an extended essay written in the mid-1930s, 'Discourse in the novel'; an extract from this essay, though not the account of language, is also included in Part II. The third discussion comes in an essay from the early 1950s, 'The problem of speech genres'. Let us take these three separate moments in turn.

In some respects the brief considerations on linguistics, included as a methodological foreword to the chapter on 'Discourse in Dostoevsky' in the 1929 book on the nineteenth-century novelist, are close to the arguments extended in *Marxism and the Philosophy of Language*. This is not surprising given the closeness in time in which the two books were written. Bakhtin makes a distinction between language as an object of study for pure linguistics, in which solely grammatical and logical relationships between words are studied and from which dialogical relationships are excluded, and language as it appears when dialogical relations (relations between speaking subjects) are included. In this latter aspect language is the topic for *metalinguistics*; linguistics alone is inadequate for analysing language as a dialogical phenomenon.

It is immediately clear that this distinction is cognate with that between *theme* and *meaning* in Volshinov's book, in that there is the same fundamental differentiation between language in its repeatable aspect (the topic for linguistics), and the particular linguistic utterance which carries and enacts relationships between actual people. But the choice of term for the study of language in its dialogic actuality – 'metalinguistics' – implies an interesting difference from *Marxism and the Philosophy of Language*, indeed an ambivalence that marks not only the relations between Bakhtin and Voloshinov but Bakhtin's writing considered on their own. For 'metalinguistics' implies that the appropriate terms for the study of language are beyond linguistics; it implies almost a repudiation of systematicity when studying the multiple relations between people which are realized in language. If this line of argument is pushed far enough, Bakhtin emerges as an anti-systematic thinker, prepared to acknowledge the role of a systematic linguistics in its place, but allotting only a small and preparatory place to it. One way of understanding Voloshinov, by contrast, is to see him as wishing to extend the area in which systematic considerations apply, not merely to the area of linguistic regularity narrowly conceived, but out to the social interactions in which utterances take on their force. This ambivalence also marks Bakhtin's other writing on language.

'Discourse in Dostoevsky' may be cognate with some aspects of Voloshinov's writing, but Bakhtin makes his argument, about the dialogic existence of language, with particular force. Language appears here as the site or space in which dialogic relationships are realized; it manifests itself in discourse, the word oriented towards another. The usefulness of this account of language for literary analysis begins to become clear; in novels in particular various kinds of dialogical relationship can be traced in the varying ways in which discourse represents and includes the words of author and character. An exemplary analysis along these line can be found in the extract from 'Discourse in Dostoevsky' reproduced on pp. 157–94).

If we turn now to the extended essay that Bakhtin wrote in the mid-1930s, 'Discourse in the novel', we find a similar, independently inter-esting account of language, which is then extended to inform an account of the novel. The contrast with the explicitly Marxist vocabulary of Voloshinov is also apparent. But the absence of much of this explicit Marxist vocabulary from 'Discourse in the novel' by no means betokens a retreat from the radically socializing project embarked upon by Voloshinov. Indeed, if anything the reverse is the case, since the conception of language offered in the later study by Bakhtin himself is more thoroughly 'sociological' than in the explicitly Marxist book. In the latter, the shift into the world of social values is made through 'evaluative accent' and hence ideology; since all uses of language are interlocutory, that is they occur between people, it follows that they are all ideological. Bakhtin does not draw substantially upon the category of 'ideology' but instead insists upon the multiplicity of social languages that make up the apparent unity of a national language; any utterance therefore takes place between language users who are socially marked in the very language they use. Thus the pragmatics of Voloshinov is certainly a social one but the 'society' consist of the multiple interlocutors between whom utter-ances occur; while for Bakhtin these interlocutors are more thoroughly socialized in conception since they speak in particular social languages.

And indeed this difference indicates one of the fundamental shifts between Voloshinov and Bakhtin. We have noticed how the former divided the history of linguistics between two fundamental tendencies: 'individual expressivism' and 'abstract objectivism'. This distinction reappears in 'Discourse in the novel' as between 'unitary' and 'individual' accounts of language; but these terms are in fact less centred on a critique of linguistics and are beginning to move towards being aspects of language itself. Thus Bakhtin produces a dynamic account of language which sees it pulled in opposite directions: centripetally, towards the unitary centre provided by a notion of a 'national language'; and centrifugally, towards the various languages which actually constitute the apparent but false unity of a national language. Bakhtin's word for these various languages is 'heteroglossia' (*raznorecie*, literally 'multi-speechedness'); it is a word he coins himself to allude to the multiplicity of actual 'languages' which are at any time spoken by the speakers of any 'language'. These are the languages of social groups and classes, of professional groups, of generations, the different languages for different occasions that speakers adopt even within these broader distinctions. At one end of the scale heteroglossia can allude to large dialectal differences which can produce mutual unintelligibility and indeed are hard to distinguish from different languages as such; while at the other end of the scale it can allude to the distinguishing slang of one year to the next and even the slogan of the hour.

This is a luminous conception which is helpful in considering several related questions with respect to language, though it is not without its problems. In the first place it undoes the rigid Saussurean distinction between synchrony and diachrony. The conception of language as dynamically pulled between centre and periphery, between unitary national forces and heteroglossia, at once describes the tensions that are holding together and pulling apart a language at any one time, and also the same forces which, in given social, economic, political, artistic and educational histories, are producing the multiple changes that constitute the history of a language. These dynamic forces are not simply linguistic ones; they are produced by historical forces that are external to language but which act partly in language. Each and every utterance, in Bakhtin's account, is intersected by these forces, realizes itself only by virtue of participating at once in the 'normative-centralizing system of unitary language' (DI 272) and contributing to living heteroglossia.

This may be considered a restatement of Voloshinov's distinction between *theme* and *meaning*, in that it again sees an utterance as produced by a combination of the normative (existing *in potentia* only) and the occasional. But it is a greatly historicized restatement, for the normative clearly does not, in the great European languages at any rate, exist *in potentia* only, but has an active and powerful presence as an imposed standard which some people may even actually speak. So here we encounter a difficulty with this account of language; not in the notion of heteroglossia, but in the normative or unitary alternative pole, which has to do double duty both as the system of norms which permits actual utterances to be made (though of course utterances are not contained by this system), and as the actually existing standard versions of the language which are such a prominent factor in the history of the major European languages. The difficulty arises, I believe, insofar as the notion of the normative retains traces of the Saussurean *langue*; if this notion is retained, each and every language that makes up the heteroglossia must itself have its own system of norms. This can only be true, as Voloshinov insists, abstractly; what is much more interesting is the competition and contradictions that exist between the various elements of the hetero-glossia and within which every utterance has to locate itself. Thus when Bakhtin asserts that 'the utterance not only answers the requirements of its own language as an individualized embodiment of a speech act, but it answers the requirements of heteroglossia as well' (DI 272), this can be understood as describing the transition from the system of norms to the non-normative use of that system in the production of an actual utter-ance; but it can also be understood as describing the participation of every utterance in the dynamics of a language in tension, so that every utterance involves a taking of sides in all the multiple conflicts and negotiations that constitute the politics of language.

It is this second emphasis which is especially helpful in considering some of the questions of historical linguistics that have preoccupied linguists since the nineteenth century. The motor of linguistic change, in this conception, becomes the very conflicts and contradictions that make up a 'language', conflicts that are socially and politically marked so that some versions of the language enjoy prestige and others do not. It would be possible to rewrite the history of English, for example, not as an account of the evolution of Received Pronunciation, but as a succes-sion of tension-filled heteroglossia, in each of which there are various languages struggling for dominance, as the result of which struggles the languages adopt new models, are transformed variously towards and away from the centre as social and political history dictates. The processes that characterize contemporary language use – the phenomena of prestige and reverse prestige, the strongly supported pull towards a normative language created by education and the national media, the equally strong centrifugal pulls of social, geographical, ethnic and generational differentiation – have all been processes which, *mutatis mutandis*, have characterized language throughout its history. These phenomena are perhaps less familiar to English speakers in England than they are elsewhere, given the exceptionally monoglot character of England and the powerful mythology that has been created around the prestige form of English spoken in England. But if you are an English speaker in Wales, Scotland or Ireland; if you are an English speaker in America; if you are an Italian speaker, who knows that it has been estimated that only five per cent of the population of Italy spoke what was designated as the national standard version of the language at the time of unification in 1861; if you are one of the majority of the world's population who speaks a non-prestige version of your 'national' language or indeed don't speak that language at all, you will know the sharp and sometimes bitterly conflictual tensions that surround every word you speak. But you may also know the pleasures that come from negotiating the heteroglossia in which you find yourself: the pleasures of solidarity and self-assertion that can come from the proud use of stigmatized forms, and the heady pleasures that can come from switching from one language to another so that none is permitted the final say.

This general conception of language permits Bakhtin a fine restatement of pragmatics (DI 276–7). In this account, the word comes to its user already marked by its history, bearing the traces of its previous uses, which any speaker or writer must either continue, deflect, or contest. There is no neutral language; the world does not speak its own meanings, but can only be alluded to by means of a socially marked language. Again, examples are easy to find from the obviously contentious domain of politics or social policy; but Bakhtin's most radical point is that such a heteroglossic history marks all language uses, and not just whether you refer to 'car thieves' as 'joy-riders' or 'perpetrators of crimes against motor vehicles'. Consider, in an example that has a long history behind it in radical discourse, the histories that lie behind the words in English for kinds of meat: beef, mutton and pork are descended from French, the language of the Norman lords who ate the meat, while cow, sheep and pig are Germanic words, the language of the people who actually looked after the animals. Or consider the words for everyday household objects, that often have multiple alternatives in the 'trade' which makes them – such as the bewildering variety of names for different kinds of nail (rounds, ovals, pins, brads, and so on), or light bulbs ('lamps'), or the different parts of doors. Every use of these words involves a negotiation which positions the user with respect to the social history that lies behind them.

[37]

Bakhtin's account of language here comes, as we have seen, in an essay called 'Discourse in the novel'; it is not an accident that his most extended consideration of language under his own name should occur in an essay on the novel, because the novel is the literary form above all which takes advantage of the multiplicity of language he describes. But we recall that for Bakhtin and Voloshinov no word can be spoken without an evaluative accent, without an attitude adopted towards that of which it speaks. This applies to the word of Bakhtin himself; it is clear that Bakhtin does not merely describe language as heteroglossic, he celebrates it. In Voloshinov's account, Saussure's 'abstract objectivism' is not simply a scientific mistake with no consequences outside science, but is actually in active alignment with the unifying centripetal forces of language. Just so, Bakhtin's account is in active alliance with the multiple, decentralizing heteroglossic forces he describes. And this is the foundation for the account of the novel that he provides in this essay, for the novel is the form which not only takes advantage of heteroglossia, but, when it is most authentically itself, is the form which exploits, celebrates and revels in the multiplicity of language. In the next chapter we shall turn to Bakhtin's various accounts of the novel; before doing so we must look at his later essay on language, 'The problem of speech genres'.

In one respect this essay is an eloquent restatement of the character-istic theme of both Voloshinov and Bakhtin, namely the inadequacy of any linguistics which is abstracted from the realities of real verbal (or written) interchange. Thus much of the essay is devoted to distinguishing between the *sentence* and the *utterance*. The former is one of the funda-mental unities of language for linguistic study; but the real basic unity of language in actual communication is the utterance, which may be made up of a single sentence but equally may be made up of a single word or exclamation ('Ah!') or of a large number of sentences together. Any attempt at a complete study of language would address itself to the utterance, and thus have to describe, in addition to merely grammatical features, the relation of the utterance to its context, its speaker's 'plan' or 'speech will', and above all its location in a dialogue. This means that the utterance must be seen as itself a response – the speaker is not Adam, Bakhtin asserts, 'dealing only with virgin and still unnamed objects, giving them names for the first time' (SG 93). And in addition every utterance expects a response, in which the listener is not merely passive but actively assimilates or challenges the preceding word.

These aspects of the essay restate in an especially clear form some of the main themes of the writing of Bakhtin with respect to language. But the essay contains a distinctive argument that marks a real advance on the earlier positions, which is his attempt to sketch a theory of genre for everyday speech as much as for writing. Such a theory stands between, as it were, language abstractly considered and the myriad utterances that people actually make. For these utterances are not produced merely out of all the possibilities that language makes available; they are rather formed in accordance with many genres which determine the way that people speak in different circumstances. Bakhtin insists on the heterogeneity of such genres, and includes the following list as examples of them:

> short rejoinders of daily dialogue (and these are extremely varied depending on the subject matter, situation and participants), everyday narration, writing (in all its various forms), the brief standard military command, the elaborate and detailed order, the fairly variegated repertoire of business documents (for the most part standard), and the diverse world of commentary (in the broad sense of the word: social, political). (SG 60)

He distinguishes between primary and secondary genres (broadly speaking between spoken and written genres), but sees the primary genres – the multiple and diverse modes of everyday speech – as every bit as historical as the great genres of the history of writing. That is, there is a history behind the forms even of the most casual or intimate exchange. 'Utterances and their speech types, that is, speech genres, are the drive belts from the history of society to the history of language' (SG 65).

This notion of speech genres is an attempt to formalize one of Bakhtin's (and Voloshinov's) central insights into language – namely its social nature, the fact that the utterance only exists between people who occupy particular places in a network of social relationships. It is because of this that the speech genre connects the history of society to the history of language, because the evolution of linguistic forms is tied to changes to social relations. This is most obvious, perhaps, in the changes that occur in modes of address; the genre of greetings evidently reflects relative positions in a social hierarchy and such changing matters as conventions of politeness. So in one sense we can see this essay as another exercise in Bakhtin's 'metalinguistics', for it too insists on the inadequacy of linguistics if it is restricted to the bare study of language outside of the social relations in which it occurs. But here the emphasis falls not on any opposition to systematicity in the study of language, but rather on the attempt to think further the historically formed genres that shape the patterns of all our speech. Yet this does not point to any sense of restriction of what can be said; Bakhtin emphasizes not only the variety of speech genres but also that a command of these genres is a condition of our free use of them and thus our adaptability and responsiveness to the unrepeatable situation of the utterance.

Bakhtin's central emphasis in this essay is on primary speech genres, rather than on those secondary genres like the novel that draw on the multiplicity of speech but redirect them to make part of another utterance. In the following chapter we shall look at his various accounts of the novel, which draw, in various and sometimes conflicting ways, on the accounts of language that we have discussed.

2
Bakhtin on the novel

An initial difficulty in discussing Bakhtin's various writings on the novel is created by their variety, for his multiple books and essays on this topic form the very substance of his work. The majority of this work was written in the years between the late 1920s and the early 1940s when, for much of the time, Bakhtin was in internal exile and without access to the usual resources of scholarship. In addition he was politically suspect and had little expectation of publication. Perhaps because of these unpropitious circumstances the various essays and books that we shall be considering in this chapter do not always cohere as systematic works of exposition. But then Bakhtin is not a systematic writer, preferring to work by suggestion, accumulation of material, and repetition of the same material in different contexts. As a result, there is not one but several Bakhtinian accounts of the novel, which certainly share some fundamental views, but which emerge with very different emphases.

Bakhtin's writing on the novel can be initially grouped into four main areas. There is first the book on Dostoevsky (1821–81) published in 1929, and republished after substantial revision and expansion in 1963. This has been translated into English as *Problems of Dostoevsky's Poetics*. Broadly speaking, Bakhtin claims in this book that Dostoevsky's novels are distinctively polyphonic, that is, they grant the voices of the main characters as much authority as the narrator's voice, which indeed engages in active dialogue with the characters' voices. The second main group of writings is made up of the unpublished 'essays' of the 1930s and 1940s (some of which are actually the length of short books), eventually published in 1975, and most of which appear in English translation in *The Dialogic Imagination*. These share a common concern with the relations between the novel and language, and offer several different accounts of the novel's generic roots. The third area is made up of the lost book on the *bildungsroman* – the manuscript of which Bakhtin famously smoked during the War when cigarette papers were unobtainable. Finally, there is the work on Rabelais and carnival, which Bakhtin submitted for his doctorate – unsuccessfully – in the 1940s but which was not published until the 1960s. This is translated into English as *Rabelais and His World*. In this book, Bakhtin locates Rabelais' work in the tumultuous festive life of the Renaissance carnival; but the carnival and folkloric roots of many of the modern novel's predecessors become a major concern of Bakhtin in the 1930s, and notions of carnival infiltrate many of his other writings, including the book on Dostoevsky. This whole area of Bakhtin's thinking is so important that I will devote a separate chapter to it. But first let us take the two other recoverable areas of his work, beginning with the book on Dostoevsky.

I

The substantial claim of the 1929 version of the book, which persists in modified form in the revised edition, is that Dostoevsky invented the polyphonic novel; that is, that his novels are organized in a profoundly different way from those that precede them, with the narrator renouncing the right to the last word and granting full and equal authority to the word of the characters. 'The chief characteristic of Dostoevsky's novels', Bakhtin writes, is 'a plurality of independent and unmerged voices and consciousnesses, a genuine polyphony of fully valid voices' (PDP 6). In these novels, therefore, unlike the novels of, for example, Tolstoy, there is no 'surplus' of artistic vision beyond the ken of the characters which organizes them and finally explains them. On the contrary, there is no finalizing, explanatory word; the voices of the characters and that of the narrator engage in an unfinished dialogue. On the one hand, then, the polyphonic novel is to be distinguished from implicitly authoritarian forms of novelistic organization which retain the final word for the narrator. But on the other hand this is not to be seen as a simple abdication of responsibility – polyphony does not mean relativism, which grants life to the differing discourses of the characters only by failing to engage with them. Rather, the dialogue of the polyphonic novel is authentic only insofar as it represents an engagement in which, in various ways, the discourses of self and other interpenetrate each other.

This is the basis for a powerful and illuminating account of Dostoevsky, but its significance clearly does not end there, for, as with so many of Bakhtin's descriptions, there is an evident evaluative accent in all that he writes about polyphony, which takes consideration of the issues raised well beyond Dostoevsky's novels alone. For polyphony operates as a true aesthetic description: that is, it not only describes a particular aesthetic object and distinguishes it from other aesthetic objects; it also provides a basis for evaluating those aesthetic objects. As a result it is impossible to read *Problems of Dostoevsky's Poetics* without recognizing that its terms are applicable to many other novelists; that it provides a way of distinguishing many of the great European novels of the last three centuries. Moreover, the notion of polyphony restates, in Bakhtin's own very characteristic accents, some of the major aesthetic problems that go back as far as Plato. In particular, it addresses the fundamental question of narrative authority, which has partially resurfaced in twentieth-century criticism in English in discussions of 'showing' rather then 'telling', and discussions over the 'discursive hierarchy' – the view that realist novels are made up of a hierarchy of discourse, with the narrator's discourse at the top speaking the language of unproblematic truth. So the issues raised by the question of polyphony have a wide general significance.

In the first place, this aesthetic has a strong and evident ethical imperative. In effect, Bakhtin celebrates Dostoevsky for affirming the moral and existential irreducibility of the *other* – as he writes, 'to affirm someone else's "I" not as an object but as another subject – this is the principle governing Dostoevsky's worldview' (PDP 10). The significance of this imperative is evidently important, not least in the context of the repressive politics of Stalinism. Bakhtin insists that, for Dostoevsky *as an artist*, the human being cannot be finally explained, 'that there is always something that only he himself can reveal' (PDP 58). Thus Dostoevsky is not interested in 'explaining' his characters in social–historical terms, but rather in provoking them to ultimate revelations of themselves in extreme situations, which are never closed or resolved. It is important to recognize, however, that this is an aesthetic account and not a moral or ethical treatise; the point for Bakhtin in these moral considerations is that they enter into the way the novels are constructed, dictating the way, for example, Dostoevsky relates character to plot, or the way that dialogue and the characters' speech enter the novel.

This ethical imperative is central to Bakhtin's account of Dostoevsky, and to the aesthetic of polyphony more generally. Yet it should not be confused with a more familiar liberal individualism, which is as alien to Bakhtin as it is to Dostoevsky. Paradoxically, though the individual human being retains the irreducible moral status I have described, that human being's consciousness cannot be conceived as existing in isolation. Just as the individual cannot be the source of a language, for the utterance always only occurs *between* people, so the individual consciousness is equally intersubjective. This is a challenging notion; as Bakhtin cryptically put it in his notes for rewriting the Dostoevsky book, 'A single consciousness is *contradictio in adjecto* [a contradiction in terms]. Consciousness is in essence multiple' (PDP 288). Bakhtin provides some explanation for this assertion by insisting that consciousness can only realize itself, however provisionally, in dialogue with the other. We might add to this by recalling Voloshinov's conception of 'inner speech', the notion that consciousness is constituted by multiple words that carry with them the traces of a myriad other consciousness – carried there by the multiple words that are the constitutents of consciousness (see pp. 18–19). So in Bakhtin's conception, Dostoevsky's novels are inhabited, not by the many independent individuals of classical liberalism, but by characters whose truth only emerges in contact with, or anticipation of, another's truth. 'Two voices is the minimum for life, the minimum for existence' (PDP 252).

The aesthetic of polyphony has important implications also for the way that novels are constructed – implications, that is, to do with the way that part relates to whole in any novel. It is convenient to approach these questions by way of their opposite, the monologic novel from which the polyphonic novel is primarily to be distinguished. In this case, the principle by which the novel is completed, by which its various parts are integrated, is easy to recognize; it is the author's overarching consciousness, which can see through and 'place' the consciousnesses of the characters, reconcile their differences where necessary, and bring them to a conclusive resolution. None of these conditions obtain for the polyphonic novel as Bakhtin conceives it. Here the novel is understood more as a process that never achieves a resolution. It thus opens on to the future rather than seeking to explain the past. Dostoevsky's novels, in this account, exemplify a kind of writing in which, because the author denies himself the final word, no integration can be suggested or achieved in a word of wisdom above the battle. Thus Bakhtin equally rejects the dialectic as a way of conceiving the structure of the novel, for the dialectic is a way of recognizing conflict and contradiction only to resolve them ultimately. The dialectic might be appropriate to the monologic novel, providing just that ultimate and final perspective in which dialogue is abolished, but Bakhtin rejects it for Dostoevsky, and thus rejects any reading of the novels which sees them as evolutionary or progressive.

This is in many ways an attractive general account, both of the structure of Dostoevsky's novels and in its capacity as a general aesthetic. It coincides with some more familiar twentieth-century or modernist notions about the novel, which have similarly repudiated the so-called 'objective' narrative stances of many nineteenth-century novelists. Yet it is worth asking both whether it is true of Dostoevsky, and indeed whether it could possibly be true of any novelist. Moreover, it is equally important to ask whether it is desirable for it to be true: whether, that is, polyphony is as ideal as perhaps it sounds. Ambivalence on this point, futhermore, takes you to some crucial difficulties at the very heart of Bakhtin's whole notion of the dialogic. The account depends upon the insistence that no single voice, above all not that of the narrator, is afforded any priority in Dostoevsky's novels. Bakhtin thus has to make a strong distinction between Dostoevsky as an artist and as a journalist; he does not deny that outside of the novels the novelist has strong and particular views and commitments which are expressed in his letters and journalistic writings; but when these views enter the novels, they are dialogized, become one word among many possible words. Now while it is certainly true that, thanks to Bakhtin, we can see that Dostoevsky's novels go to extraordinary lengths to grant authority to the word of his characters, it is hard to agree that no effort is made to sort them into some kind of hierarchy. It would be a strange reading of *The Brothers Karamazov*, for example, that did not recognize the massive weight of authorial authority lying behind the discourses of the elder Zossima and Alyosha, or the intense unease surrounding Ivan's anguished atheism. These overarching commitments remain over and above the internal dialogization to which they are subject within the novel, and are strikingly reinforced by the structure of the book, by the narrative outcomes (however inconclusive), in short by the whole overall force of the novel. If this were *not* the case, then the book would indeed become a relativistic one, specifically disclaimed by Bakhtin.

Even if this were conceded with respect to *The Brothers Karamazov*, and indeed Dostoevsky's novels more generally, it might still be felt that other novels achieve the polyphony that Bakhtin celebrates. Perhaps novels can be placed upon a scale, with polyphony at one extreme and monologism at the other; Dostoevsky may be near the polyphonic end of the spectrum, while other novelists – Joyce, perhaps, or even Dickens – are still nearer. But in fact it is impossible to imagine a novelist who does not sort the words of his or her characters into some sort of hierarchy of significance; if they did not do so they would indeed be in danger of falling into just that relativizing indifference from which Bakhtin is so keen, rightly, to dissociate Dostoevsky. And it may be that that is a condition of their interest; the effort to negotiate your way through the multiple words of the world involves, for the novelist, both the pluralistic respect which Bakhtin finds so strikingly in Dostoevsky, and a simultaneous effort at understanding, placing in relation, even synthesis. The general problem here is analogous to one that eventually arises with Bakhtin's and Voloshinov's account of linguistic pragmatics. There comes a moment when the recognition of a fact about language – that an utterance only acquires meaning in relation to the utterance of an other – takes on the status of a moral command: all utterances ought to anticipate the word of the other. In an analogous way, Bakhtin's recognition that in Dostoevsky's novels the words of the characters are highly dialogized – that is, they are shot through with anticipations of, and rejoinders to, the word of an other – leads him to insist that the whole novel ought therefore to be dialogic, ought not to give priority to one dominant voice, attitude or idea. The whole notion of polyphony, therefore, requires careful thought both as a description of the ways novels actually work, and as an aesthetic ideal.

However, it produces a powerful typology of prose, in one of the strongest chapters in *Problems of Dostoevsky's Poetics*, entitled 'Discourse in Dostoevsky'. Bakhtin is rather given to typologies, but their value, it seems to me, lies not in the detailed application of the categories he produces so much as in recognizing the principles that underlie them. Thus, in the present instance, Bakhtin divides up novelistic prose into three broad categories:

I   Direct, unmediated discourse directed exclusively towards its referential object, as an expression of the speaker's ultimate semantic authority
II Objectified discourse (discourse of a represented person)
III Discourse with an orientation towards someone else's discourse (double-voiced discourse) (PDP 199).

Both the second and third categories are further subdivided, with an especially baroque profusion of subcategories of double-voiced discourse, it being the kind of writing which especially characterizes Dostoevsky and in which Bakhtin is especially interested. But even on the basis of this simplified version of the typology, you can see some of the characteristic advantages and difficulties of Bakhtin's thinking. For although this may appear to be a straightforward and even commonsensical division of different kinds of writing (analogous to familiar distinctions like those between direct and indirect speech), in fact it is also simultaneously an evaluatively charged set of distinctions. Thus the first broad division connects with the linguistics in equating the claim to speak directly about the referential object with a claim to authority. Similarly, the second broad division, 'objectified discourse', speaks a strong aesthetic and ideological aversion on Bakhtin's part, for into this category come all those kinds of writing which acknowledge social and historical diversity only to 'place' it either in socially typifying or alternatively individualizing ways, without any authentic dialogic engagement. For as he asserts earlier in the chapter, the mere presence of linguistic diversity does not make for a polyphonic novel; 'what matters is the *dialogic angle* at which these styles and dialects are juxtaposed or counterposed in the work' (PDP 182).

But it is the third division that shows both Bakhtin's strong preference and his analytical imaginativeness and ingenuity. Into this division come a whole variety of different categories, in all of which two or more voices can be heard – the voice of the narrator and the voice of the character, sometimes also the voice of a third interlocutor. They appear in many different mutual relations – of stylization, parody, hidden polemic, and so on. I am doubtful whether some of Bakhtin's distinctions can be sustained in any very hard and fast way, but the point is not to give the reader or critic some elaborate set of pigeon-holes into which stretches of novels can be slotted, but to provide some vocabulary for understanding the diverse ways in which the immersion of novelistic prose in a multiplicity of voices can be understood. Thus Bakhtin will make particular use of his subcategory 'hidden internal polemic' in discussing those sections of Dostoevsky's novels in which the speaker is engaged in an implicit argument with some external figure. It is for just these situations that Bakhtin develops such concepts as the word 'with a sideward glance' or with a 'loophole'; categories which indicate the presence of an interlocutor in even the most private-seeming discourse. The value of the analyses which Bakhtin's notion of novelistic discourse provides can be judged from the extract from *Problems of Dostoevsky's Poetics*, reproduced in Part II, in which Bakhtin analyses discourse in Dostoevsky's short novels.

It is in this area of 'double-voiced discourse' that some of the most interesting questions provoked by Bakhtinian criticism arise, questions which lead us back to the whole general aesthetic of polyphony and thus connect the most minute local analysis of prose to the most fundamental aesthetic issues. In particular, these matters turn on the extent to which the different varieties of double-voiced discourse suggest a narrative authority beyond that of the character. In some cases they evidently do so; most parody, and much irony, allows the reader to assume a position of secure knowledge beyond the word of the character whose speech is parodied or ironised. Thus parody and some kinds of irony can in fact be the local forms of discourse in which monologism is secured. By contrast, other forms of double-voiced discourse provoke a much more radical insecurity in the reader, when one can certainly recognize that the character's word is dialogized and enjoys no ultimate authority, but one cannot locate the angle from which the dialogization is coming. In this situation, no position of secure knowledge can be inferred, and no secure resting place can be found from which the word, the attitude or the idea can be judged. These are among the characteristic effects of modernist writing, but Bakhtin's achievement is to have located them not in some idealist notion of 'textuality' (as in some versions of post-structuralism) but in the specific relations that govern author, character and interlocutor.

II

It might be still felt, however, that these relations are insufficiently socially marked in the Dostoevsky book, and certainly from the perspective of the writings, of the 1930s and early 1940s – especially 'Discourse in the novel' – this would seem to be the case. In turning to these writings from *Problems of Dostoevsky's Poetics* one can notice a similar shift to the one we observed in the shift from Voloshinov's linguistics in *Marxism and the Philosophy of Language* to Bakhtin's account of language in 'Discourse in the novel'. In both cases there is a transition from a more abstract conception of the sociality of discourse, where the presence of the social is sufficiently indicated by the intersubjectivity of language, to a more substantively socio-historical account, where the speakers of the word, either in life or in art, are located as socially marked in class, generational, professional and regional terms. In the case of the poetics of the novel this is partly a result of turning attention away from Dostoevsky, who of the great nineteenth-century Russian novelists is the one who is perhaps least interested in locating his characters in social and historical terms, as Bakhtin is at some pains to insist. But this change of attention is itself symptomatic of a more general shift, produced, it may be, out of the underground engagement ('hidden polemic') with Marxism that marks Bakhtin's whole career.

On the other hand, these essays, now mostly gathered, in English, in *The Dialogic Imagination,* do not themselves add up to any coherent system, and indeed both provide multiple accounts of the history of the novel and point to different aesthetic emphases in doing so. I wish to discuss four main areas in connection with these essays: the large categorical distinction which Bakhtin draws between the novel and poetry; the various accounts he gives of the predecessors of the modern novel in the ancient world and the Renaissance; the notion of the 'chronotope'; and the critical use that he makes of the notion of 'heteroglossia'.

One of the most surprising and controversial distinctions that Bakhtin draws is between the novel and poetry, both epic poetry in the essay 'Epic and novel', and lyric poetry more intermittently elsewhere. For this too is an evaluatively charged distinction, in which the formally attractive features of the novel – its stylistic and linguistic variety, its openness to the world-in-process of the present – are juxtaposed to the monologic stylistic elevation and fixation on the past of epic poetry. In this account, the novel is not so much a genre as an anti-genre, which defines itself by its incessant polemics with the fixed genres that seek to fix and mono-logize the word. The principal generic opponent in this ceaseless struggle is the epic, so we have yet another axis of distinction, juxtaposing the epic on one side – elevated, stylistically fixed, incapable of laughter – against the novel on the other – low, stylistically mobile and diverse, serio-comic. This axis of distinction roughly aligns with that between the monoglossic and the heteroglossic, intelligible in terms of the historical and social forces that both unite and divide a language.

The difficulty with this line of argument is apparent; crudely put, if you are impressed by Bakhtin's account of the novel, it becomes impossible to enjoy epic poetry also. This is a real difficulty, since it makes manifest the profound connection in Bakhtin's aesthetic between artisitic and evaluative questions, so that any merely eclectic reply – many people surely do enjoy both epic poetry and the novel – remains unsatisfactory. But actually, not many people do enjoy both the novel and epic poetry, in the sense that the novel has certainly displaced the epic as the characteristic modern genre. So while the difficulty remains for those of us who continue to enjoy Homer or Milton, it has effectively been solved historically in favour of the novel. This 'solution', moreover, is exactly part of Bakhtin's point; the strong aspect of an essay like 'Epic and novel' is precisely its substantive historical character, locating the history of genres in the history of nations just as the history of language needs to be. And indeed, this is the same history, for the epic is one of those forces which is aligned with the centripetal forces of linguistic and national authority, associated as it has always been with celebrating an heroic national past, from the *Iliad* and the *Aeneid* through *The Song of Roland* even to a striking contemporary version of the epic in Derek Walcott's *Omeros*. And the novel's generic hostility to the elevation of the epic – canonical case, *Don Quixote* – is not some abstract generic principle of subversion, but itself springs from active social forces which constantly pull the language away from that national centre and seek to overturn particular authorities.

Bakhtin makes a further distinction between the novel and lyric poetry on yet another axis. Lyric poetry is above all the genre, for Bakhtin, of direct subjective expression, in contrast to the always mediated or dialogized voices of the novel. This is nearer to an unmarked generic contrast than the distinction between the novel and epic, though there is an undoubted suspicion on Bakhtin's part of the lyric, insofar as it assumes the possibility of direct speech. Thus he writes in 'Discourse in the novel': 'All direct meanings and direct expressions are false, and this is especially true of emotional meanings and expressions' (DI 401). This is an unsettling position to take, seeing authenticity not in the apparent directness of lyric but in the socially located but therefore necessary obliqueness of the novel. But in general Bakhtin does not see the novelistic as preying upon the lyric as it does upon epic; rather, in some generic predecessors of the novel, like Menippean satire, prose can assimilate the lyric to make it one voice among others. On the other hand, lyric is not immune to the historic dominance of the novel as a genre. Thus many lyric poets have themselves been novelized; Bakhtin's best example here is the Byron of *Don Juan*, a poem that displays all the characteristics of the novel as it is described at least in 'Epic and novel'.

In general, then, though there remain some difficulties with the prescriptive consequences of these distinctions, the large generic contrasts drawn by Bakhtin point to a substantive history outside of writing to which writing nevertheless contributes, and which manifests itself in part in language. Immediately related to these generic distinctions is Bakhtin's effort, in a number of places, to trace the generic origins and distinctiveness of the novel itself. Unlike many 'historians of the novel',

Bakhtin does not confine his attention to the modern period, but sees the generic history of the novel stretching back into antiquity – indeed, back into untraceable folkloric roots. His notion of generic history and persistence is in fact an uncompromising one, being what one could more properly call epochal rather than historical. That is, he is not interested, in this context, in the particularities of individual schools, trends or writers, but rather in the transmission of those apparently stable features of genres which persist across striking historical differences. Thus he writes in the book on Dostoevsky that 'We emphasize again that we are not interested in the influence of separate individual authors, individual works, individual themes, ideas, images – what interests us is precisely the influence of the *generic tradition itself* which was transmitted through the particular authors' (PDP 159). This is a surprising statement from someone who, in his linguistics, had gone to such pains to attack the emphasis on *langue* at the expense of *parole* – and this is a comparison which Bakhtin makes himself. Yet one's surprise may be somewhat mitigated if it is realized again that the underlying continuity of genre – its *langue*, if you will – is not constituted in the abstract but depends upon the material persistence of forms of social life which enable it; above all, in a stress that becomes increasingly apparent in Bakhtin's writings in the 1930s, in the ongoing activities of carnival, which enjoy a real continuity between the ancient world and the Renaissance. So Bakhtin relates a prehistory of the novel in the ancient world which sees generic predecessors not only in the prose Greek romances and such works as Apuleius' *The Golden Ass*, but also in the Menippean satire, which in his account is a protean form which directly evinces the influence of carnival. Similarly in the Renaissance, some writing partakes directly in the carnival life that surrounds it, sufficiently so to transmit that generic inheritance at a second remove to succeeding novelists even when the popular life which at first sustained it had itself mostly disappeared.

However, this is a story that Bakhtin tells in many different ways. In 'Epic and novel', as we have seen, the stress falls upon the generic distinction of the novel from the epic. In 'From the prehistory of novelistic discourse' it falls upon the massive if little known 'parodic–travestying' forms that accompany the serious genres throughout antiquity and into the Renaissance, even going so far as to suggest that the major European literary languages were created out of the parodic dissolution of official language and culture in the Renaissance. In *Problems of Dostoevsky's Poetics* – that is, the rewritten version, not the first 1929 edition – we get the strongest statement of the association of historic carnival, and carnivalized forms of writing, with the growth of the novel. This may seem a surprising context, for if there is one central strand of argument in the book on Dostoevsky that seems counter-intuitive it is the association of the author of *Crime and Punishment* or *The Brothers Karamozov* with the carnivalesque. In 'Discourse in the novel' Bakhtin draws a broad distinction between two lines of development, arbitrarily designated the First and Second Lines. In this account, the First Line of development, though it is aware of heteroglossia as a background, broadly excludes it from its own stylistic organization, or at least seeks to organize it hierarchically. By contrast, the Second Stylistic Line revels in heteroglossia, embodying its diversity in diverse characters. In short, in this account Bakhtin tends to draw a line within the history of the novel which elsewhere appears as a generic contrast to the novel as a whole. Finally, in 'Forms of time and of the chronotope in the novel', he gives yet another account of this history using a quite different set of categories.

Bakhtin, as we have already seen, is profuse in coining new terms, but 'chronotope' is actually not one of his coinages; he took the term from a lecture he heard from the biologist A. A. Ukhtomsky in 1925. This is indicative of the wide intellectual interests shared by Bakhtin and the members of his circle in the 1920s – they were keen that their philosophy and their aesthetics should be cognate with contemporary developments in science like relativity theory. But the use Bakhtin makes of the term is distinctive: he makes it serve as the basis for a wide-ranging history of the novel, which he connects with the very broadest changes in the social and material history of Europe; yet, unlike most of his other writings of this period, the connection is not primarily made through the forms of language.

'Chronotope' (literally, 'time-space') is a mobile term which alludes to the way time and space are together conceived and represented. This has been done in distinct and characteristic ways in different kinds of writing, permitting different characteristic narratives and relying upon some characteristic motifs. Bakhtin provides a series of accounts of different novels and related forms, starting again with the Greek romances, seeking to show how they are organized around particular interrelated conceptions of time and space. Thus in his account of the 'adventure time' – the manner of conceiving the time in which the adventures happen – of the Greek romance, time is empty, outside biographical, social or natural significance; it is a hiatus in which adventures occur.

Space is similarly abstract. Characteristically in these stories the hero does not develop, and his fully-formed person is simply subjected to a series of ordeals which demonstrate his fidelity, courage, and so on. Thus the motif of the trial is a marked feature of these romances. Or moving on to the 'novels' of Apuleius and Petronius, which Bakhtin characterizes as 'the adventure novel of everyday life' (DI III), he can talk of the chronotope of the road, in which the course of an individual's life is fused with his actual spatial course or road. In Apuleius' *The Golden Ass*, the hero is transformed into an ass, has many adventures, then is turned back into human shape before being purified. Thus there are indeed remnants of the 'adventure-time' of the earlier romances, but they are subsumed under the higher logic of the metamorphosis, which speaks to real crises in the hero's life and effects a real transformation. The events upon the road are thus suffused with a lasting significance for the hero. Bakhtin thus provides a way of talking about narrative which links the metaphoric significance of the 'path of life' with the actual narrative progression of the hero of such a novel, suggesting also the folkloric roots of this protean chronotope, which has of course persisted well beyond its paradigmatic expression in *The Golden Ass*.

This is an interesting and suggestive way of analysing narratives, but the interest of 'Forms of time and of the chronotope in the novel' does not end here. Accompanying Bakhtin's account of differing chronotopes in the history of the novel – which culminates in an extended account of the chronotope of Rabelais, but with many suggestions for more modern novels – is the notion that transformations in the chronotope, or in people's basic conceptions of time and space, are to be explained by historic transformations in their mode of life. Bakhtin devotes a substantial section of the essay to the Rabelaisian chronotope, which he sees as located in folkloric conceptions of time. This conception of time – fundamentally generative, creating and dissolving in the manner of the productive forces of nature itself – springs from what Bakhtin describes as the 'pre-class, agricultural stage in the development of human society' (DI 206). Rabelais rediscovers this chronotope in response to the dissolution of medieval society, and it serves as the basis for his extraordinary grotesque images; but fragments of this chronotope, which springs from the earliest reaches of human social life as it is present to us in writing, are present in reduced and truncated forms throughout the history of the novel subsequent to Rabelais. The inescapable context of these transformations is the history of class society.

So we have here yet another 'history of the novel', in which we can recognize the same main characters, from Apuleius to Rabelais, who figure in Bakhtin's other histories, but in this story they have substantially different roles. Now they become the bearers of metaphorically realized conceptions of time and space, conceptions formed in historically changing modes of life, but which are transmitted by writing and thus persist beyond their originating mode of life. This general account certainly connects with other aspects of Bakhtin's thinking, in particular his ideas on generic persistence, but 'Forms of time and of the chronotope in the novel' makes a distinctive emphasis in the overall run of the writings of the Bakhtin circle, though chronotopic analysis figures strongly in the remaining fragments of the book on the *bildungsroman* or novel of education.

By contrast, the last in this group of writings from the 1930s and early 1940s, 'Discourse in the novel', displays the fullest and richest connections between Bakhtin's (and Voloshinov's) linguistics and his aesthetics of the novel. This essay, like the chronotope one, is not really an essay at all, but is the length of a short book, and it too works in suggestive and multiple ways. It is in this account that the notion of 'heteroglossia' receives its most extended definition, and comes to play a key role in the aesthetics of the novel. In short, the novel emerges as the form which best exploits the heteroglossic tendencies of language, so that the novelistic and the heteroglossic become in effect synonymous. Bakhtin provides a series of analyses of particular passages from novels, showing how the types of double-voiced discourse that they display emerge from the heteroglossic variety of their moments of origin. But, like the discourse typology to be found in the Dostoevsky book, this is far more than a neutral set of categories which enable you to do stylistics under another guise. Rather, Bakhtin is celebrating the novel insofar as it aligns itself with the centrifugal forces of language and becomes a mobile, linguistically various, anti-dogmatic, relativizing and dialogistic form.

As we have seen, one way of distinguishing the 'polyphonic' novel from the way the novel emerges from the pages of 'Discourse in the novel' is to recognize that the status of the characters' word alters; it is emphatically a social word in the later essay. The character becomes the bearer of a language, one of the many languages whose struggle and competition make up what we know as a national language. So in a novel characters and their language inevitably enter the animated struggle that marks the competition between languages in any heteroglossia. At times this conception is taken to an extreme; the point of characterization seems only to become its capacity to carry a language into the novel. Thus Bakhtin writes:

> If the subject making the novel specifically a novel is defined as a speaking person and his discourse, striving for social significance and a wider general application as one distinctive language in a heteroglot world – then the central problem for a stylistics of the novel may be formulated as the problem of *artistically representing language, the problem of representing the image of a language.* (DI 336)

This starts from familiar ground; the novel is a space in which characters ('speaking persons') try to give their discourse greater weight in relation to the other discourses that make up a heteroglossia. But it becomes almost paradoxical in suggesting that characters are quite subordinate to the language that they speak, so that a stylistics of the novel must concern itself primarily with the mutual interactions of different languages. The novel emerges from this emphasis not so much as the humanistic polyphony of *Problems of Dostoevsky's Poetics*, as a repetition in miniature of the very heteroglossia on which it draws, where the motivation for characterization is the representation of a language. In this conception, a language is not symptomatic of a person, but a person is a bearer of a language, with the specific set of social and ideological valuations that it entails.

This general description of the novel has its normative features, so that though Bakhtin sees the novel as exploiting heteroglossic variety, he has to acknowledge, in his notion of the two Lines of Development, that only certain novels can be said to conform fully to this aesthetic ideal. This conception of the novel also pitches Bakhtin into some general aesthetic problems, to do with questions of authorship and architectonics, and again he resolves them with a different emphasis from that which marks the Dostoevsky book. Because the interest here is above all in language, Bakhtin makes a distinction between the narrator's language and the author's intention. It is the narrator's language which enters into the body of the novel, and is set into active competition with the languages of the characters. But behind this, Bakhtin is insistent that the reader should sense an author's intention distinct from that of the narrator. Yet this is an insistence that can be inflected in different ways. On the one hand it can point to an account of the 'author', the 'narrator' and 'intention' similar to that of Wayne Booth, who similarly sought to distinguish between narrator and what he called the 'implied author' as a way of distinguishing different levels of narrative authority in novels.[1] On the other hand, Bakhtin can inflect his account to provide, not a *more* secure way of talking about narrative authority but a *less* secure way, or at least a way that revels in the freedom that comes with the donning of a mask:

> All forms involving a narrator or a posited author signify to one degree or another by their presence the author's freedom from a unitary and single language, a freedom connected with the relativity of literary and language systems; such forms open up the possibility of never having to define oneself in language, the possibility of translating one's own intentions from one linguisitc system to another, of fusing 'the language of truth' with 'the language of the everyday', of saying 'I am me' in someone else's language, and in my own language, 'I am other'. (DI 315)

We saw earlier, in the opposition of the novel to lyric poetry, Bakhtin's distrust of direct expression; here, we have a powerful account of the obverse of that distrust – a delight in the artistic possibilities produced by the mobile linguistic variety of the novel. While not disowning the realm of intention – Bakhtin is never an anti-intentionalist thinker – this position does not locate ultimate artistic truth in intention; indeed, it does not locate *ultimate* artistic truth anywhere, for there is no last word to be spoken. Rather, the provisional truth that does emerge from the novel is inextricably fused with the local and particular evaluations implied in 'the language of the everyday', inextricably grounded, that is to say, in historical particularity. But unlike other historicizing accounts of the novel which restrict it by tying it down with historical explanations, in Bakhtin's account the necessary entry into a historically particular language is the condition of the novel's, and indeed our own, freedom – for we can only ever take on meaning in dialogue with other equally grounded particularities (i.e. people). It is *because* the word of the author has to pass through the word of another, in Bakhtin's conception of the novel, that the novel grants you freedom.

Since, in this conception, the novel is the form that exploits heteroglossia most fully, Bakhtin can take the opportunity for yet another set of generic distinctions between the novel and other forms of writing. Here the distinction to be drawn is between artistic and extra-artistic prose such as everyday, rhetorical or scholarly writing. It is not that such forms are not dialogized, for they do indeed respond to what has already been said and anticipate rejoinders, as they have to take their part in the multiple and conflictual to and fro of language. But they are externally dialogized, they necessarily take their part in the life of a language as completed words within themselves. The novel, by contrast, is so to speak dialogized to the second degree, the dialogization entering internally into the novel's own discourse and acting from within. As opposed to the inert and given dialogization of the narrowly poetic genres, the novel activates the always already dialogized word and makes it an element of its own artistic life.

In one especially interesting section of 'Discourse in the novel' Bakhtin comes at these questions from another perspective, from that of the individual's own 'ideological becoming', or to put it in a more familiar vocabulary, from the perspective of the growth of the individual's belief-system. He draws a distinction between *authoritative discourse* and *internally persuasive discourse*. Authoritative discourse is that which may not be challenged, and so has the status of taboo; it seeks to withdraw beyond dialogue, to surround itself with an uncrossable exclusion zone. Bakhtin's persistent example is religious dogma, but acknowledged scientific truth or an authoritative political dogma may equally be examples of authoritative discourse. Such discourse may only enter consciousness whole and entire, by contrast with internally persuasive discourse, which is in a constant state of renegotiation, flux and extension. The internally persuasive word starts out as the word of another, in competition with other words that have similarly been internalized; the process of ideological becoming is one in which these different words are more and more thoroughly assimilated, brought into contact each with the other, made more thoroughly one's own though never becoming wholly so and thus always remaining in some sense double-voiced.

This is very interesting as an account of the process of individual growth and socialization, quite apart from its implications for aesthetics. Indeed, it is a reformulation of some of Voloshinov's notions from *Freudianism: A Marxist Critique*. But its interest in this context is that Bakhtin relates the complex process of the assimilation and negotiation of internally persuasive discourse to the construction of novels, for with only a slight change of emphasis the processes by which such discourse is handled become potentially artistic categories. In experimenting with the possibilities of a discourse we may fuse its words with the image of a person; we set one word against another; we may rebel against a discourse; in all these cases some of the characteristic moves of novelistic creation are already present in embryo. So we see here Bakhtin approaching the same nexus of questions from quite a different angle. Elsewhere in the essay he is concerned with heteroglossia and the capacity of the novel to assimilate it, and with the various formal characteristics that mark the novel's assimilation of the heteroglot variety and competition of language. Here, he considers the individual's assimilation of this variety, and how the complex negotiation and creative speculation that mark the internalization of the word can lead, with small changes of orientation, to the production of novels.

III

Problems of Dostoevsky's Poetics, and the essays now gathered together in *The Dialogic Imagination*, together represent a rich and varied account of the novel, and its location in the historically varied to and fro of language. But, as we have seen, this variety is itself a problem, for the various accounts, though they evidently share the same set of concerns, do not cohere in any systematic way. Indeed, the problem is more acute than this, for some of the discrepancies amount to contradictions, so much so that one sympathetic expositor of Bakhtin's work, Tzvetan Todorov, considers the general account of the novel to be simply incoherent. The general problem is this: the account provided of the novel is at once a substantive historical one, which locates the novel in particular linguistic and discursive situations, and a more abstract, ahistorical account, which sees the novelistic as a universal relativizing principle which battens upon and subverts all discursive authority. The oscillation between these two poles produces the typical phenomenon that 'novelness' can at times seem to be a characteristic of all novels, and at other times seem to distinguish some novels from others. Another way of putting this problem is to say that there is an implicit essentialism in Bakhtin's notion of the novel, whereby the extraordinary range and variety of novels is in danger of being reduced to one particular version.

The problem is not an easy one to resolve, and indeed is the kind of difficulty that besets any category that makes at once a general claim of a relativizing kind and seeks to retain a historical dimension. Similar difficulties beset the terms 'modernist' or 'writerly' when opposed to their polar opposites 'realist' or 'readerly' in certain kinds of post-structuralist critical discourse. In both cases the validated critical term only takes on its meaning when positively juxtaposed to its opposite – 'writerly' is valued *because* it unsettles the certainties of 'readerly' writing, 'modernist' is good *because* it upsets the orderly discursive hierarchy of 'realism'. But these terms always run into difficulties when they lose their specific historical location and are projected across the range of literary history. 'Modernist' is the most flagrant example, critics having found 'modernist' characteristics in writing long before the modern period. Similarly with the 'novel' for Bakhtin. It too is a notion that preys upon various discourses of authority, be they called epic, monologism, or the various serious genres that dominate at different periods of history. Yet the novel too has a substantive historical location, not perhaps as specific as 'modernism' yet sufficiently so to justify a phrase like the progressive 'novelization' of modern society in Europe, so that we can recognize, for example, that the Europe of the late nineteenth century grants much greater authority to the popular novelized word than the the Europe of the late seventeenth century. Is it possible to make sense of this oscillation, or are we faced with an unresolvable instability, caused by the very nature of the term, always battening on and subverting the word of authority and therefore always parasitic on it? Is no secure resting ground for the novel ever, in principle, to be found?

I do not think the difficulties are resolved if the discrepancies and contradictions in Bakhtin's various accounts are reconciled by stressing the more abstract or ahistorical version of them. This is the solution of Holquist and Clark in the biography, where they write that 'Bakhtin assigns the term "novel" to whatever form of expression within a given literary system reveals the limits of that system as inadequate' (p. 276). In one sense this is an elegant resolution of the problem, but it misrepresents Bakhtin in that only some of his more occasional and extreme statements approach this degree of abstraction, and the conceptual simplification and reduction it manages is achieved only at the cost of abstracting novels out of their various particular histories and making them all symptoms of one overarching ahistorical principle. It is to make Menippean satire, for example, as much an example of novelness as the nineteenth-century novel, though indeed perhaps Dostoevsky would remain a novelist on this version and Tolstoy would not. Some other, less essentialist resolution is required that respects historical, and indeed generic, specificities more closely.

One way forward here is to draw a distinction between the historical and the epochal. An historical account is one that indeed locates the novel in a set of historically specific circumstances, but which are immediately contemporary to it. An epochal account, by contrast, locates the novel in the widest reaches of time, on a time-scale which stretches way beyond its here and now. Bakhtin himself draws a similar distinction between what he calls 'great time' and 'small time'. If the latter is 'the present day, the recent past, and the forseeable future', the former, 'great time', is the 'infinite and unfinalized dialogue in which no meaning dies' (SG 169). He operates at both levels of explanation. His accounts are undoubtedly historical in that they locate the novel in particular dispositions of language, both everyday and literary language. The fullest and profoundest of such historical acts of location is the book on Rabelais, the topic of our next chapter, but the Bakhtin of 'Discourse in the novel' is historical in this sense also, in that the account he gives of individual novels such as *Little Dorrit* locates them in historically specific heteroglossic situations. (This account appears in extract 4 of Part II.) Yet these accounts draw upon epochal forces also. We have seen how, in describing the generic predecessors of the novel, Bakhtin is ready to allude to the centuries-long processes which prepare for its advent; indeed how, in his account of the Rabelaisian chronotope, he can find its origins in pre-class agricultural society. If genres do indeed have such an epochal existence, it is fair to ask what active social forces sustain them, or, to put the question in more Bakhtinian terms, to ask who speaks the generic word? In particular, if the novel is a genre which destroys genre, if it is a principle which saps the authority of all literary systems – as indeed it is at one pole of Bakhtin's thinking – then what epochal forces sustain that principle?

One strong answer to this question is 'carnival', by which would be meant not only the specific carnival festivities of early modern Europe, but the active festive life that marks the ancient world and of which early modern carnival is indeed a continuation. So, at this broad or epochal level of generality, there is a profound link between two disparate-seeming areas of Bakhtin's thought, between his ideas on language and the novel on one hand, and carnival on the other. At this relatively abstract but not ahistorical level, the novel can be thought of as the form which most exploits the heteroglossic potential that is present in all languages that come from all but the most isolated and homogenous societies. But the specific social and institutional form which enables and anticipates the activity of the novel is the epochal force of carnival. However, this is indeed an epochal answer, and the different emphases, in the different histories of the novel suggested by Bakhtin, remain. In addition, it is an answer directed to the generic origins of the novel, which does no more than provide a context for the substantive historical and discursive locations that characterize so much of his writing about particular writers and particular books.

As for this more substantively historical way of conceiving of the novel, this can in turn be inflected in different ways. In the book on Rabelais, as we shall see, Bakhtin locates the writing in a very wide-ranging survey of the particular festive forms of Rabelais' France; he makes a similar move in 'Forms of time and of the chronotope in the novel', in tracing the chronotope that underlies much of Rabelais' grotesque imagery to a very ancient but specific mode of life. In other words, one way of understanding the particularities of Rabelais' writing is to see it as drawing on and transforming the social forms that surround it, and then transmitting them forward even when those forms themselves have disappeared. Elsewhere, and especially in 'Discourse in the novel', Bakhtin locates the novel rather differently, though because this book-length essay does not have the thoroughness or completeness of the book on Rabelais, it has more the status of providing methodological suggestions than completed analyses. But the account of heteroglossia, and the particular analyses he does provide of for example *Little Dorrit*, are indeed very suggestive of the way the novel is located in the discursive to and fro of a particular society at a particular time. In this perspective, the novel is an active intervention in that struggle, seeking to re-accent the other's word, to parody, subvert, overcome, accede to, or argue with that other word in multiple, different, but traceable ways.

Both these accounts, then, in locating the novel historically, provide links outwards from the text to the linguistic, literary and social life that surrounds it. They are profoundly anti-formalist therefore, if by formalist is meant an attempt to understand the character and evolution of literature by internal literary criteria alone. This is not more than you might expect from a writer who even if he did not write *The Formal Method in Literary Scholarship*, was certainly very close to its author. But to say that these accounts are anti-formalist does not mean that they are indifferent to form. On the contrary, the crucial mediating category for Bakhtin is genre, which is precisely the category which enables him to cross between the epochal origins of the novel and its specific historical manifestations. But if Bakhtin is very alert to form in this broad generic sense, he is equally alert to form at the most minute local level of writing also, providing analyses of the discursive particularities of novels based upon more than one typology of prose. If the emphases of *Rabelais and*

His World and 'Discourse in the novel' are outwards from the text to the discursive and social forms that surround it, then this kind of local analysis tends to be upon the 'internal dialogization' of writing, a characteristic that Bakhtin sometimes claims to be distinctive of artistic prose. Though it need not be confined to 'internal' textual analysis, since the other word anticipated in the character's word or to which that word is a rejoinder need not come from within the novel, this kind of local textual analysis can certainly lend itself to a more internal or intrinsic kind of criticism.

Well, what are we to make of this wide-ranging and diverse critical engagement with the novel? There is certainly no gainsaying its ambition, for in one aspect it locates the history of the novel in no less than the broadest sweep of the social and cultural history of Europe from the ancient world through to the twentieth century, and does so in a way that disposes the novel in significant relation to the histories of the major European languages and to other forms of writing. This ambition is by no means the least attractive feature of Bakhtin's writing, even if it does encourage some rather heady generalizations about the history of Europe. But as we have seen, alongside the epochal dimension is a very much more historically specific account of the location of novelistic writing, and this too has some distinctive and attractive features.

Above all, Bakhtin's historicism has two great advantages. First, it manages to be socially and historically specific without being reductive. Unlike some other historicizing accounts of literature, especially simplified Marxist ones, Bakhtin's does not see the novel in a passive, 'reflecting' relation to the history that surrounds and produces it. On the contrary, as we have seen, the novel is conceived as an active intervention in the heteroglossia in which it lives and moves. But equally, Bakhtin has not abandoned altogether the notion of representation; the novel has not been cut loose from its moorings in history as more formalist stresses on the *activity* of language and literature tend to do. A useful contrast here is with the great Marxist critic and philosopher Georg Lukacs, whose work Bakhtin almost certainly knew. In Lukacs' anxiety to demonstrate the profound epistemological worth of novels such as those of Balzac – to prove, that is, that these novels provided *knowledge* of the history of post-Revolutionary France – he eventually came to value them only in the dimension of knowledge, and failed to show how they differed generically from history books in their capacity as novels. And Bakhtin avoids Lukacs' reductiveness in another, more humanistic way also. For one of Lukacs' ways of insisting upon the historical nature of novels is to insist upon the socio-historical typicality of the characters who inhabit them. Bakhtin does not deny this typicality, but maintains, in a key passage in 'Epic and novel', that the truth of a character cannot be exhausted by such socio-historical location – there is always some surplus, some element of their humanity which is not to be finally explained and which thus permits their orientation towards the future:

> An individual cannot be completely incarnated into the flesh of existing sociohistorical categories. There is no mere form that would be able to incarnate once and forever all of his human possibilities and needs, no form in which he could exhaust himself down to the last word, like the tragic or epic hero; no form that he could fill to the very brim, and yet at the same time not splash over the brim. (DI 37)

This is not to deny the validity of socio-historical explanation of character, only to deny its exhaustiveness. And if you find its humanism unappealing, it should be possible to give it a more materialist slant by accounting for that human 'surplus' which splashes over the categorical brim by recognizing the multiplicity of social determinations which make the individual a complex meeting-place of social forces. Once again we meet that distinctive Bakhtinian double emphasis: both the ethical stress on the irreducibility of the individual and the recognition of the complex social determinations that make the individual unique.

The second main advantage of Bakhtin's historicism is that it does not seal the novel into its moment of origin, always a danger in historicizing accounts of literature. For historical distance, in this account, may be seen as only a more extreme form of the distance that always divides a speaker from an interlocutor in any dialogue. No two interlocutors ever coincide precisely; the act of understanding always involves the effort to understand the other's word, to re-accent that other word, to assimilate it 'into a new conceptual system, that of the one striving to understand' ('Discourse in the novel', DI 282). And this is the condition of the historical life of the literature of the past; as Bakhtin writes in 'Discourse in the novel', 'Every age re-accentuates in its own way the works of its most immediate past. The historical life of classic works is in fact the uninterrupted process of their social and idological re-accentuation' (DI 421). The condition of this 're-accentuation' is not that the writing should be prised loose from its historical moorings but that it should speak them most thoroughly.

As I have insisted throughout this chapter, Bakhtin offers no mere scholarly account of the novel but an actively engaged aesthetic. It is an aesthetic that is attractive in its anti-authoritarianism and its pluralism, seeing the novel as the form which most persistently overturns the claim to speak with the voice of authority and to say the final word. Bakhtin's anti-authoritarianism gets its fullest expression in the work on Rabelais and carnival, which we have constantly been anticipating in this chapter and which provides the central topic of the next.

3
Bakhtin's carnival

Bakhtin's book on Rabelais and carnival, translated into English in 1968 as *Rabelais and His World*, provides some of his most exciting and controversial writing. It continues to be controversial now – one of Bakhtin's first translators and influential promoters in the American academy, Caryl Emerson, has written that 'the weakest, least consistent, and most dangerous category in Bakhtin's arsenal is the concept of "carnival"'.[1] And it was certainly controversial in a Russian academy intimidated by Stalinism, so much so that though the work on the thesis on which the book is based was completed in 1940, it was not examined until 1947, no degree was awarded until 1951 (and that after some controversy), and it was not published as a book until 1965.

The book marks Bakhtin's most extensive attempt to locate the work of a particular writer in the popular cultural forms that surround him, above all those of carnival. This comes to mean a great deal more than the few weeks of festivity that precede Lent in the festive calendar of early modern Europe. Bakhtin acknowledges this extension by talking of the 'carnivalesque' to refer to the varied popular–festive life of the Middle Ages and the Renaissance (RW 217–8). But it is possible to go further than this, and talk of carnivalized writing, that is, writing which has taken the carnival spirit into itself and thus reproduces, within its own structures and by its own practice, the characteristic inversions, parodies and discrownings of carnival proper. We begin this chapter with an account of the argument of the book, before assessing it and its possible uses outsides of the immediate question of its relevance to Rabelais.

I

For the first thing that strikes any reader of *Rabelais and His World* is that the book's range extends well beyond its ostensible immediate topic. It is not because of what it has to say on Rabelais, interesting though that is, that the book has been translated into so many more languages than any other book of Rabelais criticism. Indeed, the book's topic extends even beyond the popular–festive life of early modern Europe upon which, Bakhtin shows, Rabelais draws so copiously; it provides a powerfully charged account of the transition to modernity in the culture of the Continent. In brief, the historical institution of carnival and its related popular–festive forms become the key for unlocking a crucial theme of European cultural, social and personal history from the Middle Ages onwards. In this view, the Renaissance sees the flowering of a gay, affirmative, and militantly anti-authoritarian attitude to life, founded upon a joyful acceptance of the materiality of the body – though Bakhtin does not of course assert that this is the only attitude to life to be found at that time. Subsequent European history witnesses the fragmentation of that whole attitude, indeed its suppression and dispersal, under the baleful influences of rationalism and modernity from the seventeenth century onwards.

This general history is based upon a reading of Rabelais' great sixteenth-century novel, which traces its massive reliance on popular–festive forms. In this account, *Gargantua*, *Pantagruel* and the other two books of the novel (1532–51) emerge as the high point in a centuries-long process which has prepared the carnival imagery on which Rabelais draws, and which he can mobilize against the official culture of the Middle Ages. The subsequent difficulties of the literary tradition in knowing how to deal with Rabelais – a topic which forms an important element of Bakhtin's book – suggest powerfully the evanescence of that Renaissance moment. For subsequent writers have failed to see the gay and affirmative aspect of Rabelais' insistence upon the materiality of the body, and in their various failures have borne implicit testimony to the fragmentations and suppressions which have fallen upon European high culture since the Renaissance.

This is to take up the book in some of its widest implications for cultural and social history, and it should perhaps be said that these implications are not made explicit in any sustained and systematic way. Nevertheless, the book undoubtedly articulates an aesthetic which celebrates the anarchic, body-based and grotesque elements of popular culture, and seeks to mobilise them against the humourless seriousness of official culture. Rabelais is Bakhtin's supreme example of this aesthetic, but he often mentions, alongside him, his only slightly later contemporaries Cervantes and Shakespeare. Bakhtin makes the transition from popular–festive life to the writing of Rabelais via some interesting key notions in his book, which are at once aesthetic notions – that is, they can be used to describe aspects of writing – but which are also rooted in the tumultuous institution of the carnival. The most important of these linking categories is the notion of *grotesque realism*, a luminous conception which alludes to those aspects of Rabelais' writing (but not only his) which emphasize the material and the bodily. Rabelais is famous, after all, as the writer who celebrates the body which eats, digests, copulates, and defecates, but who does so in a wild, exaggerated and groteseque way. But this grotesque realism is not Rabelais' invention; it is rather to be understood as the literary expression of a central attitude in popular culture, expressed most evidently in the life of carnival with its feasting, Feasts of Fools, games-playing and symbolic inversions. This attitude is to be traced to what Bakhtin calls 'the collective ancestral body of all the people' (RW 19), that is to the epochally prepared ground of carnival images and festive forms which is no less than the material and bodily continuity of human life.

'The essential principle of grotesque realism', Bakhtin writes, 'is degradation' (RW 19), but he is also insistent that this degradation is not merely a negative process. On the contrary, Bakhtin stresses the ambivalence of carnival imagery and its use in Rabelais. The degradation enacted in carnival and in carnivalized writing – the incessant reminders that we are all creatures of flesh and thus of food and faeces also – this degradation is simultaneously an affirmation, for even 'excrement is gay matter' (RW 175), linked to regeneration and renewal. This stress on the ambivalence of carnival imagery, and the resulting ambivalence of Rabelais and other such carnivalized writing, is one of the central emphases of the book, and is one of the principal ways in which Bakhtin links these remarkable aspects of Renaissance culture to an epochally established attitude to life.

Related to this conception of grotesque realism is a distinction that Bakhtin draws between the 'grotesque body' and the 'classical body'. This is another of his evaluatively charged distinctions, and, like all of his aesthetic preferences, is linked to some of his profoundest philosophical predispositions. Where the body of classical art is an achieved and completed thing – rounded and finished, with the perfection of, say, the Apollo Belvedere – the grotesque body of Rabelais and the kind of art which he represents appears unfinished, a thing of buds and sprouts, the orifices evident through which it sucks in and expels the world. It is a body marked by the evidence of its material origin and destiny; Bakhtin gives as an example of the grotesque body, drawn from outside Rabelais' writing, terracotta figurines from Kerch which show senile pregnant hags – 'It is ambivalent. It is pregnant death, a death that gives birth' (RW 25). Samuel Beckett's own grotesque image from *Waiting for Godot* (1956) – 'They give birth astride of a grave' – appears here with its valuations reversed, its bleak futility transformed and made to sound as an affirmation. The grotesque body celebrated by Bakhtin, which appears in artistic forms and periods way beyond Rabelais and the sixteenth century, is a body in which becoming rather than completion is evident, a body whose openness to the world and the future is emphatically symbolized by the consuming maws, pregnant stomachs, evident phalluses and gargantuan evacuations that make it up. Bakhtin's discussion of the grotesque body is reproduced in Part II.

Underlying the various aesthetic discussions that make up the large part of *Rabelais and His World*, then, is Bakhtin the philosopher of becoming, though it is a very material and bodily becoming, far removed from the bloodless niceties of academic philosophy. One name he gives to this celebration of the uncompleted is 'gay relativity' (RW 11), an attitude in which all the official certainties are relativized, inverted or parodied. This gay relativity, this ambivalence in which affirmation springs from degradation, is the context in which to place the various striking formal features which Bakhtin describes in Rabelais' writing, and which find their appropriate context in the popular–cultural life which surrounds him in the sixteenth century: the language of the market-place, banquet imagery, the grotesque body, and the images of the 'material bodily lower stratum' (such is the rather awkward English translation of Bakhtin's *material'no-telesny niz*, rather more succinctly rendered in French as *le bas corporel*). In all these instances Bakhtin traces a pattern in which extensive analogues can be found for Rabelais' writing in carnival and popular–cultural forms contemporary to him; common to both Rabelais' writing and the carnival forms is an attitude in which the high, the elevated, the official, even the sacred, is degraded and debased, but as a condition of popular renewal and regeneration.

It needs to be emphasized that despite the length of *Rabelais and His World* Bakhtin does not seek to provide a comprehensive and completed analysis of Rabelais' novel. This is especially the case because he practically ignores the Third and Fourth Books. We saw that in his writings on the novel more generally he did not seek to provide a systematic exposition with a series of fully developed exemplary analyses, but worked instead by accumulation of material and suggestion. In a similar way, even in this extended monograph, Bakhtin's analysis of Rabelais does not take the reader systematically through the novel, but works by the suggestive alignment of material and the defamiliarization of its elements by extending and redescribing their appropriate context. Thus his analyses tend to decompose the surface unity of the text, only to recompose it leaving the reader with an extraordinarily enriched sense of the depths of historic life on which it draws and the range of popular– cultural practice to which it alludes. An excellent example of the strengths of this analytic method is provided by the account that Bakhtin gives of the prologue to *Pantagruel*, in the chapter entitled 'the language of the marketplace'. The account is based upon the striking combination of praise and abuse that marks the prologue – praise of course for his own book and abuse for those who disbelieve anything they will read in it. But this rather mechanical opposition is complicated by the irony that Bakhtin detects in both the praise and abuse, so that both are simul- taneously praising and abusing, demonstrating the characteristic ironic ambivalence of the market-place which can make praise into an insult and abuse into a gesture of friendship. Behind this ambivalence we can see, of course, the wider ambivalence of popular–festive life as Bakhtin has described it. He pauses particularly over a pint of tripe that Rabelais offers to anyone who can find a book to match his own:

> Is this nothing? Then find me a book in any language, in any branch of art and science that possesses such virtues, properties and prerogatives. Find it, I say, and I will buy you a pint of tripes! (Rabelais, *Pantagruel*, Prologue)

Bakhtin makes this tripe the bearer of an extraordinarily rich nexus of allusions, the food *par excellence* of grotesque realism, for it is at once food to be devoured and the devouring belly itself, the flagrant embodiment of corporeality which points to death and the means of sustenance which point to life. The swing from the mock-serious tone of the praise of his own book to the comic offer to buy tripe becomes, in this account, a characteristic swing of grotesque realism in which the play of the upper and lower sphere is set in motion.

Bakhtin produces comparable accounts of many other elements of the prologue, of the simultaneous praise and abuse, of its 'billingsgate' (the English translator's inspired equivalent of, literally, 'market-place abuse'), and of the series of diseases wished upon non-believers in the book at the conclusion of the prologue. These accounts resemble associative excur- sions into the wealth of late medieval and Renaissance popular culture;

they are emphatically not explications of symbolism or imagery. Rather, they seek to demonstrate Rabelais' inevitable reliance upon a vocabulary which has gathered its force elsewhere, in the market-place or central arena in which carnival is enacted, and which thus carries with it the epochal mentality which carnival continues.

Bakhtin draws heavily upon traditions of nineteenth and early twentieth-century scholarship which have gone to great lengths to demonstrate Rabelais' reliance upon written sources. These show – though it is anyway apparent from reading Rabelais' novel – that *Gargantua* and *Pantagruel* are immersed in learned culture, be it the learning of the medieval schools in medicine and law, the rediscovered classics which inspired contemporary humanism, or the comic literature of *facetiae* and learned parodies which abound in the Middle Ages. But this does not detract from Bakhtin's central point about Rabelais' reliance upon popular culture since, he argues, many of the written sources upon which Rabelais draws – and not just the obviously comic genres – were already carnivalized, already carried within them the leaven of popular–festive forms. The text of Rabelais' novel, in short, appears as a site in which multiple cultural forms combine – forms that are either directly carnivalistic or which bear at one or more removes the traces of carnival energies.

II

I hope that the attractions of this whole position are plain. One immediate advantage is that it gives a name, carnival or the carnivalesque, to a range of otherwise dispersed activities and cultural forms which can now be seen to have real and historical connections – from Brueghel's famous picture of *The Battle of Carnival and Lent*, through a substantial proportion of Renaissance drama, to Gulliver pissing on the palace in Lilliput to put out the fire, or right through to the writing of Milan Kundera and his mobilization of the joke against the official pieties of Stalinism. You can extend the list almost at will, though there is of course the evident danger of losing Bakhtin's careful historical specificity if you do so. Some large questions nevertheless remain, to do with both the political and ideological direction of this whole position and with how sustainable it is in scholarly terms. Is it, in the words of Lionel Gossman, an ex-admirer of *Rabelais and His World*, 'with its hysterical celebration of the body, of the grotesque, of carnival … a surrender to romantic *Lebensphilosophie* [philosophy of life] in one of its cruder guises'?[22] And even if we answer no to this question, we need still to ask, simply, whether Bakhtin's book is true.

One sophisticated response to this last question sidesteps it neatly by asserting that the truth of *Rabelais and His World* to Rabelais and sixteenth-century France is irrelevant, because the whole book is best read as a coded attack on the cultural situation of Russia in the 1930s under Stalin – or, to use a more Bakhtinian vocabulary, the book is to be read as a hidden polemic against the regime's cultural politics. There is an evident force to this reading. Bakhtin's account of carnival may have been partly prompted by the Bolshevik intellectual Lunacharvsky's account of laughter and comic writing which sees it as the merest safety-valve for social tensions. The regime's grip on cultural policy tightened significantly after 1934 when 'socialist realism' was officially promulgated as the only permissible aesthetic for the novel; much of Bakhtin's account of grotesque realism may be seen as an implicit rejoinder to this. Equally, his insistence at various points that the realism of Rabelais is of a particular, non-abstracting and non-typifying kind, may be a reply to Lukacs (see chapter 2). Bakhtin had almost certainly read Lukacs; the latter was emphasizing, in his writings in the late 1930s, the centrality of the category of the socio-historical type for any Marxist aesthetics of the novel. Finally and above all is Bakhtin's attempt to mobilize, at the conceptual level only of course, the rumbustious popular life of the carnival against the official but murderous pieties of Church and State in Renaissance Europe – laughter 'does not build stakes', he writes (RW 95). This may undoubtedly be seen as a rejoinder to cultural life under Stalinism, which sought to recruit an anodyne version of the 'folk' to buttress its peculiar combination of terror and moral uplift. My invocation of Milan Kundera may not have been so ahistorical after all.

Yet for all the force of this reading, its limitations are evident also. To read the book exclusively in this light obviously and immediately robs most of the scholarship of its point. And even if, more circumspectly, no more than an analogy is drawn, there is a danger of this analogy ignoring the historical element in Bakhtin's argument. Part of his case, after all, is that the historical conjuncture which produces Rabelais is a particular one; since the Renaissance we have witnessed a fragmentation of the alignment between popular–festive forms and a critical anti-authoritarian spirit. Carnival, therefore, in the particular sense in which Bakhtin uses the word and despite his willingness to extend its range of meaning, is not a transhistorical phenomenon. We can perhaps get some confirmation of this from the very writer whom I have quoted to demonstrate the continuing aptness of Bakhtin's notions, Milan Kundera. Despite the laughter that he directs against the pieties and stupidities of Stalinist rule in Czechoslovakia both before and after 1968, that laughter does not seem to me to have the positive regenerating force that Bakhtin ascribes to carnival laughter, but is rather produced in a sardonic and negative key. The synthesis that Rabelais and sixteenth-century represent has indeed broken down.

Whatever weight you attach to this reading of the book, however, it is not thereby absolved of the usual responsibilities of scholarly accuracy, or indeed of more important intellectual responsibilities to provide a sustainable account both of Rabelais, and of the more general cultural and social history which it offers. Let us start by examining the account that Bakhtin provides of Rabelais, working out to look at the estimate he gives of carnival and the carnivalesque, and concluding with the most general questions of social and cultural history and anthropology which the book suggests.

As we have already seen, Bakhtin does not seek to provide an exhaustive account of Rabelais' writing – indeed any such effort to give the last word on a topic is inherently suspect, for it would imply a fixity in interpretation, futile if only because it is always waiting to be undone by the next reader. Moreover, Bakhtin's topic is not so much the text of *Gargantua* and *Pantagruel* as such, as the relations between this text and the surrounding popular–cultural forms. Both of these considerations mean that the primary value of his analyses lies in the way they provide an enriched sense of the historical density of the text of Rabelais, rather than any final assessment of its meaning. Nevertheless, there is an interpretation implied of Rabelais' book, which at the very least emphasizes its immersion in popular culture at the expense of its clear commitments to the learned humanist culture that was equally contemporary to it.

There has been considerable disagreement on whether Bakhtin does or does not overemphasize the role of carnival forms in Rabelais; or perhaps this should be put the other way, if you accept the force of Bakhtin's local analyses, to ask whether he does or does not under-emphasize the role of humanism.[3] It is certainly not the case that Bakhtin ignores these elements; at several moments in the book he acknowledges the influence of learned or élite culture on the novel, for example when he concedes the classical inspiration of Gargantua's education by Ponocrates, or the Thélème episode (RW 30), or when he acknowledges that 'Thélème is essentially a humanist utopia' (RW 431). But these are little more than passing concessions and do not alter the balance of the book which is overwhelmingly towards playing up the popular cultural elements and playing down the influence of élite culture. Bakhtin wrote *Rabelais and His World* in unpropitious circumstances and, evidently, in ignorance of much twentieth-century Rabelais scholarship. It may be that he gives a one-sided account of Rabelais. But its value lies not in the overall view he provides of Rabelais but in the analytical decompositions and recompositions that he effects on the body of the text.

Bakhtin himself has an interesting way of bringing this question into focus. Towards the end of the book he asks whether the 'last word' of Rabelais is to be found in his commitment to humanism, or in his immersion in popular–festive forms (RW 453–4). If the reply is the former, then this does indeed become a last word, a reply that seals Rabelais into the Renaissance by virtue of its intelligent but limited progressiveness. If, on the other hand, Rabelais' last word is his commitment to the gay relativity of popular laughter, then that opens a perspective towards the distant future, for the utopianism of that popular laughter looks ultimately beyond the present to that far future. Bakhtin, in short, seeks to find a historical ground for his own, and perhaps our own, engagement with the laughter of Rabelais.

But this reply raises its own problems, which are to do with the very assessment of carnival and the carnivalesque, to which we must now turn. For the strongest objections to Bakhtin's celebration of the forces of carnival depend not on the accuracy or otherwise of his account of Rabelais, but on whether or not carnival did have or could have the liberating energies which he attributes to it. This is a large historical question on which there is a substantial body of discussion. But the most common objection to Bakhtin's view of carnival as an anti-authoritarian force that can be mobilized against the official culture of Church and State, is that on the contrary it is part of that culture; in the typical metaphor of this line of argument, it is best seen as a safety-valve, which in some overall functional way reinforces the bonds of authority by allowing for their temporary suspension. This is a view we have already seen articulated by Lunacharvsky. Olivia's defence of Feste in *Twelfth Night* can be aptly quoted in this context: 'There is no slander in an allow'd fool, though he do nothing but rail'. So this is the question – can Bakhtin's effort to celebrate the anarchic and anti-authoritarian energies of carnival be simply deflected by seeing them as the antics of an 'allow'd fool'?

[73]

This is not a question to be decided by an appeal to general principles, and the evidence gathered by modern historians of early modern European popular culture – obviously unavailable to Bakhtin – certainly does not run strongly in his favour.[4] One initial and important point that needs to be made is that popular–festive forms were not only the cultural property of the 'people' in the narrow modern sense, but were shared and used by all ranks in society before the seventeenth century. What distinguished the literate, in a largely pre-literate society, was not their exclusion from popular–cultural forms but their participation, in addition, in a second, learned and élite, culture. Indeed, Peter Burke has suggested that one of the characteristics of the early modern period is the gradual withdrawal of the nobility from popular–cultural forms, but certainly in the sixteenth century, when Rabelais was writing, there is evidence of widespread participation by the noble élite in carnival, including well-known and powerful people who actually wrote plays, songs and farces to be performed at carnival time. So we have to be wary of any account of carnival which sees it too simply as expressing popular resentments, if by popular is meant the peasants and artisans who made up the bulk of early modern European society.

Furthermore, it is hard to accede to a version of carnival which stresses its capacity to invert hierarchies and undermine boundaries, without at the same time recalling that many carnival and carnival-like degradations clearly functioned to reinforce communal and hierarchical norms. Part of the festivities of the Roman carnival, for example, included the ritual degradation of Jews, who were forced to participate in races through the streets of the city. One of the main aims of the *charivari*, a carnivalesque ritual which involved such activities as loud satirical singing outside individuals' houses, and their enforced parade seated backwards on a donkey, was to degrade people who had transgressed community sexual norms – its typical victims were widows or widowers who married partners younger than themselves, scolds, and husbands who allowed themselves to be beaten by their wives. (The Skimmington ride in *The Mayor of Casterbridge* is a descendant of English versions of charivari.) The carnival inversions, the world-turned-upside-down of these festivities, were clearly not aimed at loosening people's sense of the rightness of the rules which kept the world the right way up, but on the contrary at reinforcing them.

Even Bakhtin's generous notion about laughter, that it cannot be made to serve the purposes of dogmatic intolerance and violence – that 'it does not build stakes' – does not withstand the evidence to be found in the murderous religious struggles of sixteenth-century France. Many of the degradations, acts of violence, murders and massacres perpetrated by Catholics and Protestants on each other were accompanied by carnival-esque activity, as in Macon where was played the 'farce of Saint Point'. This involved going with some ladies after a party to the prison where Protestants were locked up, freeing them, getting the ladies to chat to them, and then drowning them.⁵ Carnival may not be the source of such violence, but its forms certainly accompanied it; laughter may not build stakes, but those sent to the stake sometimes went with laughter ringing in their ears.

The most fully documented case in which carnival became the focus of acute social tensions concerns the carnival at Romans in south-east France, in 1580, some fifty years after Rabelais began writing *Gargantua*.⁶ Here, both sides in a situation of fraught class conflict sought to use carnival festivities to further their social aims. The popular party were, it seems, planning to consolidate the partial gains they had already won; while the urban petty nobility and bourgeoisie certainly took the occasion to organize a bloody suppression, which included killing the leader of the popular party while he was still dressed in his bear costume. The interest here is not only that carnival forms could be used as a cover for, indeed the means of, violent social struggles, but that its forms were available to both sides; indeed, the side that made most efficient use of carnival festivity was the party of authority. Le Roy Ladurie's analysis of these events shows not only that carnival was the occasion in which deep-seated antagonisms came to a head, but also that the very carnival activities could be used as symbolic means of expressing these social and political antagonisms. Thus, in a typical way, the activities of feasting and processions, games and competitions, were organized by different festive societies, whose complex social differentiation and symbolic allegiances were used in different ways. The carnival at Romans, therefore, suggests not that the carnivalesque has one univocal social or political meaning, but that it provides a malleable space, in which activities and symbols can be inflected in different directions.

Something like this is the conclusion also of Natalie Zemon Davis, who has shown the widespread occurrence of cross-dressing – especially men dressed as women – in carnival or carnivalesque activities, but also in riots, in early modern France. She concludes that 'comic and festive inversion could *undermine* as well as reinforce … assent through its connections with everyday circumstances outside the privileged time of carnival and stage-play.'[7] Here specifically for women, but also for other subordinated groups in Renaissance Europe, carnival was a mixed blessing, to be used certainly to underline symbolically communal hierarchies, but also providing a space in which they might be overturned.

This, then, is a large and significant caveat that needs to be placed against Bakhtin's celebration of popular–festive forms as liberatory and anti-authoritarian. This substantial adjustment has indeed been made by writers basically sympathetic to Bakhtin, such as Peter Stallybrass and Allon White, who, in *The Politics and Poetics of Transgression*, accuse him of utopianism in his excessively indulgent account of popular culture.[8] This seems to me to be correct, though it might have been more appropriate to characterize Bakhtin's attitude as 'populism', for this would also help to distinguish between Bakhtin's own populist estimate of carnival, and his explicit discussion and celebration of the utopian expressions that are such a vital part of it. Yet Bakhtin uses 'utopian' in a very particular way. In at least some of his formulations, it is not that carnival looks forward to some distant prospect of social perfection, but that the space of carnival has already realized it. Carnival becomes a time outside time, 'a second life of the people, who for a time entered the utopian realm of community, freedom, equality, and abundance' (RW 9). The very language that people speak is altered, to allow a familiarity and fraternization impermissible at other times. When it enters writing, the carnival spirit offers a liberation from 'all that is humdrum and universally accepted' (RW 34), and Bakhtin, in an implicit glance at Freud, even suggests that it liberates people 'not only from external censorship but first of all from the great interior censor' (RW 94).

If this is utopianism, it gives expression to a popular utopianism quite distinct from Sir Thomas More's humanist utopia, to which Rabelais alludes. This is much more the utopianism of the Land of Cockaigne, a popular mythical land where piglets run about with apples in their mouths ready for the cooking, roast geese fly with carving knives conveniently at the ready in their backs, and barrels of ale are made without those inconvenient stoppers in their bungholes. Bakhtin's opposition to the bloodless utopias of rationalism is apparent; in *Problems of Dostoevsky's Poetics* he associates utopianism with monologism, and, echoing Engels, repudiates 'utopian socialism, with its faith in the omnipotence of the conviction' (PDP 82). But here, in the Rabelais book, he gives a fine and philosophical expression to the realm of freedom represented by feasting, laughter and familiarity; this may exaggerate these utopian elements in carnival forms but Bakhtin does not invent them. If there is a difficulty with this it is that the utopian imagination expressed in the Land of Cockaigne all too evidently bears the marks of its social and historical origin; like the magic porridge pots and gigantic turnips of folk tales, these are myths that plainly spring from a society of scarcity, able to imagine utopia only in terms of the comical excess of what it lacks. Perhaps it is a reflection of Russia's exceptional path of historical development, leapfrogging from feudalism to a kind of communism in less than a lifetime, that Bakhtin should find imaginative sustenance in the utopian forms of the pre- and early modern world rather than in the utopias of the enlightenment. But at all events, we must now turn to the general social and historical anthropology implied by the book, for it certainly involves a powerful nostalgia for the world of carnival and some dismay at the forces of modernity, rationality and enlightenment which displaced it.

For Bakhtin may be seen, in one respect at least, as exemplifying a particular aspect of twentieth-century thought in rejecting the positive evaluation attached to the progress of rationality and enlightenment; here he resembles for example the French 'archaeologist of knowledge', Michel Foucault, who gives a series of bleak analyses of some of the characteristic rational institutions of the modern world such as the prison and the mental hospital. But just to announce the comparison is to suggest its inadequacy; where Foucault's world is ruled by the inescapable processes of power, Bakhtin's worldly medium is altogether more benign. It is precisely access to a sense of the benign that carnival promises; in the last resort, the celebration of the 'material principle' in man provides a defence against 'cosmic terror' (RW 335–6). Yet this is to take just one emphasis from *Rabelais and His World* – to make it sound, indeed, like that romantic *Lebensphilosophie* which Gossman accused it of. Elsewhere in the book Bakhtin is careful to insist that, in Rabelais at least, the emphasis on biological life leads to consciousness of historical time. He makes this argument by reverting to the kind of analysis he used in the essay on the chronotope; he juxtaposes the 'vertical' sense of space characteristic of the hierarchical world view of the Middle Ages, which at its limit excludes a sense of time, to the 'horizontal' sense of the onwardness of time created by the downward movement into the life of the earth and the body characteristic of Rabelais' writing. Historical consciousness, therefore, is borne out of the sense of biological life and is distinct from it; both are present in Rabelais (RW 401–6; but see also extract 5, pp. 248–53).

Nevertheless, there is a point to the contention that Bakhtin's nostalgia for the world of carnival is a nostalgia for an ultimately religious attitude to life – despite his protestations to the contrary, and his evident relish in watching carnivalesque discrownings of official religion. In this context it is worth recalling that Bakhtin did not come across the phenomena of carnival single-handed; Sir James Frazer, in *The Golden Bough* (1890–1915), had already sought to assimilate the rituals of carnival to his worldwide anthropology of vegetation myths, which are perhaps the origin of the pattern of degradation and regeneration that Bakhtin traces in carnival. Yet Bakhtin is not interested in origins, or not interested only in them; unlike Frazer his topic is the continuing uses to which carnival is put, and his orientation is not to the past but to the future. At all events it is possible to take very different emphases from *Rabelais and His World*. One can see in it a nostalgia for a possibly religious attitude to life which takes consolation from cosmic terror in the celebration of the material con-tinuities of the body. Alternatively one can see the institution of the carnival as providing a particular synthesis of, indeed, epochal attitudes to the body with anti-authoritarian practices (making that large caveat about the political direction of carnival which we saw to be necessary) – a synthesis peculiar to early modern Europe and which has subsequently been fragmented and suppressed.

And it is indeed from this second perspective that some of the most interesting attempts have been made to carry forward Bakhtin's analyses into substantial accounts of the social and cultural history subsequent to Rabelais. Clearly carnival on its own is too special a topic to provide a comprehensive social or cultural history, but used as a topos, or recurrent organising image, it can become a very useful key to understanding the transition to modernity. This is the method of Stallybrass and White in *The Politics and Poetics of Transgression*, where the authors use the notion of carnival, and its successive displacements and repressions, as a way of unlocking a history which is at once social, cultural and personal. We have already noticed how Stallybrass and White criticize Bakhtin for the excessively positive valuation he gives to carnival; this is reflected in their more general argument, which draws on the historical sociology of Norbert Elias to provide a cognate account of the 'civilizing process'. This is very much more ambivalent than Bakhtin about the value to be attached to the repressions of the body effected in the transition to 'civilization', that is, he is prepared to see gain as well as loss in the process. Similarly, Terry Castle, in *Masquerade and Civilisation: The*

Carnivalesque in Eighteenth-Century English Culture and Fiction, has used the notion of the carnivalesque, as it manifests itself in the specifically English and privatized masquerade, as a means to understand some of the crucial changes in eighteenth-century society, and the eighteenth-century novel.[9] Castle is responding to, and giving a local demonstration of, Bakhtin's account of the secular decline in the carnivalesque attitude, and its replacement by the uniform, fixed and hierarchical world-view of rationalism and bureaucracy, seeing the peculiar nostalgia evoked by masquerade as part of the more general pathos that is now attached to that vanished world-view.

These are merely two examples of the way that Bakhtin's more general account of the history of carnival, and its implications for social and cultural history, has been taken up. In neither case are the authors uncritical of Bakhtin; *Rabelais and His World* clearly cannot provide a comprehensive social history on its own, and nor would any of Bakhtin's admirers claim that it could. Nevertheless, it does provide a richly suggestive topos, one which condenses many crucial and highly contested aspects of European history over the last five centuries: attitudes to the body; popular culture and élite attempts to regulate it; sexual norms and their transgressions. The controversy over Bakhtin's notion of carnival and the powerful positive charge he attaches to it reflects the energies that are still engaged in those various attempts at regulation, contestation and repression.

III

These, then, are some of the opportunities created by Bakhtin's account of carnival and the carnivalesque, some of the problems created by it, and some of the caveats that need to be entered against his celebration. However, we are still left with a striking piece of criticism, and in this section I wish to concentrate on the central *aesthetic* conception of *Rabelais and His World*, that of grotesque realism. In Bakhtin's text this accompanies a general account of the grotesque, and is focused on a discussion of the grotesque body; moreover, some interesting interpretative methods spring from it.

One of the central oppositions of Bakhtin's book is that between the classic and the grotesque. In announcing this opposition Bakhtin disclaims any preference for one over the other; he presents himself more as a neutral cultural historian intent on describing a hitherto insufficiently studied area of cultural activity which, despite the scant attention and indeed depreciation it has received, in fact includes a vast area of folk culture and its successors in European writing. But this disclaimer needs to be taken with a pinch of salt; we have already seen how the grotesque body appeals to Bakhtin as the philosopher of becoming, and though we certainly should not imagine that he repudiates all 'classic' art, there is nevertheless a strong positive evaluation to be read in his accounts of the grotesque and grotesque realism.

Let us begin with the more general category. By the grotesque Bakhtin alludes, in the first instance, to that characteristic strain in archaic and folk art, by no means confined to Europe, that represents the body as unbounded, in transformation, materially linked to its past and its future, in which to use Bakhtin's own language, 'the inner movement of being itself was expressed in the passing of one form into another, in the ever incompleted character of being' (RW 32). Bakhtin's philosophical preferences are of course evident in this way of characterizing the grotesque; existence is not to be thought of as ever completed but always in the process of becoming. So the grotesque is to be seen as the aesthetic expression of that attitude to life which also underlies the carnival, an attitude founded upon the biological continuity of the body of the people. It is the *people's* body because Bakhtin is insistent that in folk art up to the Renaissance this perception of life, and its artistic expression in the grotesque, is not private, has not settled upon the individual body of the bourgeois subject – that is a development of the seventeenth century and after. Indeed, he suggests that the successive transformations of the grotesque in the history of European writing are symptomatic of this cultural change, for in periods subsequent to the Renaissance, and especially in Romanticism, there is undoubtedly a tremendous interest in the grotesque but this has become private, 'subjective' grotesque, has lost its gay and affirmative character as it has become fixated upon the biological *individual*, rather than collective biological life.

Bakhtin does not draw a sharp line to distinguish his more general category of the grotesque from its more particular manifestation in grotesque realism, but given his insistence upon *degradation* as its characteristic aesthetic activity, it seems clear that the negative or critical moment of the grotesque has become more prominent here. While Rabelais of course provides him with most of his examples, he actually introduces the concept more by way of *Don Quixote*. It is, naturally, in the figure of Sancho Panza that grotesque realism gets its fullest expression, and Bakhtin makes that figure the centre of a complex set of equivalences:

> Sancho's materialism, his potbelly, appetite, his abundant defecation, are on the absolute lower level of grotesque realism of the gay bodily grave (belly, bowels, earth) which has been dug for Don Quixote's abstract and deadened idealism. One could say that the knight of the sad countenance must die in order to be reborn a better and a greater man. (RW 22)

Grotesque realism can here be seen as a kind of artistic practice which moves both from the upper to the lower level of the biological body and from heaven to earth; indeed these two movements are equivalent. At its best and most inclusive, grotesque realism can bring these different aspects together, for that is the condition of it being as much regenerative as degrading. But this has not happened in the history of European writing; indeed, Bakhtin suggests that the synthesis is beginning to break down in *Don Quixote* itself, and that simultaneous with the conception of the body of grotesque realism in the novel is another conception in tension with it, a conception which is already incipiently private and individual. This means that Bakhtin is tracing, within the text of Cervantes' novel, two conflicting and historically divergent conceptions of the human body.

We can get a sense of the usefulness of the notion of grotesque realism with respect to writing perhaps more familiar to English-speaking readers, by considering *Gulliver's Travels* in this context. This is a text whose aesthetic is indeed centrally characterized by degradation, by a downward movement into the material and the bodily. The reader is constantly confronted by the body presented in all sorts of grotesque and exaggerated ways, be it the body of Gulliver seen from the perspectives of the tiny Lilliputians, or the still more grotesque bodies of the gigantic Brobdignagians seen in horrific close-up. But from the perspective of the sixteenth century Swift's eighteenth-century grotesque appears an almost purely negative affair, scarcely retaining any of that regenerative laughter which Bakhtin claims as so important to the mode. True, the Lilliputians look up in awe at Gulliver's genital organs as they pass beneath his legs, and his urine does put out the palace fire just as Gargantua's urine is regenerative – in fact it's the source of the River Rhone; but in general Swift's grotesque is motivated by a powerful strain of disgust. When the Yahoos shower Gulliver with excrement in the voyage to the Houyhnhnms, this is definitely not 'gay matter'. So although we can see a clear continuation of grotesque realism in Swift's writing, the regenerative synthesis of Rabelais appears to have broken down in it.

This is perhaps a too insistently chronological reading, too determined to place Swift in a developmental sequence and thus seeing him too much as a sympton of an underlying process rather than seeing *Gulliver's Travels* as a distinctive achievement in its own right. Nevertheless, there is an illumination to be gained from locating writers in terms of some wider cultural and social history – perhaps, indeed, this is the only justification of such a critical practice. And grotesque realism is certainly an illuminating conception for a range of art not governed by the demands of classical proportion.

The aesthetic focus of grotesque realism is of course the grotesque body. Not only does this notion illuminate a central strand in the history of representations of the body, it also has important implications for the way we understand the historical consciousness of it. In the words of Laurie Finke, a critic who has used the distinction between the classical body and the grotesque body in work on medieval mystical writing,

> Bakhtin's terms call into question our usually biologistic understanding of the "body". Ordinarily we attribute to the body an *a priori* material existence without considering how our experience of our bodies is organised by cultural representations of them. Such representations are not universal but have historical specificity.[10]

Seen from this perspective, the grotesque body not only figures in representations, it has also structured the most apparently intimate and 'given' elements of historical consciousness, namely our very sense of our own body. Once again we begin to see a perhaps surprising affinity between Bakhtin and the work of Michel Foucault, who in writing on the history of sexuality has sought to undermine common-sense ahistorical ideas concerning the given persistence of biological experience. This is a useful comparison up to a point, but again Bakhtin's emphases are positive ones; unlike Foucault he makes no effort to attack one's sense of the authenticity of one's own experience. If this general orientation towards the notion of the grotesque body is adopted, it helps to counter too biologistic an interpretation of *Rabelais and His World*. There certainly is an insistence upon the biological continuity of human life as a locus of value in the book, as we have repeatedly seen; but the notion of the grotesque body suggests how that underlying attitude receives its particular historical manifestation.

If we glance back at Bakhtin's comments on Sancho Panza, we can get a further idea of the fecundity of the interpretative practice that Bakhtin's use of 'grotesque realism' now yields. We saw there how Sancho's body became the locus, in Bakhtin's account, of at least two equivalent movements, or better to say two versions of the same downward movement: from the upper to the lower bodily stratum, and from the upper to the lower regions of the medieval hierarchy. This dual downward swing is characteristic of grotesque realism as Bakhtin describes it in Rabelais, and enables him to produce some extraordinary analyses, based upon the complex sets of homologies that flow from establishing the equivalence. One of the most striking interpretations in this manner is of chapter 13 of *Gargantua*, the famous chapter in which Gargantua describes the various experiments he has made to find the best method of wiping his arse. He finally settles upon the downy neck of a goose, for the warmth and downy sensation is communicated from the bum-gut through the intestine to the heart and the brain. This is made the occasion of a remarkable analysis by Bakhtin, who sees in the downward and upward movements of the body an equivalence with a degrading and parodic reascent in medieval theology. He secures this interpretation by means of an appeal to the comic folkloric topography of Europe, which has several sites known as entrances to hell but which are also vulgarly known as the 'holes' of ... Saint Patrick, Seville, and so on. It should be stressed that this is not a reversion to an interpretative attitude to Rabelais which sees his text as a kind of secret code that has to be broken in order to get at a hidden meaning. On the contrary, the grotesque body in this chapter remains a body and its arse remains an arse. However, it becomes, in Bakhtin's text, the site of a wide-ranging interpretative practice which can align it with the liberatory demystifications of theological parody and even, in the resolute opposition to religious mystification, the beginnings of the scientific attitude.

Not all readers will be persuaded by the interpretative ambition shown by Bakhtin here and in similar passages elsewhere in the book. Others may want to push his analytic method in another direction. If the grotesque body is a site upon which medieval religious and social hierarchies can be symbolically inverted, it is surely right to point out that the body as Bakhtin describes it is predominantly gendered as female. It is the body of generation, and the swellings that indicate this are its breasts and pregnant belly; it is the metaphoric equivalent of mother earth, to which the degradation of grotesque realism returns. So, although this is an interpretative possibility that is certainly not followed out by Bakhtin, the grotesque body may be a way of mapping not only the social and religious hierarchies of medieval and Renaissance culture, but of mapping gender hierarchies also and valuations that run through them.

Bakhtin makes grotesque realism the starting-point in the development of realism 'of grand style' – by which he means, in addition to Rabelais, Cervantes and Shakespeare, such writers as Stendhal, Balzac, Hugo and Dickens (RW *52*). When divorced from that origin, he asserts, realism becomes static, empirical, socially typifying. We may see here yet another generic history of the novel, again with only a doubtful connection to the various other histories of the novel that Bakhtin produced in the 1930s and early 1940s. However, it is to these more general connections, of Bakhtin's writing on carnival to his other writing, and its use in contemporary critical discourse, that we must address our attention in the final section of this chapter.

IV

At a high level of abstraction, it is certainly possible to assimilate 'carnival' to the 'novelistic'. One contemporary writer, Graham Pechey, has articulated this connection especially well:

> Any sociopolitical project of centralisation or hegemony has always and everywhere to *posit itself against* the ubiquitously decentralizing (centrifugal) forces within ideology. 'Carnival' is the name Bakhtin gives to these forces in so far as they find expression in consciously parodic representations across a range of signifying practices; 'the novel' is the name he gives to their entry into the forms of *writing* at any time in history but most influentially in the case of Rabelais and the line of comic fiction descending from him.[11]

This seems to me to be a very helpful line of argument. It has the signal merit of locating both carnival and the novel (understood in its more general sense) firmly in the socio-political arena, in the actual struggles over meaning that determine both the minutiae and the general direction of 'signifying practices'. In this respect it makes a real advance over those attempts to assimilate both carnival and the novel as Bakhtin uses them to a more socially unspecific notion of 'play'; this more politically naïve kind of libertarian euphoria renders the negations of carnival ultimately harmless by dissociating them from their historic specificities as part of a more general principle of semiotic play – they become merely 'fun'. But Pechey achieves his assimilation at some cost, notably the loss of considerable historical specificity on his own part. Above all, the central difficulty of attempts to assimilate too closely carnival and the novel is that in *Rabelais and His World* Bakhtin traces a secular decline in the carnival spirit since the sixteenth century, yet it is precisely this period which has seen the most pronounced 'rise of the novel'.

This is an intractable difficulty, only partially resolved by Bakhtin's own attempt, in the second edition of the book on Dostoevsky, to trace polyphony in the novel to the epochal generic survival of carnival forms which valorize subordinate voices. The difficulty is ultimately this. Bakhtin uses two powerful synthetic notions, 'carnival' and 'novel', which at a certain level of abstraction are clearly related, since both are characterized by the inversion and undoing of hierarchical or centripetal discourses. Yet each notion is not only or even predominantly an abstract principle; their intelligibility depends upon their substantial allusion to actual historic practices. And the practices to which they allude actually obtained over very different historical time-scales, so that they have, so to speak, very different historical centres of gravity. Moreover, the logic of the argument in *Rabelais and His World* is that carnival – structurally similar to 'novel' – has declined just as actual novels have become the dominant form of writing, that is to say in secular terms from the seventeenth century onwards.

I do not have a resolution of this difficulty to propose. However, it is important to recognize that this is not just a purely conceptual matter, a case of an academic anomaly that needs to be sorted out in order to lend Bakhtin's system the appearance of internal coherence. These are, in fact, substantial historical questions, which concern actual social practices and their transposition into writing. Above all, they concern the source of the social energy that gets articulated in the novel, in societies and historical periods where carnival is no more than a memory, however important its embodiment in generic terms. Any resolution of this difficulty, therefore, will spring not from the letter of Bakhtin's writing, in a vain attempt at reconciling its various parts, but from its spirit, which constantly seeks to dissolve the actuality of writing in the actuality of the social practices, written and otherwise, which surround it.

Bakhtin's book on Rabelais was the first of his books to be translated into West European languages, and consequently the notion of carnival is the one that has longest been in circulation in the West. This has perhaps led to some distortions in the perception of Bakhtin as a thinker. But it also means that 'carnival' has had time to be used in all sorts of different contexts, way beyond those in which the notion appears in Bakhtin's own writing. One area in which the notion of carnival has been especially productive has been in thinking about the theatre, despite Bakhtin's own expressed antipathy to drama. This dislike is at first sight surprising; it might be felt that the philosopher of dialogism would be especially sympathetic to that form in which dialogue most naturally appears. But this is not the case, and for two main reasons. The first concerns what Bakhtin claims is the thinness of dramatic language, which makes all its characters speak in the same voice. Here Bakhtin sounds as though all drama were written by Racine. A more substantial objection, which makes drama into another of the 'others' of the novel in the manner of the epic or lyric poetry, is the organization of the languages in drama; in particular, drama does not allow for the dialogic interpenetration of one language by another which is enabled in the novel by the simultaneous presence of the narrator's overarching language along with the language of the characters (DI 266). Notwithstanding this expressed antipathy, we have noticed how Bakhtin included Shakespeare in his trio of Renaissance avatars of grotesque realism, and the carnivalesque evidently animates not only his theatre but that of other Renaissance dramatists, such as the Jonson of *Batholomew Fair*, as well. Indeed, one of the finest pieces of Shakespearean criticism in the last half century, C. L. Barber's *Shakespeare's Festive Comedies*, provides some striking analogues to Bakhtin, above all in his situation of Shakespeare's writing in popular–festive forms.[12] But the fullest account of Renaissance theatre to be written in explicitly Bakhtinian terms is undoubtedly Michael Bristol's *Carnival and Theater*, which gives a nuanced account of the presence of carnival forms in Shakespeare's theatre.[13]

If I have not conveyed the attractiveness, fecundity and excitement of Bakhtin's account of carnival, I have not achieved one of my main aims in writing this chapter. It has given a new name to otherwise diverse and historically separate cultural activities – and thus defamiliarized them, made them strange by placing them in a new context. It has drawn attention to a distinctive aesthetic, grotesque realism, and gone some way to providing the appropriate terms for its understanding. Above all, in celebrating the popular–festive forms of the carnival, Bakhtin has captured some of their spirit, and propelled into the none-too-carnivalesque pages of academic criticism and literary history a distinct flavour of the travestying and relativizing impulses that animated the Renaissance market-place. It may be, as Terry Eagleton has somewhat sardonically remarked, that carnival is a notion that is particularly likely to appeal to academics, excited at the prospect of parodies and subversions in thought that they would certainly not contemplate with equanimity in life.[14] But if carnivalized academic writing is hard to imagine, this may be because its writers are too reluctant to contemplate the loss of authority that would follow.

If there is a contemporary literary position which has made the presence or absence of authority, including its own, a central topic, it has tended to be called deconstruction. Bakhtin has been recruited both as an anticipator of deconstruction and as a sufficient rejoinder to it. I have tried to show, in my discussion of carnival, that, like the novel, it is a term with a particular historic centre of gravity, but which is nevertheless capable of a more general or abstract formulation. My own preference, let it be said, is for a more historicizing emphasis; the triumph of *Rabelais and His World*, it seems to me, is to expand the appropriate context for *Gargantua* and *Pantagruel* in sometimes breathtaking ways. But the context remains a historical one; if Bakhtin's practice is deconstructive, it liberates the sign not into some ahistorical free place but into the specific freedoms won for it by the rituals and festivities of carnival. But this is to anticipate the following chapter, which will examine more closely the implications of Bakhtin's thinking when considering the relations of writing to the social practices, including other writing, which surround it.

4
Bakhtin and contemporary criticism

As we have seen, Bakhtin is a wide-ranging, imaginative and suggestive writer, but he is not a systematic one. The difficulties of constructing a 'system' out of his work – even if one should conceive such a misplaced ambition – are of course compounded if one takes 'Bakhtin' to include Voloshinov and Medvedev as well. So his value to us now is certainly not that of a ready-made interpretative system which can be 'applied' to a range of writing, to solve the various intellectual challenges and difficulties which have, to some degree, transformed the way we think about language and literature over the last twenty-five years. Yet his particular intellectual trajectory, and the extraordinary history in which it occurred, lend a remarkable weight to the various and sometimes contradictory positions to be found in the writing of Bakhtin and his circle. As a result, they press upon the diverse intellectual currents of Europe and America from unexpected directions, dialogizing in turn New Critical formalism, structuralism, Marxism, deconstruction and some versions of historicism. In this chapter I wish to give an outline of that dialogue, recognizing not only its evident material limitations – a thorough attempt to interanimate Bakhtin and the intellectual history of the West is of course way beyond the scope of such a book as this – but also recognizing that in principle such a dialogue can never be completed, must always be provisional while there remains the chance for another voice to join it.

However, the point of looking at these various 'isms' is not a sterile exercise in intellectual history. The recent changes and transformations in intellectual life have not been driven only internally, but by the changes in social and political life of the society that surrounds the academy. If this is obvious with respect to the changing fortunes of Marxism, it is equally so in the case of formalism, structuralism and deconstruction. These can be seen as attempts to formulate, in the appropriate formal languages, the profound divisions and alienations that characterize modern society – not least the division between the academy itself and the society in which it plays an ambivalent part. Given the extraordinary cultural politics of Russia in the 1920s, 1930s and 1940s; given the remarkable route to modernization taken by the Soviet Union; given the exceptional social importance of the Russian intelligentsia – given all these it is hardly surprising that Bakhtin should arrive at opposite emphases in considering the linguistic, aesthetic and socio-historical problems at the heart of recent and contemporary debates. We extract Bakhtin from this difficult and complex history at our peril, yet this is the condition of making him speak. And indeed, this paradox suggests just the most valuable of his insights – the Janus face of the speaking subject, immersed in a multiple past, speaking a language bearing ineradicable and pervasive traces of that past, yet turned towards the future, towards an interlocutor whose response cannot be guaranteed.

One reason why Bakhtin should appear to anticipate some of both structuralism and deconstruction is because of his engagement with Russian formalism in the 1920s, for this intellectual orientation itself anticipated some of the characteristic stresses of structuralism as it manifested itself in the study of literature. Above all, both formalism and structuralism tend to play up the autonomy of the art-work, understood in terms of the distinctive laws which produce it. Medvedev criticizes this severely, seeking to return writing, in the Marxist idiom of *The Formal Method in Literary Scholarship*, to the ideological milieu of its society. The book which makes this move most spectacularly, of course, is *Rabelais and His World*, first published in 1965. Its assimilation in the West thus coincides with the move from structuralism to post-structuralism in France, and one of the prime movers in that transition was Julia Kristeva, profoundly influenced by Bakhtin's work on carnival. In short, it is possible to see the intellectual history of Paris as following, at a forty-year interval, the intellectual history of Mikhail Bakhtin, and indeed being partly prompted by it.

One way of understanding structuralism is to see it as an attempt to apply the Saussurean model of language to matters which are not purely linguistic – in the relevant case, to literature. In this model, it will be recalled, an underlying system or *langue* is the condition by which any individual word or utterance has meaning, so that the object of study becomes this underlying system rather than the individual word. If this model is 'applied' to domains other than language the results can be surprising, and can be made to eat away at some of the common-sense assumptions that sustain our ideas of such matters as authorship and the relation of language to external reality. In particular, an emphasis on the underlying code of a piece of literature, be it understood as a code either specific to that one piece of literature or shared with other writing, undermines two natural-seeming assumptions: that the author of a piece of writing is the originator of its meanings, and that it refers in a mapping or 'isomorphic' way to the world beyond it. How can we make Bakhtin speak to these two questions?

What is at stake in the debate about authorship is the question of whether, in considering the history of writing, you afford primacy to large, relatively impersonal and intersubjective phenomena such as 'codes' or 'discourses', or to the agents who use them. In certain extreme formulations, the primacy of discourse over its agents is such as to dissolve any notion of authorship altogether, making the question one of accounting for how, in writing since the Renaissance, it has been necessary to invent an 'author function' as a way of grounding and limiting discursive heterogeneity.[1] In this perspective, large and impersonal 'discourses' form the appropriate object of study; historically writing has not always been signed, so it becomes a matter of historical inquiry as to when and why people began to feel the need to assign writing to 'authors' – to invent an 'author function'. On the other hand, it has been a characteristic emphasis, at least since Romanticism, to seek to explain writing as an emanation of an individual subjectivity, to make the individual author the source of all meaning. If the debate is understood in this way, it begins to resemble the opposition between what Voloshinov described as 'abstract objectivism' and 'individualistic subjectivism' (see chapter 1, pp. 24–8), and it might be possible to effect a similar synthesis, in the domain of writing, to the one he tentatively offered in the domain of language more generally. And indeed, it is possible to see the outline of such a resolution in Voloshinov, in which the historicity and sociality of discourse remains central, but in which its users – writers – are able to inflect, negotiate and redirect the discourses at their disposal in particular and at least partially intended ways.

But it is not necessary to work only from first principles in this way, because Bakhtin himself alludes to structuralism, especially in his late notes now published under the title 'Towards a methodology for the human sciences' (SG 159–72). It is inappropriate to deduce too much from these late notes because of the cryptic form in which they appear, but what Bakhtin does say bears strongly on this question of authorship. In the context of structuralism, he asserts that he is 'against enclosure in a text', and contrasts this enclosure with his own attitude: 'But I hear *voices* in everything and dialogic relations among them' (SG 169). And he also insists that 'this personalism is not psychological, but semantic' (SG 170). Against the textual enclosure of structuralism Bakhtin opposes the 'voice', understood not in psychological but in linguistic terms. The speaking voices in a text are not to be abstracted, but they are *speaking* voices, carrying the 'image of a language', to use that formulation from 'Discourse in the novel' (DI 336).

Moreover, there are discussions of the question of authorship scattered throughout Bakhtin's writing – and indeed it is a constitutive category of the extended unpublished essay from the early 1920s, 'Author and hero in aesthetic activity', which may perhaps be seen as the philosophical starting-point of Bakhtin's career. In this early essay, aesthetic activity is grounded in the relationship between self and other, in particular the self of the author and the other of the hero. But these are not two conceptual unities or givens; rather there is a non-coincidence between the self which experiences and the self which writes – in the neo-Kantian idiom of the essay, 'the *subiectum* of lived life and the *subiectum* of the aesthetic activity which gives form to that life are in principle incapable of coinciding with one another' (AA 96). So even in this early essay, the author is the indispensable starting-point for Bakhtin's considerations on writing, but he or she is not conceived in a unitary way. In later writing, this splitting of the author within the author will become a matter of the various languages competing with each other even within the apparently unitary self. Bakhtin will not abandon the author, in the manner of some versions of structuralism, but he will radically socialize the way the author needs to be conceived.

There is an especially interesting discussion of these matters in a passage we have already glanced at from 'Discourse in the novel', where the question of authorship arises in the context of a discussion of the various languages that make up the novelistic text (reproduced on pp. 206–9). If none of these languages can be taken directly as expressing the author's view of the world – if, indeed, in the examples Bakhtin cites, these languages are specifically attributed to a narrator – is it possible to locate an author in or behind these languages? Bakhtin speaks of a 'posited author', that is, of a position of narrative authority beyond that of the specified narrator but to which the reader can only gain access through that other's language. In that respect the author's intentions are always refracted through one or more historically specific languages, and the author is above the battle, playing off one language against another.

In this conception, authorship is not a function of the discourse but a condition of it; yet, although it becomes a realm of freedom, the condition of this freedom is an entering into historicity by taking on the language of another. The characteristic double Bakhtinian stress re-emerges here as elsewhere: at once on the historically specific, the immersion in the here and now which all use of language entails, and on the real if partial freedom that is bestowed by the very uniqueness and specificity of every linguistic and literary occasion.

In the matter of authorship, then, a characteristic structuralist position appears as a version of 'abstract objectivism', as a version, in short, of idealism. But this does not, of course, mean that Bakhtin embraces the opposite, 'individualistic subjectivist' position with respect to authors; he still retains his insistence on the sociality and historicity of the discourses which authors set in motion. A similar point can be made with respect to the question of reference. Unlike some typical structuralist and post-structuralist positions, Bakhtin's attention to the activity of language itself does not entail any reduction in the capacity of language to refer – indeed, his insistence that all words are spoken with an evaluative accent is meaningless if torn from the context to which those evaluations make reference. This is not to make Bakhtin into a 'realist' critic, concerned only to see writing in the dimension of knowledge. Rather, it is to recognize that the effort he makes to ground writing in the sociality of language is accompanied by no idealist abandonment of writing's location in a world of particulars, made up of such things as authors and objects referred to. He briefly formulates this location in *Problems of Dostoevsky's Poetics*:

> Dialogic relationships are absolutely impossible without logical relationships or relationships oriented toward a referential object, but they are not reducible to them, and they have their own specific character ... Logical and semantically referential relationships, in order to become dialogic, must be embodied, that is, they must enter another sphere of existence: they must become *discourse*, that is, an utterance, and receive an *author*, that is, a creator of the given utterance whose position it expresses. (PDP 184)

Bakhtin therefore remains interested in *dialogic* relationships, that is, his specific object of enquiry is the interrelationship between socially and historically grounded languages. But these relationships cannot exist in a vacuum, and depend for their existence upon those phenomena which have been the objects of enquiry of traditional philosophy and literary criticism, that is, upon logical structures within writing, upon ties between that writing and the world, and upon actually existing individuals known as authors. While it is certainly the case that we cannot talk about the world without using an evaluatively charged word, a word that carries with it a whole social history, that does not mean that we cannot talk about the world. Nor does it mean that reference to the world is no more than an illusory support to the internal dynamic of our speech, which would be an extreme but typical post-structuralist position.

Insofar, then, as Bakhtin, through Voloshinov, provides a critique of Saussure, it is not surprising to find that his own thinking about such matters as authorship and reference runs profoundly counter to attempts to draw out the supposed implications of Saussure in these areas. Moreover, because Bakhtin never conceives matters in purely epistemological terms – that is, he is always concerned to subsume matters of knowledge into dialogic relationships – he always provides emphases that run counter to the 'epistemologism' of much post-Saussurean thinking, even or perhaps especially when such thinking imagines itself to be providing a critique of epistemology. We can see this clearly if we juxtapose Bakhtin's thinking about the novel and heteroglossia with an interesting, mildly deconstructive account of the realist novel, provided by Colin MacCabe, which seeks to specify a tradition within the novel as 'classic realist'.[2] In this argument, parallel in many ways with Bakhtin's hostility to 'monologic' novels, the novel is conceived as a 'discursive hierarchy', which disposes the speech of the characters beneath the truth-speaking discourse of the narrator. Thus the speech of the characters is opaque, to be read not for what it tells us about the world beyond it but for what it tells us about the characters who speak it; while the speech of the narrator, making due allowances for such artistic strategies as irony, is transparent, opening directly onto the world. Typical examples of 'classic realist' texts in this position are the novels of George Eliot, said to be made up of a discursive hierarchy in which her capacity to speak the truth of what she writes is persistently and ostentatiously displayed, while the speech of her characters is carefully and conscientiously 'placed' in historical and socially typifying terms. The contract to such 'classic realist' writing is modernist writing in the style of say Joyce, who celebrates precisely the 'revolution of the word', the incapacity of language ever to settle into a fixed or truth-speaking position.

The parallels between this position and Bakhtin's criticism of monologism should be apparent; and indeed, since such accounts are written in the knowledge of Kristeva's writings on the novel, it may be that they bear witness, at several removes, to Bakhtin's influence. But the differences in emphasis are just as important. In the first place the focus of the argument is very different. For those who criticize the 'classic realist' text, the focus remains a predominantly epistemological one, concerned to show the impossibility of the 'truth-speaking' authorial voice escaping the same deconstructive considerations which afflict all language. For Bakhtin, by contrast, the focus is at once ethical and social, in which the objection to the monologic 'discursive hierarchy' is that it represents a politically unacceptable arrogation of authority. Second, the alternative, the valued other, is very different also. For the Bakhtin of the Dostoevsky book, the alternative to monologism is of course polyphony, which does not mean a simple celebration of the other's word but a responsible engagement with it – though of course with no attempt to arrogate the final word. Even the Bakhtin of the book on Rabelais, who might be thought to be nearest to endorsing a 'revolution of the word', celebrates the upturnings and discrownings of carnival not in the name of some abstract Oedipal principle but because of their popular character and their historically prepared particularity.

If Bakhtin can be said to effect a deconstruction of the apparent unities of authorship, or the apparent obviousness of reference, it is always towards the heterogeneity of the historical process, and never towards the paradoxes that can be generated by considering epistemology in the abstract. The same historical engagement distinguishes his thinking on the set of problems now brought together under the heading of 'intertextuality', a term coined by Julia Kristeva out of her engagement with Bakhtin in the 1960s – though she soon came to regret some of the uses to which the term was put. We can distinguish two broad areas to which this term alludes. On the one hand it alludes to a fact of writing – that it is made up of a mosaic of fragments of other writing, drawing on, redirecting and reinflecting the myriad discourses that circulate in any society at any time. On the other hand, 'intertextuality' alludes to the radical implications that might be drawn from this – and which certainly are drawn by Kristeva herself – for our very notions of subjectivity. Let us take each of these two broad areas in turn.

In the first instance, we can see the insight into the intertextual nature of writing being pulled in two opposite directions. One of these is towards 'source study', either of a very traditional kind, in which no effort is made to undermine the autonomy of any particular text, but the various 'sources' on which it draws are made to appear, or in which some relationship of competition is postulated between any text and some 'precursor' text. There is nothing wrong with this kind of criticism except that it does not go nearly far enough. In the opposite direction lies the notion of 'textuality'. This seeks to do away with our common-sense ideas of authors and texts, and replace them with a sense of the underlying productiveness of writing itself; from the perspective of 'textuality' any actual text is merely a particular density among a myriad codes or discourses, whose origins cannot be traced and which stretch to the horizon in all directions. The Bakhtinian notion of heteroglossia marks a qualitative move forward from both these alternatives. It radically transforms the question of sources, making them a matter not just of individual influences or borrowing, but of the socially located languages that each and every text manages in its own particular way. And the social location of heteroglossia equally undoes the unstoppable indeterminancy of 'textuality'. This is in part because, as we have seen, Bakhtin is prepared to retain a notion of reference, of the text's relation to the world around it, which must, at the very least, act as a kind of anchor for any utterance, giving it some location in time and space. More importantly, however, Bakhtin, by means of the notion of heteroglossia, locates the utterance in the to and fro of active social forces, pulling back and forth in competition with each other and expressing their antagonisms in and through language. What grounds the aesthetic utterance is not finally its relation to the world beyond it, but the fact that it is always already in that world, acting in its own manner with the materials – the socially marked languages – appropriate to it.

But what of the more radical version of intertextuality, adumbrated by Julia Kristeva out of her engagement with Bakhtin in the 1960s – when the books on Rabelais and Dostoevsky were available but not the major writings of the 1930s including 'Discourse in the novel'? Here is her first formulation of what she calls 'an insight first introduced into literary theory by Bakhtin':

> any text is constructed as a mosaic of quotations; any text is the absorption and transformation of another. The notion of *intertextuality* replaces that of intersubjectivity, and poetic language is read as at least *double*.[3]

This is to take one possible emphasis from Bakhtin and draw out its implications provocatively. In this version, the very notion of subjectivity is dissolved, in the first instance with respect to aesthetic activity alone but eventually with respect to any subjectivity; we are not subjects so much as sites in which the various interactions and transpositions of the multiple texts of society are effected. Kristeva enjoys playing with the paradoxes such a view can generate, especially with respect to authorship:

> The writer's interlocutor, then, is the writer himself, but as reader of another text. The one who writes is the same as the one who reads. Since his interlocutor is a text, he himself is no more than a text rereading itself as it rewrites itself.[4]

This is enjoyably excessive, but it will not do just to dismiss it, for it may be considered cognate with some of the paradoxes that Bakhtin's writing can generate even when it remains in its own idiom. In particular, a similarly vertiginous sense of an unstoppable regress can be created by considering the dialogic nature of the utterance; the word is never your own word, but always in part the word of another, for whom in turn the word is never their own. If torn from the social location in which dialogue occurs, Bakhtin too can be made to sound as though we all speak in a hall of mirrors.

Kristeva later reformulated her notion of intertextuality in the light of some impatience with the way it had been taken up, though this later version was still developed directly out of her engagement with Bakhtin:

> The term *inter-textuality* designates this transposition of one (or of several) system(s) of signs into another; but because this term has often been understood in the banal sense of 'source-criticism' of a text, we will rather use the term *transposition*, which has the advantage of specifying that the passage from one signifying system to another demands a new articulation of the thetic (*thetique*) – of the enunciative and denotative positioning. If it is admitted that any signifying practice is a transposition of diverse signifying systems (an inter-textuality), it will be understood that its 'site' of enunciation and its denoted 'object' are never unique, full and identical to themselves, but are always plural, burst apart, susceptible to tabular models. Polysemy thus also appears as the result of a semiotic polyvalence, of belonging to diverse semiotic systems.[5]

One example she gives of such a transposition from one signifying practice to another, indicating her apparent closeness to Bakhtin at this point, is the transposition of the scene of carnival into a written text. Once again Kristeva draws upon what is genuinely there in Bakhtin but develops it in directions which are uncongenial to his thinking – or at least, towards a terminus which is negative rather than positive. Her first conclusion develops from the notion of 'transposition' – the fact that all signifying occasions represent the transformation of one or several signifying practices. This notion becomes the starting-point for a deconstruction of the apparent unity of the 'enunciative and denotative positioning', so that the first terminus of her argument is to undo the apparent unities of writer and referential object. We have already seen that Bakhtin may be happy to concede this but that he goes on from there to insist that complex relationships are nevertheless possible between writer, character and topic. The second large conclusion which she draws from the fact of intertextuality is that it provides an explanation of polysemy, of the capacity of any piece of writing, indeed any signifying practice, to carry out multiple and diverse meanings. This is because, in her account, all writing is multiple in its very constitution. The contrast with Bakhtin is again instructive. First, we have noted that there is a genuine effort in Bakhtin to reinstate some notion of unity even though the predominant movement is towards a celebration of polyphony, heteroglossia, and the upheavals of the carnivalesque. But more importantly than this, Kristeva effectively deracinates the signifying process, tearing it out of the dialogic encounter which is its only imaginable context for Bakhtin. Polysemy thus becomes a property of the writing, not a possible way in which the relationship between writing and reader may be negotiated. As a consequence, the production of meaning happens as a result of purely textual operations independent of historical location; the multiplicity of possible meanings in a text spring from that text and not from the multiplicity of possible occasions in which that text can be read.

Kristeva has been very influential, not least on Roland Barthes, whose *S/Z* is undoubtedly the single most extended, and virtuoso, attempt to locate a piece of writing in the multiple codes that make it up.[6] Kristeva's use of Bakhtin to develop the notion of intertextuality thus provides the occasion for some instructive contrasts between the attitudes of the Russian intellectual and those of his counterparts in the West – or at least Paris in the late 1960s. For the contrast is not so much one of scholarly method or conclusions, as of the whole philosophical, even political attitudes which inform those methods and conclusions. For Kristeva and Barthes, textuality and intertextuality provide opportunities for a peculiar notion of liberation, in which the deadening certainties of bourgeois culture, tying books to authors, words to their singular meanings, subjects to their unitary subjectivities, can be at least momentarily lifted, in favour of the joyful deferments of sense made possible by the endless switching of one code to another. Barthes' notion of *jouissance* nicely sums up this attitude – the pleasure (metaphorically sexual pleasure), to be had from the gaps and deferments of a meaning never fully completed. But Bakhtin is the philosopher, not of coming, but of becoming. That is to say, the unfinishedness which acts as a value in his writing is ultimately historical; it is a window onto the future. The historical process is never finished or completed, and as a result he does not need to imagine a version of liberation which takes you out of the historical process altogether.

One way that Bakhtin describes this location of meanings within the historical process is through 're-accentuation', especially as he uses the term in the conclusion to 'Discourse in the novel'. He seeks to find a means of describing the continued life of writing in history, starting indeed with the scholarly problem of a modern reader's capacity to recognize the presence of such all-important phenomena as parody in the writing of the past. In the absence of adequate knowledge of the dialogic background to a piece of writing, it may be impossible to recognize parody; there can be no guarantee of the continuing 'correctness' of interpretation because the dialogizing background is continually changing. This is the process which he describes as 're-accentuation', but as you might expect from Bakhtin he does not describe this process to lament the ever-growing distance from the truth. On the contrary, the process of historical re-accentuation is in fact only a continuation of the central novelistic process anyway; what an author does in writing is always to take another's word and re-accent it, give it a new valuation. Moreover, the word for Bakhtin is not inert, but living – 'and is therefore in all things true to *itself*' (DI 419). It may therefore be that under changed circumstances, against a new dialogic background, that word will come back into its own, and the parodic accent with which it was initially uttered will be appropriately discarded.

In this account, therefore, 'the historical life of classic works is in fact the uninterrupted process of their social and ideological re-accentuation' (DI 421). This seems to me to provide the basis for a rational rethinking of the classic problem besetting any historicizing account of writing, namely the difficulty of explaining how a piece of writing can persist, in powerful and meaningful ways, beyond its originating moment. There is a pervasive temptation to solve this question by invoking some ahistorical conception of human nature, which persists as a kind of substratum and

[98]

to which literature speaks. Quite apart from any general objections one might have to such a notion, it simply fails to account for the multiplicity, the diversity, the sheer downright oddness of many of the cultural artefacts, including writing, of the past. Bakhtin goes some way at least towards providing a description of what has historically happened without immediate recourse to that humanist cancelling of the problem.

To begin with, 're-accentuation' only carries on what is already happening in the process of reading. There is never a coincidence between author and reader, indeed there is never a coincidence between author and him or herself. So the scholarly fantasy of reconstructing the original moment of a text's reception as a way of discovering the truth of the text is not only a fantasy but a disabling one, if that originating moment is conceived as unitary or non-contradictory. Historical distance is thus only an extreme case of the distance that always divides reader from text, and this distance is the condition for meaningfulness, for it is precisely the space of dialogue. Moreover, that historical distance is not a barrier but may indeed be an opportunity, constantly providing new contexts in which the word may be dialogized and in which its unrealized possibilities may be made to speak. If there is some idealism in this, it is in the notion of the always-to-be-realised potential in any word (any '*living* word'). Yet it is possible to understand this in material terms also, to see the potential in the word as the product of the multiplicity of determinations that act upon it and of which it speaks. In this case, the process of re-accentuation would be one in which one contradictory and complex historical moment comes into dialogue with another, in which, in short, one historical specificity speaks to another. It is only to be expected that in these circumstances the result should be a complex negotiation of difference and similarity, of difference where you anticip- ated similarity, and vice-versa. The experience of reading writing from the past is surely just such a process, so that the effort to bracket out the historical distance and specificity, characteristic of some humanist ways of reading, is fundamentally misplaced. Engagement with the writing of the past, in this account, can retain its character of difficulty and strangeness as much as those moments of recognition and solidarity, for what it involves is the dialogue of two people who are immersed in their historically specific situations but not fully realized in them.

In contrast to the utopian, weightless and idealist fantasies of some versions of rationalism, then, Bakhtin does not envisage any exit from historical embodiment based upon some Archimedean point of rationality outside the historical process. But equally, as we saw in the chapter on the novel, he is insistent that no-one is ever fully explained by their socio-historical category – there is always some surplus of 'humanness' directed towards the future. Bakhtin is a various and complex thinker, capable of many different emphases; you may wish to engage more with the Bakhtin who insists on the socio-historical immersion than with the Bakhtin who simultaneously retains a loophole towards a realm of freedom. But it is important to recognize that he is both at once, and indeed, in his account any dialogue is premised upon both participants being caught but not trapped in the social process.

So far I have tried to engage Bakhtin with some of the characteristic questions asked by contemporary, theoretically informed criticism, espe-cially when such criticism can be thought of as being anticipated in some way by the writing of the Bakhtin circle. But one very characteristic development of contemporary literary criticism was emphatically not anticipated by Bakhtin and his fellows: the enormously increased atten-tion to questions of gender and women's oppression which has been won by the resurgence of the women's movement and feminism. This is not to say that questions of gender are absent from the writings of the Bakhtin circle – I am persuaded by the argument which suggests that no writing can ever free itself from its bodily origin, so the gendered body is bound to find its way even into the most abstract-seeming writing. We have indeed noticed that in Bakhtin's account of the 'grotesque body' of carnivalized writing questions of gender are evident. But this has not been the dominant way in which feminism has sought to engage with or dialogize Bakhtin's writing. In the fullest such effort, Dale Bauer's *Feminist Dialogics: A Theory of Failed Community,* Bauer has sought to problematize what she sees as the benign notion of the dialogic com-munity by recognizing that one of the lines of fissure in any community is the line of gender.[7] Thus the notion of heteroglossia must at least be extended to recognize that the competition of different languages must include the different languages of women. But Bauer is far from advoc-ating a simple pluralist 'adding in' of one more excluded voice; she rightly insists that to recognize such a line of fissure is also to recognize the inevitability of contestation and struggle across it, so that the character of a dialogic community is marked as much by difficulty and resistance as by benign dialogic engagement.

This seems to me to be a productive way of interanimating Bakhtin with feminism. It also points to an ambivalence that is perhaps within

Bakhtin's writing and certainly within the take-up of that writing. For it can be argued that the notion of 'heteroglossia' is one that already invokes contestation and conflict – the notion of carnival certainly does so. So from this perspective Bauer's insistence on the contestatory element that is *introduced* by feminism is pushing at an open door; that conflictual character in the competition of languages is already there in Bakhtin, though of course not with that central emphasis on gender that Bauer introduces. By contrast, it is certainly also true that dialogic interaction *is* often conceived as fundamentally benign in Bakhtin, in a way that appeals to those modern readers who wish to emphasize the ethical imperative, in Bakhtin's writing, that elevates dialogic engagement. Once again we can see that there are real grounds for those contemporary, competing, claims on Bakhtin.

Finally, we need to consider the challenge that Bakhtin's insistence upon the embodiment of the word poses to any rationalist project of knowledge. In other words, we need to ask what are the implications when you insist that all forms of knowledge about other people are fundamentally dialogues occurring between people equally grounded in particular historical languages. For one way of reading this idea is towards the destruction of any theoretical hierarchy, any attempt to sort one person's knowledge over and above another's. The antithesis, within the aesthetics of the novel, between the monologic and the polyphonic novel, is only the most extended version of a theme which recurs elsewhere in Bakhtin. In this antithesis, it will be recalled, the polyphonic novel is celebrated for the way it grants a voice to the characters of equal status to that of the voice of the narrator who claims no final word for him or her self. In the monologic novel, by contrast, such a final word is indeed claimed by the narrator, so that the voices of the characters are subordinated to it. We have here what are two contradictory impulses. On the one hand there is the impulse towards abstracted understanding, judgement, explanation and placement of others; on the other hand there is the impulse towards sympathy, solidarity and affirmation of the other's voice.

I have presented this almost as a matter of abstract knowledge, but as we have repeatedly seen in the course of this study, nothing ever appears to Bakhtin in this naked epistemological mode. In the actual studies of writing that Bakhtin provides, the positions of 'author' and 'hero' are occupied by people in such a way that for the author to arrogate a position of superior knowledge is also to arrogate a position of power amid a set of social relationships. Classically, for Bakhtin, those social relationships are both experienced and in some part realized through language, indeed the multiple languages that make up any heteroglossia. In the contemporary world, the diversity of languages has been enormously extended in the West, so that to arrogate the only position of knowledge as that of the received language of authority is to make especially unwarranted assumptions across lines of race, class and gender. But Bakhtin cannot, either, be co-opted as a simple advocate for relativism in these matters. If 'polyphony' points towards pluralism, it is not of a *laissez-faire* kind, but one which enjoins the double injunction both to engage others and to allow them their difference. In that difficult negotiation, finally unresolved by Bakhtin himself, can be traced the outline of the difficult, exciting and sometimes explosive cultural negotiations of the modern world.

Notes to Part I

Introduction

1 Katerina Clark and Michael Holquist, *Mikhail Bakhtin* (Harvard University Press, 1984).

1 Voloshinov and Bakhtin on language

1 I have in mind here much of so-called 'structuralism' in cultural studies and Levi-Strauss's anthropology.

2 The explicit attack on dialectics, as opposed to dialogue, comes in *Speech Genres and Other Late Essays*, p. 147.

2 Bakhtin on the novel

1 See Wayne C. Booth, *The Rhetoric of Fiction* (2nd edition, University of Chicago Press, 1983), especially pp. 71–6 for 'implied author'.

3 Bakhtin's carnival

1 Caryl Emerson, 'Problems with Baxtin's Poetics', *Slavic and East European Journal*, 32 (1988), 503–25, p. 520.

2 Lionel Gossman, Review of *Mikhail Bakhtin*, *Comparative Literature*, 38 iv (Fall 1986), 337–49, p. 345.

3 For an argument that Bakhtin radically underestimates the role of learned humanism in Rabelais' writing, see Richard M. Berrong, *Rabelais and Bakhtin: Popular Culture in Gargantua and Pantagruel* (University of Nebraska Press, Lincoln and London, 1986).

4 Allon White has insisted that this is not a question that can be decided in the abstract, but only by reference to the now massively accumulating historical materials. See 'The struggle over Bakhtin: Fraternal reply to Robert Young'. *Cultural Critique*, 8 (Winter 1987–8), 217–41. Two useful starting places are Peter Burke, *Popular Culture in Early Modern Europe* (Temple Smith, London, 1978), and Natalie Zemon Davis, *Society and Culture in Early Modern France* (Duckworth, London, 1975).

5 Natalie Davis, *Society and Culture*, p. 181.

6 See Emmanuel Le Roy Ladurie, *Carnival: A People's Uprising at Romans, 1579–1580*, translated by Mary Feeney (Scolar Press, London, 1980).

7 Natalie Davis, *Society and Culture*, p. 131.

8 Peter Stallybrass and Allon White, *The Politics and Poetics of Transgression* (Methuen, London, 1986).

9 Terry Castle, *Masquerade and Civilisation: The Carnivalesque in Eighteenth-Century English Culture and Fiction* (Methuen, London, 1986).

10   Laurie Finke, 'Mystical bodies and the dialogics of vision, *Philological Quarterly* 67 (1988), 439–50, p. 443.

11   Graham Pechey, 'On the borders of Bakhtin: Dialogization, decolonization', *Oxford Literary Review*, 9 (1987), 59–84, pp. 62–3.

12   C. L. Barber, *Shakespeare's Festive Comedies: A Study of Dramatic Form and Its Relation to Social Custom* (Meridian Books, New York, 1963).

13   Michael D. Bristol, *Carnival and Theater: Plebeian Culture and the Structure of Authority in Renaissance England* (Routledge, New York and London, 1989).

14   Terry Eagleton, 'Bakhtin, Schopenhauer, Kundera', in Ken Hirschkop and David Shepherd (eds), *Bakhtin and Cultural Theory* (Manchester University Press, 1989), 178–88, p. 183.

4 *Bakhtin and contemporary criticism*

1   See especially Michel Foucault, 'What is an Author', in Josue V. Harari (ed), *Textual Strategies: Perspectives in Post-Structuralist Criticism* (Methuen, London, 1980), pp. 141–60.

2   See for example, Colin MacCabe, *James Joyce and the Revolution of the Word* (Methuen, London, 1978), especially chapter 2, 'The end of a meta-language: from George Eliot to *Dubliners*', pp. 13–38.

3   Julia Kristeva, 'Word, dialogue and novel', in Leon S. Roudiez (ed), *Desire in Language: A Semiotic Approach to Literature and Art*, translated by Thomas Gora, Alice Jardine and Leon Roudiez (Basil Blackwell, Oxford, 1980), p. 66.

4   Ibid., p. 87.

5   Julia Kristeva, *La Revolution du Langage Poetique* (Seuil, Paris, 1974), pp. 59–60. My translation.

6   Roland Barthes, *S/Z: An Essay*, translated by Richard Miller (Hill and Wang, New York, 1974).

7   Dale M. Bauer, *Feminist Dialogics: A Theory of Failed Community* (State University of New York Press, 1988).

PART II

---

*Extracts from the writings of
Bakhtin and his circle*

5

V. N. Voloshinov
'Language, speech, and utterance' and 'Verbal interaction'

From *Marxism and the Philosophy of Language*, translated by Ladislav Matejka and I. R. Titunik (Academic Press, New York, 1986, pp. 65–98).

The following extract is made up of two chapters from Part II of Voloshinov's book on language. The two chapters consist of critiques of, respectively, 'abstract objectivism' and 'individualistic subjectivism', and move towards a dialectical synthesis of the two trends in linguistic thought; in such a synthesis the outline of a true science of language can at last be glimpsed. As I explained in chapter 1, 'abstract objectivism' includes the thinking of Saussure, who may indeed be thought of as the outstanding representative of this trend of thought in the twentieth century.

Part I of Voloshinov's book prepared for this more formal critique of linguistic thought by asserting some general principles. Above all, these insist that language is a social phenomenon, that it exists between people, and that it carries the values and accents – the ideology – of social beings in real situations. But the book also takes up a strand of argument from Voloshinov's book on Freud, in arguing that the formative influence of language on consciousness means that consciousness too is a social phenomenon. Thus the psyche, like the utterance, is a 'borderline' phenomenon, located between the organism and the outside world. The argument against 'individualistic subjectivism' in the following pages becomes clearer in this light.

The manner of argument by which Voloshinov proceeds in these two chapters – from critique of two opposed positions to a third, positive, conclusion – is also characteristic of Bakhtin's manner of argument, though as we have seen Bakhtin was later to repudiate the dialectic as an intellectual procedure, in marked contrast to Voloshinov's explicit claims here. One further claim of the author – that utterances, even the 'monuments' of the past, only have meaning as part of a living chain of meanings – requires that the living chain into which Voloshinov's own statements were inserted be partially reconstructed. Thus it is important to recognize that in quoting from N. Ja. Marr in 'Language, speech, and utterance', Voloshinov is claiming the support of the dominant figure in Soviet linguistics. Marr held some eccentric and now utterly discredited views on the evolution of languages. Voloshinov quotes from him in a way which supports his own line of argument that linguistics has derived from the philological study of the alien word, without acceding to the views of linguistic stages advanced elsewhere. In 'Verbal interaction', Voloshinov refers to Spitzer and the 'Vosslerites'; these were all late nineteenth-century idealist descendants of Humboldt, who stressed, against much current linguistic thought, the importance of individual creativity in linguistic change.

Language, speech, and utterance

Can language as a system of normative, self-identical forms be considered an objective fact? Language as a system of norms and the actual viewpoint on language in a speaker's consciousness. What kind of linguistic reality underlies a linguistic system? The problem of the alien, foreign word. The errors of abstract objectivism. Summary and conclusions.

In the preceding chapter, we tried to give an entirely objective picture of the two main trends of thought in the philosophy of language. Now we must submit those trends to a thorough critical analysis. Only after having done so will we be able to answer the question posed at the end of the preceding chapter.

Let us begin with critical analysis of the second trend, that of abstract objectivism.

First of all, let us pose a question: to what degree may the system of self-identical linguistic norms (i.e., the system of language, as the representatives of the second trend understand it) be considered a real entity?

None of the representatives of abstract objectivism would, of course, ascribe concrete material reality to the system of language. True, that system is expressed in material things – in signs – but as a system of normatively identical forms, it has reality only in the capacity of the social norm.

Representatives of abstract objectivism constantly stress – and it is one of their basic principles – that the system of language is an objective fact external to and independent of *any* individual consciousness. Actually, represented as a system of self-identical, immutable norms, it can be perceived in this way only by the individual consciousness and from the point of view of that consciousness.

Indeed, if we were to disregard the subjective individual consciousness vis-à-vis the language system, the system of norms incontestable for that consciousness, if we were to look at language in a truly objective way – from the side, so to speak, or more accurately, from above it, we would discover no inert system of self-identical norms. Instead, we would find ourselves witnessing the ceaseless generation of language norms.

From a truly objective viewpoint, one that attempts to see language in a way completely apart from how it appears to any given individual at any given moment in time, language presents the picture of a ceaseless flow of becoming. From the standpoint of observing a language objectively, from above, there is no real moment in time when a synchronic system of language could be constructed.

Thus *a synchronic system, from the objective point of view, does not correspond to any real moment in the historical process of becoming.* And indeed, to the historian of language, with his diachronic point of view, a synchronic system is not a real entity; it merely serves as a conventional scale on which to register the deviations occurring at every real instant in time.

So, then, a synchronic system may be said to exist only from the point of view of the subjective consciousness of an individual speaker belonging to some particular language group at some particular moment of historical time. From an objective point of view, no such system exists at any real instant of historical time. We may suppose, for instance, that while Caesar was engaged in writing his works, the Latin language was for him a fixed, incontestable system of self-identical norms; but, for the historian of Latin, a continuous process of linguistic change was going on at the very moment that Caesar was working (whether or not the historian of Latin would be able to pinpoint those changes).

Any system of social norms occupies an analogous position. It exists only with respect to the subjective consciousness of individuals belonging to some particular community governed by norms. Such is the nature of a system of moral norms, of judicial norms, of norms for aesthetic taste (there are, indeed, such norms), and so on. Of course, these norms vary: their obligatory nature varies, as does the breadth of their social compass, as does also the degree of their social significance, determined by their proximity to the basis, etc. But the nature of their existence as norms remains the same – they exist only with respect to the subjective consciousness of members of some particular community.

Does it follow, then, that this relationship between the subjective consciousness and language as a system of objective, incontestable norms is itself bereft of any objectivity? Of course not. Properly understood, this relationship can be considered an objective fact.

If we claim that language as a system of incontestable and immutable norms exists objectively, we commit a gross error. But if we claim that language, with respect to the individual consciousness, is a system of immutable norms, that such is the mode of existence of language for each member of any given language community, then what we are expressing in these terms is a completely objective relationship. Whether the fact itself is correctly constituted, whether language actually does appear only as a fixed and inert system of norms to the speaker's consciousness – that is another question. For the time being we shall leave that question open. But the point, in any case, is that a certain kind of objective relationship can be established.

Now, how do representatives of abstract objectivism themselves regard this matter? Do they assert that language is a system of objective and incontestable self-identical norms, or are they aware of the fact that this is only the mode of existence of the language for the subjective consciousness of a speaker of any given language?

No better answer can be given than the following: most representatives of abstract objectivism are inclined to assert *the unmediated reality, the unmediated objectivity of language as a system of normatively identical forms.* In the case of these representatives of the second trend, abstract objectivism converts directly into *hypostasizing abstract objectivism.* Other representatives of the trend (Meillet, for instance) have a more critical attitude and do take account of the abstract and conventional nature of the linguistic system. However, not a single representative of abstract objectivism has arrived at a clear and distinct conception of the kind of reality that language as an objective system does possess. In the majority of cases, these representatives walk the tightrope between two conceptions of the word "objective" as applied to the system of language: one in quotation marks, so to speak (from the standpoint of the speaker's subjective consciousness), and one without quotation marks (from the objective standpoint). This, incidentally, is the way that Saussure, too, handles the question – he provides no clear-cut solution.

Now we must ask: does language really exist for the speaker's subjective consciousness as an objective system of incontestable, normatively identical forms? Has abstract objectivism correctly understood the point of view of the speaker's subjective consciousness? Or, to put it another way: is the mode of being of language in the subjective speech consciousness really what abstract objectivism says it is?

We must answer this question in the negative. The speaker's subjective consciousness does not in the least operate with language as a system of normatively identical forms. That system is merely an abstraction arrived with a good deal of trouble and with a definite cognitive and practical focus of attention. The system of language is the product of deliberation on language, and deliberation of a kind by no means carried out by the consciousness of the native speaker himself and by no means carried out for the immediate purposes of speaking.

In point of fact, the speaker's focus of attention is brought about in line with the particular, concrete utterance he is making. What matters to him is applying a normatively identical form (let us grant there is such a thing for the time being) in some particular, concrete context. For him, the centre of gravity lies not in the identity of the form but in that new and concrete meaning it acquires in the particular context. What the speaker values is not that aspect of the form which is invariably identical in all instances of its usage, despite the nature of those instances, but that aspect of the linguistic form because of which it can figure in the given, concrete context, because of which it becomes a sign adequate to the conditions of the given, concrete situation.

We can express it this way: *what is important for the speaker about a linguistic form is not that it is a stable and always self-equivalent signal, but that it is an always changeable and adaptable sign.* That is the speaker's point of view.

But doesn't the speaker also have to take into account the point of view of the listener and understander? Isn't it possible that here, exactly, is where the normative identity of a linguistic form comes into force?

This, too, is not quite so. The basic task of understanding does not at all amount to recognizing the linguistic form used by the speaker as the familiar, "that very same," form, the way we distinctly recognize, for instance, a signal that we have not quite become used to or a form in a language that we do not know very well. No, the task of understanding does not basically amount to recognizing the form used, but rather to understanding it in a particular, concrete context, to understanding its meaning in a particular utterance, i.e., it amounts to understanding its novelty and not to recognizing its identity.

In other words, the understander, belonging to the same language community, also is attuned to the linguistic form not as a fixed, self-identical signal, but as a changeable and adaptable sign.

The process of understanding is on no account to be confused with the process of recognition. These are thoroughly different processes. Only a sign can be understood; what is recognized is a signal. A signal is an internally fixed, singular thing that does not in fact stand for anything else, or reflect or refract anything, but is simply a technical means for indicating this or that object (some definite, fixed object) or this or that action (likewise definite and fixed).[1] Under no circumstances does the signal relate to the domain of the ideological; it relates to the world of technical devices, to instruments of production in the broad sense of the term. Even further removed from ideology are the signals with which reflexology is concerned. These signals, taken in relation to the organism of the animal subject, i.e., as signals for that subject, have no relation to techniques of production. In this capacity they are not signals but stimuli of a special kind. They become instruments of production only in the hands of the experimenter. The grievous misconceptions and the in-grained habits of mechanistic thought are alone responsible for the attempt to take these "signals" and very nearly make of them the key to the understanding of language and of the human psyche (inner word).

Should a linguistic form remain only a signal, recognized as such by the understander, it, then, does not exist for him as a linguistic form. Pure signality is not evinced even in the early stages of language learning. In this case, too, the linguistic form is oriented in context; here, too, it is a sign, although the factor of signality and its correlative, the factor of recognition, are operative.

Thus the constituent factor for the linguistic form, as for the sign, is not at all its self-identity as signal but its specific variability; and the constituent factor for understanding the linguistic form is not recognition of "the same thing," but understanding in the proper sense of the word, i.e., orientation in the particular, given context and in the particular, given situation – orientation in the dynamic process of becoming and not "orientation" in some inert state.[2]

It does not, of course, follow from all that has been said that the factors of signalization and its correlative, recognition, are absent from language. They are present, but they are not constituents of language as such. They are dialectically effaced by the new quality of the sign (i.e., of language as such). In the speaker's native language, i.e., for the linguistic conscious-ness of a member of a particular language community, signal-recognition is certainly dialectically effaced. In the process of mastering a foreign language, signality and recognition still make themselves felt, so to speak, and still remain to be surmounted, the language not yet fully having become language. The ideal of mastering a language is absorption of signality by pure semioticity and of recognition by pure understanding.[3]

The linguistic consciousness of the speaker and of the listener-understander, in the practical business of living speech, is not at all concerned with the abstract system of normatively identical forms of language, but with language-speech in the sense of the aggregate of possible contexts of usage for a particular linguistic form. For a person speaking his native tongue, a word presents itself not as an item of vocabulary but as a word that has been used in a wide variety of utterances by co-speaker A, co-speaker B, co-speaker C and so on, and has been variously used in the speaker's own utterances. A very special and specific kind of orientation is necessary, if one is to go from there to the self-identical word belonging to the lexicological system of the language in question – the dictionary word. For that reason, a member of a language community does not normally feel himself under the pressure of incontestable linguistic norms. A linguistic form will bring its normative significance to the fore only in exceptionally rare instances of conflict, instances that are not typical for speech activity (and which for modern man are almost exclusively associated with writing).

One other extremely pertinent consideration needs to be added here. The verbal consciousness of speakers has, by and large, nothing whatever to do with linguistic form as such or with language as such.

In point of fact, the linguistic form, which, as we have just shown, exists for the speaker only in the context of specific utterances, exists, consequently, only in a specific ideological context. In actuality, we never say or hear *words*, we say and hear what is true or false, good or bad, important or unimportant, pleasant or unpleasant, and so on. *Words are always filled with content and meaning drawn from behaviour or ideology.* That is the way we understand words, and we can respond only to words that engage us behaviorally or ideologically.

Only in abnormal and special cases do we apply the criterion of correctness to an utterance (for instance, in language instruction). Normally, the criterion of linguistic correctness is submerged by a purely ideological criterion: an utterance's correctness is eclipsed by its truthfulness or falsity, its poeticalness or banality, etc.[4]

Language, in the process of its practical implementation, is inseparable from its ideological or behavioral impletion. Here, too, an orientation of an entirely special kind – one unaffected by the aims of the speaker's consciousness – is required if language is to be abstractly segregated from its ideological or behavioral impletion.

If we advance this abstract segregation to the status of a principle, if we reify linguistic form divorced from ideological impletion, as do certain representatives of the second trend, then we end up dealing with a signal and not with a sign of language-speech.

[113]

The divorce of language from its ideological impletion is one of abstract objectivism's most serious errors.

In sum, then, for the consciousness of a speaker of a language, the real mode of existence for that language is not as a system of normatively identical forms. From the viewpoint of the speaker's consciousness and his real-life practice in social intercourse, there is no direct access to the system of language envisioned by abstract objectivism.

What, then, in such a case, is this system?

It is clear from the start that that system is obtained by way of abstraction, that it is composed of elements extracted in an abstract way from the real units that make up the stream of speech – from utterances. Any abstraction, if it is to be legitimate, must be justified by some specific theoretical and practical goal. An abstraction may be productive or not productive, or may be productive for some goals and tasks and not productive for others.

What are the goals that underlie the kind of linguistic abstraction that leads to the synchronic system of language? And from what point of view may this system be regarded productive and necessary?

At the basis of the modes of linguistic thought that lead to the postulation of language as a system of normatively identical forms lies a *practical and theoretical focus of attention on the study of defunct, alien languages preserved in written monuments.*

This philological orientation has determined the whole course of linguistic thinking in the European world to a very considerable degree, and we must stress this point with all possible insistence. European linguistic thought formed and matured over concern with the cadavers of written languages; almost all its basic categories, its basic approaches and techniques were worked out in the process of reviving these cadavers.

Philologism is the inevitable distinguishing mark of the whole of European linguistics as determined by the historical vicissitudes of its birth and development. However far back we may go in tracing the history of linguistic categories and methods, we find philologists everywhere. Not just the Alexandrians, but the ancient Romans were philologists, as were the Greeks (Aristotle is a typical philologist). Also, the ancient Hindus were philologists.

We can state outright: *linguistics makes its appearance wherever and whenever philological need has appeared.* Philological need gave birth to linguistics, rocked its cradle, and left its philological flute wrapped in its swaddling clothes. That flute was supposed to be able to awaken the dead.

But it lacked the range necessary for mastering living speech as actually and continuously generated.

N. Ja. Marr is perfectly correct in pointing out this philological essence in Indo-European linguistic thought:

> Indo-European linguistics, commanding an already established and a long since fully formed object of investigation – the Indo-European languages of the historical epochs – and taking its departure, moreover, almost exclusively from the petrified forms of written languages – dead languages foremost among them – is naturally itself incapable of bringing to light the process of the emergence of speech in general and the origination of its species.[5]

Or in another passage:

> The greatest obstacle [to the study of aboriginal speech – V.V.] is caused not by the difficulty of the research itself, nor the lack of solid data, but by our scientific thinking, which is locked into the traditional outlook of philology or the history of culture and has not been nurtured by the ethnological and linguistic perception of living speech in its limitlessly free, creative ebb and flow.[6]

Marr's words hold true not only, of course, for Indo-European studies, which have set the tone for all contemporary linguistics, but also for the whole of linguistics as we know it from history. Everywhere, as we have said, linguistics is the child of philology.

Guided by the philological need, linguistics has always taken as its point of departure the finished monologic utterance – the ancient written monument, considering it the ultimate realium. All its methods and categories were elaborated in its work on this kind of defunct, monologic utterance or, rather, on a series of such utterances constituting a corpus for linguistics by virtue of common language alone.

But the monologic utterance is, after all, already an abstraction, though, to be sure, an abstraction of a "natural" kind. Any monologic utterance, the written monument included, is an inseverable element of verbal communication. Any utterance – the finished, written utterance not excepted – makes response to something and is calculated to be responded to in turn. It is but one link in a continuous chain of speech performances. Each monument carries on the work of its predecessors, polemicizing with them, expecting active, responsive understanding, and anticipating such understanding in return. Each monument in actuality is an integral part of science, literature, or political life. The monument, as any other monologic utterance, is set toward being perceived in the context of current scientific life or current literary affairs, i.e., it is perceived in the generative process of that particular ideological domain of which it is an integral part.

The philologist – linguist tears the monument out of the real domain and views it as if it were a self-sufficient, isolated entity. He brings to bear on it not an active ideological understanding but a completely passive kind of understanding, in which there is not a flicker of response, as there would be in any authentic kind of understanding. The philologist takes the isolated monument as a document of language and places it in relation with other monuments on the general plane of the language in question. All methods and categories of linguistic thought were formed in this process of comparing and correlating isolated monologic utterances on the plane of language.

The dead language the linguist studies is, of course, an alien language. Therefore, the system of linguistic categories is least of all a product of cognitive reflection on the part of the linguistic consciousness of a speaker and that language. Here reflection does not involve a native speaker's feeling for his own language. No, this kind of reflection is that of a mind striking out into, breaking trails through, the unfamiliar world of an alien language.

Inevitably, the philologist-linguist's passive understanding is projected onto the very monument he is studying from the language point of view, as if that monument were in fact calculated for just that kind of understanding, as if it had, in fact, been written for the philologist.

The result of all this is a fundamentally erroneous theory of understanding that underlies not only the methods of linguistic interpretation of texts but also the whole of European semasiology. Its entire position on word meaning and theme is permeated through and through with the false notion of *passive understanding,* the kind of understanding of a word that excludes active response in advance and on principle.

We shall see later that this kind of understanding, with built-in exclusion of response, is not at all in fact the kind of understanding that applies in language-speech. The latter kind of understanding inextricably merges with an active position taken apropos of what has been said and is being understood. The characteristic feature of passive understanding is exactly a distinct sense of the identity factor in a linguistic sign, i.e., perception of it as an artifact-signal and, in correlation with this, the predominance of the recognition factor.

Thus *dead, written, alien language* is the true description of the language with which linguistic thought has been concerned.

The *isolated, finished, monologic utterance*, divorced from its verbal and actual context and standing open not to any possible sort of active response but to passive understanding on the part of a philologist – that is the ultimate "donnée" and the starting point of linguistic thought.

Engendered in the process of mastering a dead, alien language for purposes of scientific investigation, linguistic thought has also served another, not investigatory, but instructional purpose: the purpose not of deciphering a language but of teaching an already deciphered language. Monuments were made over from heuristic documents into a classical model of language for the lecture hall.

This second basic task of linguistics – its creating the apparatus essential for instruction in a deciphered language, for codifying it, so to speak, in line with the aims of lecture-hall transmission, made a substantial imprint on linguistic thinking. *Phonetics, grammar, lexicon* – the three branches of the system of language, the three organizing centers for linguistic categories – took shape within the channel of these two major tasks of linguistics: *the heuristic and the pedagogical.*

What is a philologist?

Despite the vast differences in cultural and historical lineaments from the ancient Hindu priests to the modern European scholar of language, the philologist has always and everywhere been a decipherer of alien, "secret" scripts and words, and a teacher, a disseminator, of that which has been deciphered and handed down by tradition.

The first philologists and the first linguists were always and everywhere *priests*. History knows no nation whose sacred writings or oral tradition were not to some degree in a language foreign and incomprehensible to the profane. To decipher the mystery of sacred words was the task meant to be carried out by the priest-philologists.

It was on these grounds that ancient philosophy of language was engendered: the Vedic teaching about the word, the Logos of the ancient Greek thinkers, and the biblical philosophy of the word.

To understand these philosophemes properly, one must not forget for one instant that they were *philosophemes of the alien word*. If some nation had known only its own native tongue; if, for that nation, word had always coincided with native word or that nation's life; if no mysterious, alien word, no word from a foreign tongue, had ever entered its purview, then such a nation would never have created anything resembling these

[117]

philosophemes.[7] It is an astonishing feature: from remotest antiquity to the present day, the philosophy of word and linguistic though have been built upon specific sensibility to the alien, foreign-language word and upon those tasks which precisely that kind of word presents to the mind – deciphering and teaching what has been deciphered.

The Vedic priest and the contemporary philologist-linguist are spellbound and held captive in their thinking about language by one and the same phenomenon – the phenomenon of alien, foreign-language word.

One is sensible of one's native word in a completely different way or, to be more precise, one is ordinarily not sensible of one's native word as a word crammed with all those categories that it has generated in linguistic thought and that it generated in the philosophical-religious thought of the ancients. Native word is one's "kith and kin"; we feel about it as we feel about our habitual attire or, even better, about the atmosphere in which we habitually live and breathe. It contains no mystery; it can become a mystery only in the mouth of others, provided they are hierarchically alien to us – in the mouth of the chief, in the mouth of the priests. But in that case, it has already become a word of a different kind, externally changed and removed from the routine of life (taboo for usage in ordinary life, or an archaism of speech); that is, if it had not already been from the start a foreign word in the mouth of a conqueror-chief. Only at this point is the "Word" born, and only at this point – *incipit philosophia, incipit philologia.*

Orientation in linguistics and the philosophy of language toward the alien, foreign word is by no means an accidental occurrence or a whim on the part of linguistics and philosophy. No, that orientation is the expression of the enormous historical role that the alien word has played in the formation of all the historical cultures. It has played that role with respect to all domains of ideological creativity without exception, from the sociopolitical order to the behavioral code of daily life. Indeed, it was the alien, foreign-language word that brought civilization, culture, religion, and political organization (e.g., the role of the Sumerians with respect to the Babylonian Semites, of the Japhites to the Hellenes, of Rome and of Christianity to the barbarian peoples, of Byzantium, the "Varangians," the South Slavic tribes to the Eastern Slavs, etc.). This grandiose organizing role of the alien word, which always either entered upon the scene with alien force of arms and organization or was found on the scene by the young conqueror-nation of an old and once mighty culture and captivated, from its grave, so to speak, the ideological consciousness of the newcomer-nation – this role of the alien word led to its coalescence in the depths of the historical consciousness of nations with the idea of authority, the idea of power, the idea of holiness, the idea of truth, and dictated that notions about the word be preeminently oriented toward the alien word.

However, the philosophy of language and linguistics never were, and are still not today, objectively aware of the enormous historical role played by the foreign word. No, linguistics is still enslaved by it; linguistics represents, as it were, the last wave to reach us of the once-upon-a-time fructifying inundation of alien speech, the last residue of its dictatorial and culture-creating role.

For this very reason, linguistics, itself the product of foreign word, is far from any proper understanding of the role played by the foreign word in the history of language and linguistic consciousness. On the contrary, Indo-European studies have fashioned categories of understanding for the history of language of a kind that preclude proper evaluation of the role of alien word. Meanwhile, that role, to all appearances, is enormous.

The idea of *linguistic "crossing" as the basic factor in the evolution of languages* has been definitively advanced by Marr. He also recognized linguistic crossing to be the main factor in the solution of the problem of how language originated:

> Crossing in general, as a factor in the emergence of different language species and even types of language, being *the* source for the formation of new species, has been observed and traced throughout all the Japhetic languages, and this must be considered one of the most momentous achievements of Japhetic linguistics.... The point is that no primigene of sound language, no single-tribal language exists or, as we shall see, existed or could have existed. Language, the creation of sociality which had arisen on the basis of intertribal communication brought about by economic needs, is the accumulation of precisely this kind of sociality, which is always multitribal.[8]

In his article, "On the Origin of Language," Marr has the following to say on our topic:

> In short, the approach to this or that language in terms of so-called national culture, as the mass, native language of an entire population, is unscientific and unrealistic; the ecumenical, classless national language remains a fiction. But that is not the half of it. Just as castes in the early stages of development issue from tribes – or really from tribal formations,

that are also by no means simple in themselves – so by way of crossing, did concrete tribal languages and, even more so, national languages, come to represent crossbred types of languages, crossbred from the combination of simple elements through which, in one way or another, every language is formed. Paleontological analysis of human speech goes no further than definition of these tribal elements, but the Japhetic theory accommodates these elements in such a decisive and definitive way that the question of the origin of language is boiled down to the question of the emergence of these elements, which are in fact nothing more than tribal names.[9]

Here we can only take note of the significance of the alien word for the problem of the origin of language and its evolution. These problems exceed the scope of our present study. For us the importance of the alien word consists in its role as a factor determining philosophical linguistic thought and the categories and approaches stemming from that thought.

We shall now disregard the particularities of aboriginal thought about the alien word[10] and also the categories of the ancient philosophemes of word mentioned above. We shall attempt to note down here only those particular features in thought about the word that have persisted through the centuries and have had determinative effect on contemporary linguistic thought. We may safely assume that these are precisely the categories that have found their most marked and most clear-cut expression in the doctrine of abstract objectivism.

We shall now attempt to reformulate, in the following series of concise premises, those features of cognizance of the alien word that underlie abstract objectivism. In doing so, we shall also be summarizing our preceding exposition and supplementing it at certain crucial points.[11]

1. *The factor of stable self-identity in linguistic forms takes precedence over their mutability.*
2. *The abstract takes precedence over the concrete.*
3. *Abstract systematization takes precedence over historical actuality.*
4. *The forms of elements take precedence over the form of the whole.*
5. *Reification of the isolated linguistic element to the neglect of the dynamics of speech.*
6. *Singularization of word meaning and accent to the neglect of its living multiplicity of meaning and accent.*
7. *The notion of language as a ready-made artifact handed down from one generation to another.*
8. *Inability to conceptualize the inner generative process of a language.*

Let us consider briefly each of these features of the system of thought dominated by the alien word.

1. The first feature needs no further commentary. We have already pointed out that understanding one's own language is focused not on recognizing identical elements of speech but on understanding their new, contextual meaning. The construction of a system of self-identical forms may then be said to be an indispensable and vital stage in the process of deciphering an alien language and handing it on.

2. The second point, too, is clear enough on the basis of what has already been said. The finished monologic utterance is an abstraction, in point of fact. Concretization of a word is possible only by way of including that word into the actual historical context of its original implementation. By propounding the isolated monologic utterance, all those ties that bind an utterance to the full concreteness of historical generation are torn away.

3. Formalism and systematicity are the typical distinguishing marks of any kind of thinking focused on a ready-made and, so to speak, arrested object.

This particular feature of thought has many different manifestations. Characteristically, what undergoes systematization is usually (if not exclusively) someone else's thought. True creators – the initiators of new ideological trends – are never formalistic systematizers. Systematization comes upon the scene during an age which feels itself in command of a ready-made and handed-down body of authoritative thought. A creative age must first have passed; then and only then does the business of formalistic systematizing begin – an undertaking typical of heirs and epigones who feel themselves in possession of someone else's, now voiceless word. Orientation in the dynamic flow of generative process can never be of the formal, systematizing kind. Therefore, formal, systematizing grammatical thought could have developed to its full scope and power only on the material of an alien, dead language, and only could have done so provided that that language had already, to a significant degree, lost its affective potency – its sacrosanct and authoritative character. With respect to living language, systematic, grammatical thought must inevitably adopt a conservative position, i.e., it must interpret living language as if it were already perfected and ready-made and thus must look upon any sort of innovation in language with hostility. Formal, systematic thought about language is incompatible with living, historical understanding of language. From the system's point of view, history always seems merely a series of accidental transgressions.

4. Linguistics, as we have seen, is oriented toward the isolated,

monologic utterance. Linguistic monuments comprise the material for study, and the passively understanding mind of the philologist is brought to bear on the material. Thus all the work goes on within the bounds of some given utterance. As for the boundaries that demarcate the utterance as a whole entity, they are perceived faintly or sometimes not at all. Research is wholly taken up in study of immanent connections on the inside territory of the utterance. Considerations of the utterance's external affairs, so to speak, remain beyond the field of study. Thus, all connections that exceed the bounds of the utterance as a monologic whole are ignored. One might well expect, then, that the very nature of an utterance's wholeness and the forms that the wholeness may take are left outside of linguistic thought. And indeed, linguistic thought goes no further than the elements that make up the monologic utterance. The structure of a complex sentence (a period) – that is the furthest limit of linguistic reach. The structure of a whole utterance is something linguistics leaves to the competence of other disciplines – to rhetoric and poetics. Linguistics lacks any approach to the compositional forms of the whole. Therefore, there is no direct transition between the linguistic forms of the elements of an utterance and the forms of its whole, indeed, no connection at all! Only by making a jump from syntax can we arrive at problems of composition. This is absolutely inevitable, seeing that the forms making up the whole of an utterance can only be perceived and understood against the background of other whole utterances belonging to a unity of some particular domain of ideology. Thus, for instance, the forms of a literary utterance – a literary work of art – can only be understood in the unity of literary life, indissolubly connected with other kinds of *literary* forms. When we relegate a literary work to the history of language as a system, when we regard it only as a document of language, we lose access to its forms as the forms of a literary whole. There is a world of difference between referring a work to the system of language and referring a work to the concrete unity of literary life, and that difference is insurmountable on the grounds of abstract objectivism.

5. Linguistic form is merely an abstractly extractable factor of the dynamic whole of speech performance – of the utterance. Abstraction of that sort is, of course, perfectly legitimate within the range of the specific tasks linguistics sets for itself. However, abstract objectivism supplies the grounds for the reification of the linguistic form, for its becoming an element supposedly extractable in actuality and supposedly capable of an isolated, historical existence of its own. This is completely under-

standable: after all, the system as a whole cannot undergo historical development. The utterance as a whole entity does not exist for linguistics. Consequently, the elements of the system, i.e., the separate linguistic forms, are all that is left. And so *they* must be what can undergo historical change.

History of language, then, amounts to the history of separate linguistic forms (phonetic, morphological or other) that undergo development despite the system as a whole and apart from concrete utterances.[12]

Vossler is perfectly right in what he says about the history of language as conceived by abstract objectivism:

> Roughly speaking, the history of language, as it is given to us by historical grammar, is the same sort of thing as a history of clothing would be, which does not take the concept of fashion or the taste of the time as its point of departure, but provides a chronologically and geographically arranged list of buttons, clasps, stockings, hats, and ribbons. In historical grammar, such buttons and ribbons would have names like weak or strong *e*, voiceless *t*, voiced *d*, and so on.[13]

6. The meaning of a word is determined entirely by its context. In fact, there are as many meanings of a word as there are contexts of its usage.[14] At the same time, however, the word does not cease to be a single entity; it does, not, so to speak, break apart into as many separate words as there are contexts of its usage. The word's unity is assured, of course, not only by the unity of its phonetic composition but also by that factor of unity which is common to all its meanings. How can the fundamental poly-semanticity of the word be reconciled with its unity? To pose this question is to formulate, in a rough and elementary way, the cardinal problem of semantics. It is a problem that can only be solved dialectically. But how does abstract objectivism go about it? For abstract objectivism, the unity factor of a word solidifies, as it were, and breaks away from the fundamental multiplicity of its meanings. This multiplicity is perceived as the occasional overtones of a single hard-and-fast meaning. The focus of linguistic attention is exactly opposite that of real-life understanding on the part of the speakers engaged in a particular flow of speech. The philologist-linguist, when comparing different contexts in which a given word appears, focuses his attention on the identity factor in its usage, since to him what is important is to be able to remove the word from the contexts compared and to give it definition outside context, i.e., to create a dictionary word out of it. This process of isolating a word and fixing its

meaning outside any context takes on added force when comparing different languages, i.e., when trying to match a word with an equivalent word in another language. In the process of linguistic treatment, meaning is constructed, as it were, on the border of at least two languages. These endeavours on the linguist's part are further complicated by the fact that he creates the fiction of a single and actual object corresponding to the given word. This object, being single and self-identical, is just what ensures the unity of meaning. The fiction of a word's literal realia promotes to an even greater degree the reification of its meaning. On these grounds, the dialectical combination of the unity of meaning with its multiplicity becomes impossible.

Another grave error on the part of abstract objectivism is to be seen in the following. The various contexts of usage for any one particular word are conceived of as all lying on the same plane. These contexts are thought of as forming a series of circumscribed, self-contained utterances all pointed in the same direction. In actual fact, this is far from true: contexts of usage for one and the same word often contrast with one another. The classical instance of such contrasting contexts of usage for one and the same word is found in dialogue. In the alternating lines of a dialogue, the same word may figure in two mutually clashing contexts. Of course, dialogue is only the most graphic and obvious instance of varidirectional contexts. Actually, any real utterance, in one way or another or to one degree or another, makes a statement of agreement with or a negation of something. Contexts do not stand side by side in a row, as if unaware of one another, but are in a state of constant tension, or incessant interaction and conflict. The change of a word's evaluative accent in different contexts is totally ignored by linguistics and has no reflection in its doctrine on the unity of meaning. This accent is least amenable to reification, yet it is precisely a word's multiaccentuality that makes it a living thing. The problem of multiaccentuality ought to be closely associated with the problem of multiplicity of meanings. Only provided that they are associated together can the two problems be solved. But it is exactly this association that the basic principles of abstract objectivism utterly preclude. Linguistics has thrown evaluative accent overboard along with the unique utterance (*parole*).[15]

7. According to the teaching of abstract objectivism, language is handed down as a ready-made product from generation to generation. Of course, the representatives of the second trend understand the transmission of the language legacy, transmission of language as an artifact, in meta-

phorical terms, but still, in their hands, such a comparison is not merely a metaphor. In reifying the system of language and in viewing living language as if it were dead and alien, abstract objectivism makes language something external to the stream of verbal communication. This stream flows on, but language, like a ball, is tossed from generation to generation. In actual fact, however, language moves together with that stream and is inseparable from it. Language cannot properly be said to be handed down – it endures, but it endures as a continuous process of becoming. Individuals do not receive a ready-made language at all, rather, they enter upon the stream of verbal communication; indeed, only in this stream does their consciousness first begin to operate. Only in learning a foreign language does a fully prepared consciousness – fully prepared thanks to one's native language – confront a fully prepared language which it need only accept. People do not "accept" their native language – it is in their native language that they first reach awareness.[16]

8. Abstract objectivism, as we have seen, is incapable of tying together the existence of language in its abstract, synchronic dimension with the evolution of language. Language exists for the consciousness of the speaker as a system of normatively identical forms, but only for the historian as a process of generation. This excludes any possibility for the speaker's consciousness to be actively in touch with the process of historical evolution. The dialectical coupling of necessity with freedom and with, so to speak, linguistic responsibility is, of course, utterly impossible on these grounds. A purely mechanistic conception of linguistic necessity holds sway here. No doubt this feature of abstract objectivism, too, is connected with its subconscious fixation on dead and alien language.

All that remains is for us to summarize our critical analysis of abstract objectivism. The problem we posed at the beginning of the first chapter – the problem of the actual mode of being of linguistic phenomena as a specific and unified object of study – was incorrectly solved by abstract objectivism. Language as a system of normatively identical forms is an abstraction justifiable in theory and practice only from the standpoint of deciphering and teaching a dead, alien language. This system cannot serve as a basis for understanding and explaining linguistic facts as they really exist and come into being. On the contrary, this system leads us away from the living, dynamic reality of language and its social functions, notwithstanding the fact that adherents of abstract objectivism claim sociological significance for their point of view. Underlying the theory of abstract objectivism are presuppositions of a rationalistic and mechanistic world outlook. These presuppositions are least capable of furnishing the grounds for a proper understanding of history – and language, after all, is a purely historical phenomenon.

Does it follow from this that the basic positions of the first trend, the trend of individualistic subjectivism, are the correct ones? Perhaps individualistic subjectivism has succeeded in grasping the true reality of language-speech? Or perhaps the truth lies somewhere in the middle, representing a compromise between the first and second trends, between the theses of individualistic subjectivism and the antitheses of abstract objectivism?

We believe that in this instance, as everywhere else, the truth is not to be found in the golden mean and is not a matter of compromise between thesis and antithesis, but lies over and beyond them, constituting a negation of both thesis and antithesis alike, i.e., constituting a *dialectical synthesis*. The theses of the first trend also do not hold up under critical examination, as we shall see in the next chapter.

Let us at this point direct attention to the following: Abstract objectivism, by taking the system of language and regarding it as the entire crux of linguistic phenomena, rejected the speech act – the utterance – as something individual. As we said once before, herein lies the *proton pseudos* of abstract objectivism. For individualistic subjectivism, the entire crux of the matter is just exactly the speech act – the utterance. However, individualistic subjectivism likewise defines this act as something individual and therefore endeavours to explain it in terms of the individual psychic life of the speaker. Herein lies its *proton pseudos*.

In point of fact, the speech act or, more accurately, its product – the utterance, cannot under any circumstances be considered an individual phenomenon in the precise meaning of the word and cannot be explained in terms of the individual psychological or psychophysiological conditions of the speaker. *The utterance is a social phenomenon.*

It shall be our concern to substantiate this thesis in the next chapter.

Verbal interaction

Individualistic subjectivism and its theory of expression. Criticism of the theory of expression. The sociological structure of experience and expression. The problem of behavioral ideology. The utterance as the basic unit in the generative process of speech.

Approaches to the solution of the problem of the actual mode of existence of language. The utterance as a whole entity and its forms.

The second trend of thought in the philosophy of language was associated, as we saw, with rationalism and neoclassicism. The first trend – individualistic subjectivism – is associated with *romanticism*. Romanticism, to a considerable degree, was a reaction against the alien word and the categories of thought promoted by the alien word. More particularly and more immediately, romanticism was a reaction against the last resurgences of the cultural power of the alien word – the epochs of the Renaissance and neoclassicism. The romanticists were the first philologists of native language, the first to attempt to a radical restructuring of linguistic thought. Their restructuring was based on experience with native language as the medium through which consciousness and ideas are generated. True, the romanticists remained philologists in the strict sense of the word. It was, of course, beyond their power to restructure a mode of thinking about language that had taken shape and had been sustained over the course of centuries. Nevertheless, new categories were introduced into that thinking, and these new categories were precisely what gave the first trend its specific characteristics. Symptomatically, even recent representatives of individualistic subjectivism have been specialists in modern languages, chiefly the Romance languages (Vossler, Leo Spitzer, Lorch, *et al.*).

However, individualistic subjectivism also took the monologic utterance as the ultimate reality and the point of departure for its thinking about language. To be sure, it did not approach the monologic utterance from the viewpoint of the passively understanding philologist but, rather, approached it from within, from the viewpoint of the person speaking and expressing himself.

What does the monologic utterance amount to, then, in the view of individualistic subjectivism? We have seen that it is a purely individual act, the expression of an individual consciousness, its ambitions, intentions, creative impulses, tastes, and so on. The category of expression for individualistic subjectivism is the highest and broadest category under which the speech act – the utterance – may be subsumed.

But what is expression?

Its simplest, rough definition is: something which, having in some way taken shape and definition in the psyche of an individual, is outwardly objectified for others with the help of external signs of some kind.

Thus there are two elements in expression: that inner something which is *expressible*, and its *outward objectification* for others (or possibly for oneself). Any theory of expression, however complex or subtle a form it may take, inevitably presupposes these two elements – the whole event of expression is played out between them. Consequently, any theory of expression inevitably presupposes that the expressible is something that can somehow take shape and exist apart from expression; that it exists first in one form and then switches to another form. This would have to be the case; otherwise, if the expressible were to exist from the very start in the form of expression, with quantitative transition between the two elements (in the sense of clarification, differentiation, and the like), the whole theory of expression would collapse. The theory of expression inevitably presupposes a certain dualism between the inner and outer elements and the explicit primacy of the former, since each act of objectification (expression) goes from inside out. Its sources are within. Not for nothing were idealistic and spiritualistic grounds the only grounds on which the theory of individualistic subjectivism and all theories of expression in general arose. Everything of real importance lies within; the outer element can take on real importance only by becoming a vessel for the inner, by becoming expression of spirit.

To be sure, by becoming external, by expressing itself outwardly, the inner element does undergo alteration. After all, it must gain control of outer material that possesses a validity of its own apart from the inner element. In this process of gaining control, of mastering outer material and making it over into a compliant medium of expression, the experiential, expressible element itself undergoes alteration and is forced to make a certain compromise. Therefore, idealistic grounds, the grounds on which all theories of expression have been established, also contain provision for the radical negation of expression as something that deforms the purity of the inner element.[1] In any case, all the creative and organizing forces of expression are within. Everything outer is merely passive material for manipulation by the inner element. Expression is formed basically within and then merely shifts to the outside. The understanding, interpretation, and explanation of an ideological phenomenon, it would follow from this argument, must also be directed inward; it must traverse a route the reverse of that for expression. Starting from outward objectification, the explanation must work down into its inner, organizing bases. That is how individualistic subjectivism understands expression.

The theory of expression underlying the first trend of thought in philosophy of language is fundamentally untenable.

The experiential, expressible element and its outward objectification are created, as we know, out of one and the same material. After all, there is no such thing as experience outside of embodiment in signs. Consequently, the very notion of a fundamental, qualitative difference between the inner and the outer element is invalid to begin with. Furthermore, the location of the organizing and formative center is not within (i.e., not in the material of inner signs) but outside. It is not experience that organizes expression, but the other way around – *expression organizes experience*. Expression is what first gives experience its form and specificity of direction.

Indeed, from whichever aspect we consider it, expression-utterance is determined by the actual conditions of the given utterance – above all, by its *immediate social situation*.

Utterance, as we know, is constructed between two socially organized persons, and in the absence of a real addressee, an addressee is presupposed in the person, so to speak, of a normal representative of the social group to which the speaker belongs. The *word is oriented toward an addressee*, toward *who* that addressee might be: a fellow-member or not of the same social group, of higher or lower standing (the addressee's hierarchical status), someone connected with the speaker by close social ties (father, brother, husband, and so on) or not. There can be no such thing as an abstract addressee, a man unto himself, so to speak. With such a person, we would indeed have no language in common, literally and figuratively. Even though we sometimes have pretensions to experiencing and saying things *urbi et orbi*, actually, of course, we envision this "world at large" through the prism of the concrete social milieu surrounding us. In the majority of cases, we presuppose a certain typical and stabilized *social purview* toward which the ideological creativity of our own social group and time is oriented, i.e., we assume as our addressee a contemporary of our literature, our science, our moral and legal codes.

Each person's inner world and thought has its stabilized *social audience* that comprises the environment in which reasons, motives, values, and so on are fashioned. The more cultured a person, the more closely his inner audience will approximate the normal audience of ideological creativity; but, in any case, specific class and specific era are limits that the ideal of addressee cannot go beyond.

Orientation of the word toward the addressee has an extremely high significance. In point of fact, *word is a two-sided act.* It is determined equally by whose word it is and *for whom* it is meant. As word, it is precisely *the product of the reciprocal relationship between speaker and listener, addresser and addressee.* Each and every word expresses the "one" in relation to the "other." I give myself verbal shape from another's point of view, ultimately, from the point of view of the community to which I belong. A word is a bridge thrown between myself and another. If one end of the bridge depends on me, then the other depends on my addressee. A word is territory shared by both addresser and addressee, by the speaker and his interlocutor.

But what does being the speaker mean? Even if a word is not entirely his, constituting, as it were, the border zone between himself and his addressee – still, it does in part belong to him.

There is one instance of the situation wherein the speaker is the undoubted possessor of the word and to which, in this instance, he has full rights. This instance is the physiological act of implementing the word. But insofar as the act is taken in purely physiological terms, the category of possession does not apply.

If, instead of the physiological act of implementing sound, we take the implementation of word as sign, then the question of proprietorship becomes extremely complicated. Aside from the fact that word as sign is a borrowing on the speaker's part from the social stock of available signs, the very individual manipulation of this social sign in a concrete utterance is wholly determined by social relations. The stylistic individualization of an utterance that the Vosslerites speak about represents a reflection of social interrelationships that constitute the atmosphere in which an utterance is formed. *The immediate social situation and the broader social milieu wholly determine – and determine from within, so to speak – the structure of an utterance.*

Indeed, take whatever kind of utterance we will, even the kind of utterance that is not a referential message (communication in the narrow sense) but the verbal expression of some need – for instance, hunger – we may be certain that it is socially oriented in its entirety. Above all, it is determined immediately and directly by the participants of the speech event, both explicit and implicit participants, in connection with a specific situation. That situation shapes the utterance, dictating that it sound one way and not another – like a demand or request, insistence on one's rights or a plea for mercy, in a style flowery or plain, in a confident or hesitant manner, and so on.

The immediate social situation and its immediate social participants determine the "occasional" form and style of an utterance. The deeper layers of its structure are determined by more sustained and more basic social connections with which the speaker is a contact.

Even if we were to take an utterance still in process of generation "in the soul," it would not change the essence of the matter, since the structure of experience is just as social as is the structure of its outward objectification. The degree to which an experience is perceptible, distinct, and formulated is directly proportional to the degree to which it is socially orientated.

In fact, not even the simplest, dimmest apprehension of a feeling – say, the feeling of hunger not outwardly expressed – can dispense with some kind of ideological form. Any apprehension, after all, must have inner speech, inner intonation and the rudiments of inner style: one can apprehend one's hunger apologetically, irritably, angrily, indignantly, etc. We have indicated, of course, only the grosser, more egregious directions that inner intonation may take; actually, there is an extremely subtle and complex set of possibilities for intoning an experience. Outward expression in most cases only continues and makes more distinct the direction already taken by inner speech and the intonation already embedded in it.

Which way the intoning of the inner sensation of hunger will go depends upon the hungry person's general social standing as well as upon the immediate circumstances of the experience. These are, after all, the circumstances that determine in what evaluative context, within what social purview, the experience of hunger will be apprehended. The immediate social context will determine possible addressees, friends or foes, toward whom the consciousness and the experience of hunger will be oriented: whether it will involve dissatisfaction with cruel Nature, with oneself, with society, with a specific group within society, with a specific person, and so on. Of course, various degrees of perceptibility, distinctiveness, and differentiation in the social orientation of an experience are possible; but without some kind of evaluative social orientation there is no experience. Even the cry of a nursing infant is "oriented" toward its mother. There is the possibility that the experience of hunger may take on political colouring, in which case its structure will be determined along the lines of potential political appeal or a reason for political agitation. It may be apprehended as a form of protest, and so on.

With regard to the potential (and sometimes even distinctly sensed) addressee, a distinction can be made between two poles, two extremes between which an experience can be apprehended and ideologically structured, tending now toward the one, now toward the other. Let us label these two extremes the "*I-experience*" and the "*we-experience.*"

The "I-experience" actually tends toward extermination: the nearer it approaches its extreme limit, the more it loses its ideological structuredness and, hence, its apprehensible quality, reverting to the physiological reaction of the animal. In its course toward this extreme, the experience relinquishes all its potentialities, all outcroppings of social orientation, and, therefore, also loses its verbal delineation. Single experiences or whole groups of experiences can approach this extreme, relinquishing, in doing so, their ideological clarity and structuredness and testifying to the inability of the consciousness to strike social roots.[2]

The "we-experience" is not by any means a nebulous herd experience; it is differentiated. Moreover, ideological differentiation, the growth of consciousness, is in direct proportion to the firmness and reliability of the social orientation. The stronger, the more organized, the more differentiated the collective in which an individual orients himself, the more vivid and complex his inner word will be.

The "we-experience" allows of different degrees and different types of ideological structuring.

Let us suppose a case where hunger is apprehended by one of a disparate set of hungry persons whose hunger is a matter of chance (the man down on his luck, the beggar, or the like). The experience of such a declassé loner will be coloured in some specific way and will gravitate toward certain particular ideological forms with a range potentially quite broad: humility, shame, enviousness, and other evaluative tones will color his experience. The ideological forms along the lines of which the experience would develop would be either the individualistic protest of a vagabond or repentant, mystical resignation.

Let us now suppose a case in which the hungry person belongs to a collective where hunger is not haphazard and does bear a collective character – but the collective of these hungry people is not itself tightly bound together by material ties, each of its members experiencing hunger on his own. This is the situation most peasants are in. Hunger is experienced "at large," but under conditions of material disparateness, in the absence of a unifying economic coalition, each person suffers hunger in the small, enclosed world of his own individual economy. Such a collective lacks the unitary material frame necessary for united action.

A resigned but unashamed and undemeaning apprehension of one's hunger will be the rule under such conditions – "everyone bears it, you must bear it, too." Here grounds are furnished for the development of the philosophical and religious systems of the nonresistor or fatalist type (early Christianity, Tolstoyanism).

A completely different experience of hunger applies to a member of an objectively and materially aligned and united collective (a regiment of solders; workers in their association within the walls of a factory; hired hands on a large scale, capitalist farm; finally, a whole class once it has matured to the point of "class unto itself"). The experience of hunger this time will be marked predominantly by overtones of active and self-confident protest with no basis for humble and submissive intonation. These are the most favourable grounds for an experience to achieve ideological clarity and structuredness.[3]

All these types of expression, each with its basic intonations, come rife with corresponding terms and corresponding forms of possible utterances. The social situation in all cases determines which term, which metaphor, and which form may develop in an utterance expressing hunger out of the particular intonational bearings of the experience.

A special kind of character marks the individualistic *self-experience*. It does not belong to the "I-experience" in the strict sense of the term as defined above. The individualistic experience is fully differentiated and structured. Individualism is a special ideological form of the "we-experience" of the bourgeois class (there is also an analogous type of individualistic self-experience for the feudal aristocratic class). The individualistic type of experience derives from a steadfast and confident social orientation. Individualistic confidence in oneself, one's sense of personal value, is drawn not from within, not from the depths of one's personality, but from the outside world. It is the ideological interpretation of one's social recognizance and tenability by rights, and of the objective security and tenability provided by the whole social order, of one's individual livelihood. The structure of the conscious, individual personality is just as social a structure as is the collective type of experience. It is a particular kind of interpretation, projected into the individual soul, of a complex and sustained socioeconomic situation. But there resides in this type of individualistic "we-experience," and also in the very order to which it corresponds, an inner contradiction that sooner or later will demolish its ideological structuredness.

An analogous structure is presented in solitary self-experience ("the ability and strength to stand alone in one's rectitude"), a type cultivated by Romain Rolland and, to some extent, by Tolstoj. The pride involved in this solitude also depends upon "we." It is a variant of the "we-experience" characteristic of the modern-day West European intelligentsia. Tolstoj's remarks about there being different kinds of thinking – "for oneself" and "for the public" – merely juxtapose two different conceptions of "public." Tolstoj's "for oneself" actually signifies only another social conception of addressee peculiar to himself. There is no such thing as thinking outside orientation toward possible expression and, hence, outside the social orientation of that expression and of the thinking involved.

Thus the personality of the speaker, taken from within, so to speak, turns out to be wholly a product of social interrelations. Not only its outward expression but also its inner experience are social territory. Consequently, the whole route between inner experience (the "expressible") and its outward objectification (the "utterance") lies entirely across social territory. When an experience reaches the stage of actualization in a full-fledged utterance, its social orientation acquires added complexity by focusing on the immediate social circumstances of discourse and, above all, upon actual addressees.

Our analysis casts a new light upon the problem of consciousness and ideology that we examined earlier.

Outside objectification, outside embodiment in some particular material (the material of gesture, inner word, outcry), *consciousness is a fiction.* It is an improper ideological construct created by way of abstraction from the concrete facts of social expression. But consciousness as organized, material expression (in the ideological material of word, a sign, drawing colors, musical sound, etc.) – consciousness, so conceived, is an objective fact and a tremendous social force. To be sure, this kind of consciousness is not a supraexistential phenomenon and cannot determine the constitution of existence. It itself is part of existence and one of its forces, and for that reason it possesses efficacy and plays a role in the arena of existence. Consciousness, while still inside a conscious person's head as inner-word embryo of expression, is as yet too tiny a piece of existence, and the scope of its activity is also as yet too small. But once it passes through all the stages of social objectification and enters into the power system of science, art, ethics, or law, it becomes a real force, capable even of exerting in turn an influence on the economic bases of social life. To be sure, this force of consciousness is incarnated in specific social organizations, geared into steadfast ideological modes of expression (science, art, and so on), but even in the original, vague form of glimmering thought and experience, it had already constituted a social event on a small scale and was not an inner act on the part of the individual.

From the very start experience is set toward fully actualized outward expression and, from the very start, tends in that direction. The expression of an experience may be realized or it may be held back, inhibited. In the latter case, the experience is inhibited expression (we shall not go into the extremely complex problem of the causes and conditions of inhibition). Realized expression, in its turn, exerts a powerful, reverse influence on experience: it begins to tie inner life together, giving it more definite and lasting expression.

This reverse influence by structured and stabilized expression on experience (i.e., inner expression) has tremendous importance and must always be taken into account. The claim can be made that it is a matter *not so much of expression accommodating itself to our inner world but rather of our inner world accommodating itself to the potentialities of our expression, its possible routes and directions.*

To distinguish it from the established systems of ideology – the systems of art, ethics, law, etc. – we shall use the term *behavioral ideology* for the whole aggregate of life experiences and the outward expressions directly connected with it. Behavioral ideology is that atmosphere of unsystematized and unfixed inner and outer speech which endows our every instance of behavior and action and our every "conscious" state with meaning. Considering the sociological nature of the structure of expression and experience, we may say that behavioral ideology in our conception corresponds basically to what is termed "social psychology" in Marxist literature. In the present context, we should prefer to avoid the word "psychology," since we are concerned exclusively with the content of the psyche and the consciousness. That content is ideological through and through, determined not by individual, organismic (biological or physiological) factors, but by factors of a purely sociological character. The individual, organismic factor is completely irrelevant to any understanding of the basic creative and living lineaments of the content of consciousness.

The established ideological systems of social ethics, science, art, and religion are crystallizations of behavioral ideology, and these crystallizations, in turn, exert a powerful influence back upon behavioral ideology, normally setting its tone. At the same time, however, these already formalized ideological products constantly maintain the most vital organic contact with behavioral ideology and draw sustenance from it; otherwise, without that contact, they would be dead, just as any literary work or cognitive idea is dead without living, evaluative perception of it. Now, this ideological perception, for which alone any ideological piece of work can and does exist, is carried out in the language of behavioral ideology. Behavioral ideology draws the work into some particular social situation. The work combines with the whole content of the consciousness of those who perceive it and derives its apperceptive values only in the context of that consciousness. It is interpreted in the spirit of the particular content of consciousness (the consciousness of the perceiver) and is illuminated by it anew. This is what constitutes the vitality of an ideological production. In each period of its historical existence, a work must enter into close association with the changing behavioral ideology, become permeated with it, and draw new sustenance from it. Only to the degree that a work can enter into that kind of integral, organic association with the behavioral ideology of a given period is it viable for that period (and of course, for a given social group). Outside its connection with behavioral ideology it ceases to exist, since it ceases to be experienced as something ideologically meaningful.

We must distinguish several different strata in behavioral ideology. These strata are defined by the social scale on which experience and expression are measured, or by the social forces with respect to which they must directly orient themselves.

The purview in which an experience or expression comes into being may, as we know, vary in scope. The world of an experience may be narrow and dim; its social orientation may be haphazard and ephemeral and characteristic only for some adventitious and loose coalition of a small number of persons. Of course, even these erratic experiences are ideological and sociological, but their position lies on the borders of the normal and the pathological. Such an experience will remain an isolated fact in the psychological life of the person exposed to it. It will not take firm root and will not receive differentiated and full-fledged expression: indeed, if it lacks a socially grounded and stable audience, where could it possibly find bases for its differentiation and finalization? Even less likely would such an adventitious experience be set down, in writing or even more so in print. Experiences of that kind, experiences born of a momentary and accidental state of affairs, have, of course, no chance of further social impact or efficacy.

The lowest, most fluid, and quickly changing stratum of behavioral ideology consists of experiences of that kind. To this stratum, consequently, belong all those vague and undeveloped experiences, thoughts, and idle, accidental words that flash across our minds. They are all of them cases of miscarriages of social orientations, novels without heroes, performances without audiences. They lack any sort of logic or unity. The sociological regulatedness in these ideological scraps is extremely difficult to detect. In this lowest stratum of behavioral ideology only statistical regularity is detectable; given a huge quantity of products of this sort, the outlines of socioeconomic regulatedness could be revealed. Needless to say, it would be a practical impossibility to descry in any one such accidental experience or expression its socioeconomic premises.

The upper strata of behavioral ideology, the ones directly linked with ideological systems, are more vital, more serious and bear a creative character. Compared to an established ideology, they are a great deal more mobile and sensitive: they convey changes in the socioeconomic basis more quickly and more vividly. Here, precisely, is where those creative energies build up through whose agency partial or radical restructuring of ideological systems comes about. Newly emerging social forces find ideological expression and take shape first in these upper strata of behavioral ideology before they can succeed in dominating the arena of some organized, official ideology. Of course, in the process of this struggle, in the process of their gradual infiltration into ideological organizations (the press, literature, and science), these new currents in behavioral ideology, no matter how revolutionary they may be, undergo the influence of the established ideological systems and, to some extent, incorporate forms, ideological practices, and approaches already in stock.

What is usually called "creative individuality" is nothing but the expression of a particular person's basic, firmly grounded, and consistent line of social orientation. This concerns primarily the uppermost, fully structured strata of inner speech (behavioral ideology), each of whose terms and intonations have gone through the stage of expression and have, so to speak, passed the test of expression. Thus what is involved here are words, intonations, and inner-word gestures that have undergone the experience of outward expression on a more or less ample social scale and have acquired, as it were, a high social polish and lustre by the effect of reactions and responses, resistance or support, on the part of the social audience.

In the lower strata of behavioral ideology, the biological-biographical factor does, of course, play a crucial role, but its importance constantly diminishes as the utterance penetrates more deeply into an ideological system. Consequently, while bio-biographical explanations are of some value in the lower strata of experience and expression (utterance), their role in the upper strata is extremely modest. Here the objective sociological method takes full command.

So, then, the theory of expression underlying individualistic subjectivism must be rejected. *The organizing center of any utterance, of any experience, is not within but outside – in the social milieu surrounding the individual being.* Only the inarticulate cry of an animal is really organized from inside the physiological apparatus of an individual creature. Such a cry lacks any positive ideological factor vis-à-vis the physiological reaction. Yet, even the most primitive human utterance produced by the individual organism is, from the point of view of its content, import, and meaning, organized outside the organism, in the extraorganismic conditions of the social milieu. Utterance as such is wholly a product of social interaction, both of the immediate sort as determined by the circumstances of the discourse, and of the more general kind, as determined by the whole aggregate of conditions under which any given community of speakers operates.

The individual utterance (*parole*), despite the contentions of abstract objectivism, is by no means an individual fact not susceptible to sociological analysis by virtue of its individuality. Indeed, if this were so, neither the sum total of these individual acts nor any abstract features common to all such individual acts (the "normatively identical forms") could possibly engender a social product.

Individualistic subjectivism is *correct* in that individual utterances *are* what constitute the actual, concrete reality of language, and in that they *do have* creative value in language.

But individualistic subjectivism is *wrong* in ignoring and failing to understand the social nature of the utterance and in attempting to derive the utterance from the speaker's inner world as an expression of that inner world. The structure of the utterance and of the very experience being expressed is a *social structure.* The stylistic shaping of an utterance is shaping of a social kind, and the very verbal stream of utterances, which is what the reality of language actually amounts to, is a social stream. Each drop of that stream is social and the entire dynamics of its generation is social.

Individualistic subjectivism is also completely *correct* in that linguistic form and its ideological impletion are *not* severable. Each and every word is ideological and each and every application of language involves ideological change. But individualistic subjectivism is *wrong* insofar as it also derives this ideological impletion of the word from the conditions of the individual psyche.

Individualistic subjectivism is *wrong* in taking the monologic utterance, just as abstract objectivism does, as its basic point of departure. Certain Vosslerites, it is true, have begun to consider the problem of dialogue and so to approach a more correct understanding of verbal interaction. Highly symptomatic in this regard is one of Leo Spitzer's books we have already cited – his *Italienische Umgangssprache*, a book that attempts to analyze the forms of Italian conversational language in close connection with conditions of discourse and above all with the issue of the addressee.[4] However, Leo Spitzer utilizes a *descriptive psychological* method. He does not draw from his analysis the fundamentally sociological conclusions it suggests. For the Vosslerites, therefore, the monologic utterance still remains the basic reality.

The problem of verbal interaction has been posed clearly and distinctly by Otto Dietrich.[5] He proceeds by way of subjecting to criticism the theory of utterance as expression. For him, the basic function of language is not expression but *communication* (in the strict sense), and this leads him to consider the role of the addressee. The minimal condition for a linguistic manifestation is according to Dietrich, *twofold* (speaker and listener). However, Dietrich shares assumptions of a general psychological type with individualistic subjectivism. Dietrich's investigations likewise lack any determinate sociological basis.

Now we are in a position to answer the question we posed at the end of the first chapter of this section of our study. *The actual reality of language-speech is not the abstract system of linguistic forms, not the isolated monologic utterance, and not the psychophysiological act of its implementation, but the social event of verbal interaction implemented in an utterance or utterances.*

Thus, verbal interaction is the basic reality of language.

Dialogue, in the narrow sense of the word, is of course, only one of the forms – a very important form, to be sure – of verbal interaction. But dialogue can also be understood in a broader sense, meaning not only direct, face-to-face, vocalized verbal communication between persons, but also verbal communication of any type whatsoever. A book, i.e., *a verbal performance in print*, is also an element of verbal communication. It is something discussable in actual, real life dialogue, but aside from that, it is calculated for active perception, involving attentive reading and inner responsiveness, and for organized, *printed* reaction in the various forms devised by the particular sphere of verbal communication in question (book reviews, critical surveys, defining influence on subsequent works, and so on). Moreover, a verbal performance of this kind also inevitably orients itself with respect to previous performances in the same sphere, both those by the same author and those by other authors. It inevitably takes its point of departure from some particular state of affairs involving a scientific problem or a literary style. Thus the printed verbal performance engages, as it were, in ideological colloquy of large scale: it responds to something, objects to something, affirms something, anticipates possible responses and objections, seeks support, and so on.

Any utterance, no matter how weighty and complete in and of itself, *is only a moment in the continuous process of verbal communication.* But that continuous verbal communication is, in turn, itself only a moment in the continuous, all-inclusive, generative process of a given social collective. An important problem arises in this regard: the study of the connection between concrete verbal interaction and the extraverbal situation – both the immediate situation and, through it, the broader situation. The forms this connection takes are different, and different factors in a situation may, in association with this or that form, take on different meanings (for instance, these connections differ with the different factors of situation in literary or in scientific communication). *Verbal communication can never be understood and explained outside of this connection with a concrete situation.* Verbal intercourse is inextricably interwoven with communication of other types, all stemming from the common ground of production communication. It goes without saying that word cannot be divorced from this eternally generative, unified process of communication. In its concrete connection with a situation, verbal communication is always accompanied by social acts of a nonverbal character (the performance of labor, the symbolic acts of a ritual, a ceremony, etc.), and is often only an accessory to these acts, merely carrying out an auxiliary role. *Language acquires life and historically evolves precisely here, in concrete verbal communication, and not in the abstract linguistic system of language forms, nor in the individual psyche of speakers.*

From what has been established, it follows that the methodologically based order of study of language ought to be: (1) the forms and types of verbal interaction in connection with their concrete conditions; (2) forms of particular utterances, of particular speech performances, as elements of a closely linked interaction – i.e., the genres of speech performance in human behavior and ideological creativity as determined by verbal interaction; (3) a reexamination, on this new basis, of language forms in their usual linguistic presentation.

This is the order that the actual generative process of language follows: *social intercourse is generated* (stemming from the basis); *in it verbal communication and interaction are generated; and in the latter, forms of speech performances are generated; finally, this generative process is reflected in the change of language forms.*

One thing that emerges from all that has been said is the extreme importance of the problem of the forms of an utterance *as a whole.* We have already pointed out that contemporary linguistics lacks any approach to the utterance itself. Its analysis goes no further than the elements that constitute an utterance. Meanwhile, utterances are the real units that make up the stream of language-speech. What is necessary in order to study the forms of this real unit is precisely that it not be isolated from the historical stream of utterances. As a whole entity, the utterance is implemented only in the stream of verbal intercourse. The whole is, after all, defined by its boundaries, and these boundaries run along the line of contact between a given utterance and the extraverbal and verbal (i.e., made up of other utterances) milieu.

The first and last words, the beginning and end points of real-life utterance – that is what already constitutes the problem of the whole. The process of speech, broadly understood as the process of inner and outer verbal life, goes on continuously. It knows neither beginning nor end. The outwardly actualized utterance is an island rising from the boundless sea of inner speech; the dimensions and forms of this island are determined by the particular *situation* of the utterance and its *audience.* Situation and audience make inner speech undergo actualization into some kind of specific outer expression that is directly included into an unverbalized behavioral context and in that context is amplified by actions, behavior, or verbal responses of other participants of the utterance. The full-fledged question, exclamation, command, request – these are the most typical forms of wholes in behavioral utterances. All of them (especially the command and request) require an extraverbal complement and, indeed, an extraverbal commencement. The very type of structure these little behavioral *genres* will achieve is determined by the effect of its coming up against the extraverbal milieu and against another word (i.e., the words of other people). Thus, the form a command will take is determined by the obstacles it may encounter, the degree of submissiveness expected, and so on. The structure of the genre in these instances will be in accord with the accidental and unique features of behavioral situations. Only when social custom and circumstances have fixed and stabilized certain forms in behavioral interchange to some appreciable degree, can one speak of specific types of structure in genres of behavioral speech. So, for instance, an entirely special type of structure has been worked out for the genre of the light and casual causerie of the drawing room where everyone "feels at home" and where the basic differentiation within the gathering (the audience) is that between men and women. Here we find devised special forms of insinuation, half-sayings, allusions to little tales of an intentionally nonserious character, and so on. A different type of structure is worked out in the case of conversation between husband and wife, brother and sister, etc. In the case where a random assortment of people gathers – while waiting in a line or conducting some business – statements and exchanges of words will start and finish and be constructed in another, completely different way. Village sewing circles, urban carouses, workers' lunchtime chats, etc., will all have their own types. Each situation, fixed and sustained by social custom, commands a particular kind of organization of audience and, hence, a particular repertoire of little behavioral genres. The behavioral genre fits everywhere into the channel of social intercourse assigned to it and functions as an ideological reflection of its type, structure, goal, and social composition. The behavioral genre is a fact of the social milieu: of holiday, leisure time, and of social contact in the parlor, the workshop, etc. It meshes with that milieu and is delimited and defined by it in all its internal aspects.

The production processes of labour and the processes of commerce know different forms for constructing utterances.

As for the forms of ideological intercourse in the strict sense of the term – forms for political speeches, political acts, laws, regulations, manifestos, and so forth; and forms for poetic utterances, scientific treatises, etc. – these have been the object of special investigation in rhetoric and poetics, but, as we have seen, these investigations have been completely divorced from the problem of language on the one hand, and from the problem of social intercourse on the other.[6] Productive analysis of the forms of the whole of utterances as the real units in the stream of speech is possible only on the basis that regards the individual utterance as a purely sociological phenomenon. Marxist philosophy of language should and must stand squarely on the utterance as the real phenomenon of language-speech and as a socioideological structure.

Now that we have outlined the sociological structure of the utterance, let us return to the two trends in philosophical linguistic thought and make a final summing up.

R. Šor, a Moscow linguist and an adherent of the second trend of thought in philosophy of language, ends a brief sketch of the contemporary state of linguistics with the following words:

> "Language is not an artifact (*ergon*) but a natural and congenital activity of mankind" – so claimed the romanticist linguistics of the 19th century. Theoretical linguistics of modern times claims otherwise: "Language is not an individual activity (*energiea*) but a cultural-historical legacy of mankind (*ergon*).[7]

This conclusion is amazing in its bias and one-sidedness. On the factual side, it is completely untrue. Modern theoretical linguistics includes, after all, the Vossler school, one of Germany's most powerful movements in contemporary linguistic thought. It is impermissible to identify modern linguistics with only one of its trends.

From the theoretical point of view, both the thesis and the antithesis made up by Šor must equally be rejected, since they are equally inadequate to the real nature of language.

Let us conclude the argument with an attempt to formulate our own point of view in the following set of propositions:

1. *Language as a stable system of normatively identical forms is merely a scientific abstraction*, productive only in connection with certain particular practical and theoretical goals. This abstraction is not adequate to the concrete reality of language.

2. *Language is a continuous generative process implemented in the social-verbal interaction of speakers.*

3. *The laws of the generative process of language are not at all the laws of individual psychology, but neither can they be divorced from the activity of speakers.* The laws of language generation are *sociological* laws.

4. *Linguistic creativity does not coincide with artistic creativity nor with any other type of specialized ideological creativity. But, at the same time, linguistic creativity cannot be understood apart from the ideological meanings and values that fill it.* The generative process of language, as is true of any historical generative process, can be perceived as blind mechanical necessity, but it can also become "free necessity" once it has reached the position of a conscious and desired necessity.

5. *The structure of the utterance is a purely sociological structure.* The utterance, as such, obtains between speakers. The individual speech act (in the strict sense of the word "individual") is *contradictio in adjecto*.

[143]

6

M. M. Bakhtin and P. N. Medvedev
From 'Material and device as
components of the poetic construction'

From *The Formal Method in Literary Scholarship: A Critical Introduction
to Sociological Poetics*, translated by Albert J. Wehrle (Harvard
University Press, 1985, pp. 118–28).

The following extract makes up the second half of a chapter in which Medvedev
criticizes the formalist account of the relationship between *material* and *device*.
As I explained in the introduction, formalism elevated form over content in its
approach to literature, and following from this general alignment, considered
the *material* of a work of art as merely the occasion for the display of its various
devices, which are its real *raison d'être*.

In the first half of the chapter, Medvedev traces this whole orientation on the
part of the formalists to their initial enthusiasm for the avant-garde poetry of
futurism and its use of the 'transrational word', that is, poetry which verges
towards pure pleasure in sound, and towards the abandonment of sense. If you
begin with this kind of art as your notion of the typical art-object, then the other
aesthetic doctrines of formalism become more understandable. Thus when it
comes to a consideration of prose, Shklovsky's distinction between *siujhet* and
fabula appears as another version of the formalist elevation of device over
material, of the artfulness of the art-object over the material which it treats. In
this distinction, *fabula* (often translated as story) is the simple narrative, the story
as it might have happened in real time and space. *Siujhet*, by contrast, (usually
translated by 'plot') is the way that story appears in any actual novel, transformed
in the manner of its telling. *Fabula* is only the occasion, in this account, for the
various devices of the *siujhet*, such as repetition, retardation, parallelism, and so
on. Medvedev considers this whole approach to be merely the reversal of
traditional aesthetics which had considered the various technical devices of
literature as subordinate to its material – but he sees it as an enfeebling reversal,
for 'Inside out is always worse than right side out' (FM 107).

In a similar way, Medvedev criticizes the formalist Eichenbaum for the
account he gives of Gogol's *The Overcoat*. Eichenbaum claimed that the story,
which concerns a poor Civil Service copying clerk, was mere indifferent material
upon which the various devices of *skaz* could be built – *skaz* being the name
given by the formalists to denote methods of narration which bear traces of

oral forms. Medvedev protests against the arbitrariness of this whole line of argument, for neither Shklovsky nor Eichenbaum give any reasons for deciding which element of any piece of writing should be considered the *motivation* for any other. But he does recognize in this question of the relationship of the material to the device a special form of a wider problem, which is that of the relationship between meaning and the material signs that carry meaning. In the following extract, he seeks to secure that relationship by means of the notion of 'social evaluation'; in general terms this account is cognate with the account of language given by Voloshinov in the previous extract. At the conclusion to the chapter he differentiates between that general characteristic of language and its particular, specific character in the poetic work.

From 'Material and device as components of the poetic construction'

The proper formulation of the problem of the poetic construction

The problem the formalists raised and incorrectly solved has lost none of its force.

How, within the unity of the artistic construction, is the direct material presence of the work, its here and now, to be joined with the endless perspectives of its ideological meaning? How is the development of the story in the real time of performance or perception to be joined with the development of the narrative event in an ideal time that may stretch on over years?

We have seen that the formalists' solution cannot withstand criticism. They began from the false assumption that the fullness, generality, and breadth of meaning could not be included in the material here and now of the poetic construction. Their fear of meaning in art led the formalists to reduce the poetic construction to the peripheral, outer surface of the work. The work lost its depth, three-dimensionality, and fullness. Their concepts of material and device are expressions of this superficial view of the construction. Having established a reverse proportionality between meaning and artistic significance, the formalists inevitably arrived at the device, which, as the combination of indifferent material, was formalistically empty.

The problem must be solved in another way.

The problem would have been solved if the formalists had succeeded in finding an element in the poetic work which would simultaneously participate in both the material presence of the word and in its meaning,

[145]

which would serve as a medium joining the depth and generality of meaning with the uniqueness of the articulated sound. This medium would create the possibility of a direct movement from the periphery of the work to its inner significance, from external form to intrinsic ideological meaning.

It is precisely in this sense, as the quest for such a medium, that the problem of the poetic construction has always been understood.

In West European poetics at the present time, there is a particularly acute awareness of this aim. The key to the solution is most often found in the concept of the "inner form of the word." Potebnia, who continued the Humboldt tradition of "inner form" in Russia, understood and solved the problem precisely this way in his theory of the image.

The image was the medium which united the sensual concreteness of sound with the generality of its meaning. Being graphic and practically sensual, the image had something in common with the unique material datum of sound. And, being able to generalize, typify, symbolically widen its significance, it was akin to meaning.

As we have seen, the symbolists formulated the problem of the poetic construction in this same way. For them too the symbol and symbolic signification functioned to unite the external sign with internal meaning.

All of these solutions were grounded in idealism and joined with an individualistic psychological conception of ideological creation and are unacceptable to us. But they correctly marked the way toward the true solution.

It is typical that the formalists, while criticizing the symbolists and the Potebnia theory of the image, did not understand the meaning of the problem, and did not take its true center of gravity into account. This is understandable: from the very beginning they cut off meaning and oriented themselves toward the transrational word, so it was inevitable that they would miss the whole problem.

Social evaluation and its role

What, in fact, is the element which unites the material presence of the word with its meaning?

We submit that social evaluation is the element.

It is true that social evaluation is not the exclusive property of poetry. It is present in every active word to the extent that the word enters the concrete and individual utterance. The linguist does not engage in social evaluation, since he is not concerned with concrete forms of the utterance. Therefore, we do not find social evaluation in language taken as an abstract linguistic system.

What is social evaluation? What is its role in language or, more precisely, in the utterance, and what is its significance for the poetic construction?

The connection between meaning and sign [*smysl i znak*] in the word taken concretely and independently of the concrete utterance, as in a dictionary, is completely random and only of technical significance. Here the word is simply a conventional sign. There is a gap between the individuality of the word and its meaning, a gap which can only be overcome by a mechanistic linkage, by association.[1]

But the individual concrete utterance, even if it consists of only one word, is a different case. Every concrete utterance is a social act. At the same time that it is an individual material complex, a phonetic, articulatory, visual complex, the utterance is also a part of social reality. It organizes communication oriented toward reciprocal action, and itself reacts; it is also inseparably enmeshed in the communication event. Its individual reality is already not that of a physical body, but the reality of a historical phenomenon. Not only the meaning of the utterance but also the very fact of its performance is of historical and social significance, as, in general, is the fact of its realization in the here and now, in given circumstances, at a certain historical moment, under the conditions of the given social situation.

The very presence of the utterance is historically and socially significant. This presence passes from natural reality to the category of historical reality. The utterance is not a physical body and not a physical process, but a historical event, albeit an infinitesimal one. Its individuality is that of a historical achievement in the definite epoch under definite social conditions. This is the individuality of a sociohistorical act, which is fundamentally different from the individuality of a physical object or process.

But the meaning of the word-utterance is also joined to history through the unique act of its realization, becoming a historical phenomenon. For it is the given meaning which becomes the object of discussion in the here and now, and the fact that this topic is discussed in a certain way and enters the concrete purview of the speakers is completely determined by the aggregate sociohistorical conditions and the concrete situation of the given individual utterance.

[147]

Out of the enormous diversity of subjects and meanings accessible to the given social group, only a certain meaning and definite subject enter the purview of those engaged in the given type of ideological intercourse at the given time and place. An organic, historical, and actual connection is established between the meaning and act (utterance), between the act and the concrete sociohistorical situation. The material individuality of the sign and the generality and breadth of meaning merge in the concrete unity of the historical phenomenon-utterance.

This meaning is itself historical. The organic connection between the sign and meaning attained in the concrete historical act of the utterance exists only for the given utterance and only under the given conditions of its realization.

If we tear the utterance out of social intercourse and materialize it, we lose the organic unity of all its elements. The word, grammatical form, sentence, and all linguistic definiteness in general taken in abstraction from the concrete historical utterance turn into technical signs of a meaning that is as yet only possible and still not individualized historically. The organic connection of meaning and sign cannot become lexical, grammatically stable, and fixed in identical and reproducible forms, i.e., cannot in itself become a sign or a constant element of a sign, cannot become grammaticalized. This connection is created only to be destroyed, to be reformed again, but in new forms under the conditions of a new utterance.

It is this historical actuality, which unites the individual presence of the utterance with the generality and fullness of its meaning, which makes meaning concrete and individual and gives meaning to the word's phonetic presence here and now, that we call social evaluation.

Social evaluation actualizes the utterance both from the standpoint of its factual presence and the standpoint of its semantic meaning. It defines the choice of subject, word, form, and their individual combination within the bounds of the given utterance. It also defines the choice of content, the selection of form, and the connection between form and content.

The deeper and more stable social evaluations are determined by the economic existence of a class in the given epoch of its existence. One may say that the major historical aims of a whole epoch in the life of the given social group are formed in these evaluations. Other evaluations are connected with the more immediate and brief phenomena of social life and, finally, with the news of the day, hour, and minute. All these evaluations interpenetrate and are dialectically connected. The aim of the epoch unfolds in the aim of every day and even every hour. Social evaluation unites the minute of the epoch and the news of the day with the aim of history. It determines the historical physiognomy of every action and every utterance, its individual, class, and epochal physiognomy.

It is impossible to understand the concrete utterance without accustoming oneself to its values, without understanding the orientation of its evaluations in the ideological environment.

For to comprehend an utterance does not mean to grasp its general meaning, as we grasp the meaning of a "dictionary word." To understand an utterance means to understand it in its contemporary context and our own, if they do not coincide. It is necessary to understand the meaning of the utterance, the content of the act, and its historical reality, and to do so, moreover, in their concrete inner unity. Without such an understanding, meaning is dead, having become some dictionary meaning of no necessity.

Social evaluation defines all aspects of the utterance, totally permeates it, but finds its most pure and typical expression in expressive intonation.

As distinct from the more stable syntactic intonation, expressive intonation, which colors every word of the utterance, reflects its historical uniqueness. Expression is not determined by a logical scheme of meaning, but by its individual fullness and integrity and the whole concrete historical situation. Expressive intonation colors meaning and sound equally, bringing them intimately near one another in the unique unity of the utterance. Of course, expressive intonation is not obligatory, but it is the most distinct expression of social evaluation when it does occur.

In the utterance, every element of the language-material implements the demands of social evaluation. A language element is only able to enter the utterance if it is capable of satisfying these demands. It is only to express the social evaluation that a word becomes the material of an utterance. Therefore, the word does not enter the utterance from a dictionary, but from life, from utterance to utterance. The word passes from one unity to another without losing its way. It enters the utterance as a word of intercourse, permeated with the concrete immediate and historical aims of this communication.

Every utterance is subject to this condition, including the literary utterance, i.e., the poetic construction.

[149]

Social evaluation and the concrete utterance

The material of poetry is not language understood as the aggregate or system of linguistic possibilities (phonetic, grammatical, lexical). The poet does not select linguistic forms, but rather the evaluations posited in them. All the linguistic characteristics of the word that remain after the abstraction of these evaluations are not only unable to be the material of poetry, but cannot even be examples of grammar.

For instance, a linguistic example is a conditional utterance; a pure linguistic form only lends itself to symbolic designation. A linguistic form is only real in the concrete speech performance, in the social utterance.

Even the transrational word is spoken with some kind of intonation. Consequently, some value orientation can be observed in it, some evaluating gesture.

When the poet selects words, their combination, and their compositional arrangement, he selects, combines, and arranges the evaluations lodged in them as well. And the resistance of the material we feel in every poetic work is in fact the resistance of the social evaluations it contains. These existed before the poet took them, reevaluated them, renewed them, and gave them new nuances. Only a schoolboy toiling over his Latin exercise experiences linguistic resistance from material.

This deduction of Shklovskii's is typical: "The literary work is pure form.... It is not a thing, not material, but the relationship of materials."[2] As we know, Shklovskii thinks the material is indifferent in value:

> The scale of the work, the arithmetical value of its numerator and denominator, is unimportant; what is important is this relationship. Comical or tragical works, works of the world or parlor – the juxtaposition of world to world or cat to stone – all are equal.[3]

This statement, of course, is not a scholarly principle, but a paradox of the feuilleton variety, that is, a little work of art.

All of its effect is based on the value equilibrium between the words "cat" and "world," "stone" and "world," i.e., precisely on their "arithmetical value." Without the evaluations lodged in these words, there is no paradox.

For the poet, as for any speaker, language is a system of social evaluations; and the richer, more differentiated and complex it is, the more significant the work will be.

But, in any case, only that word or form in which the social evaluation is still living and perceptible is able to enter the artistic work.

Only through evaluation do the possibilities of language become real.

Why are two particular words next to each other? Linguistics only explains how this is possible. The real reason cannot be explained within the limitations of linguistic possibilities. Social evaluation is needed to turn a grammatical possibility into a concrete fact of speech reality.

Let us imagine that two inimical social groups have at their disposal the same linguistic material, absolutely the same lexicon, the same morphological and syntactical possibilities, etc.

Under these conditions, if the differences between our two social groups arise from important socioeconomic premises of their existences, the intonation of one and the same word will differ profoundly between groups; within the very same grammatical constructions the semantic and stylistic combinations will be profoundly different. One and the same word will occupy a completely different hierarchical place in the utterance as a concrete social act.

The combination of words in the concrete utterance or the literary performance is always determined by their value coefficients and the social conditions under which the utterance is produced.

Of course, our example is fictitious. For we assumed that the various evaluations were active within the bounds of one and the same ready-made language.

As a matter of fact, though, language is created, formed, and constantly generates within the bounds of a definite value horizon. Therefore, it is not possible for two significantly different social groups to have the very same language.

Only for the individual consciousness do evaluations develop within the sphere of readily available language possibilities. From the sociological point of view language possibilities themselves find their origin and development within the sphere of evaluations which necessarily form within a given social group. Even the formalist theory of the indifference of the material acknowledges this.

This theory arose as the theoretical expression of the perception of the material practised by the futurists.

The futurists began their work with a disorganized system of social evaluations.

They took words lightly, as witness their "orientation toward nonsense" and on speech "as simple as a moo." Words lost their evaluational weight, the distance between them was decreased, and their hierarchy shaken. It was as if words were taken from the idle conversations of people having nothing to do with life.

This is connected with the fact that the futurists were examples of that social group which was cast into the periphery of society, which was socially and politically inactive and rootless.

The system of evaluations which found its expression in symbolist poetry decomposed, and life did not create conditions for the formation of a new system. Where the symbolist had seen meaning, activity, a theurgical act, the futurist saw only a meaningless word, its bare linguistic possibilities consequently brought into the foreground.

The material of poetry is language, language as a system of social evaluations, not as the aggregate of linguistic possibilities.

It is obvious that the study of poetry cannot be based exclusively on linguistics,[4] although it can and should use the latter.

What is more, in studying the life of the concrete speech performance, the study of poetry has much to teach contemporary formalist linguistics.

In general, the ideological studies concerned with the life of the concrete utterance and, consequently, the actualization of language as an abstract system of possibilities, must constantly take account of linguistics. Linguistics will, of course, reach a point at which it will depart from the concrete social evaluation, as dictated by its practical and theoretical aims. But it must take the role of social evaluation into account.

Thus, the poetic work, like every concrete utterance, is an inseparable unity of meaning and reality based on the unity of the social evaluation which totally permeates it.

All the elements which an abstract analysis of a work (quite proper within its limits) can isolate – phonetic composition, grammatical structure, thematic elements, and so on – all these elements are united by and serve social evaluation.

It is social evaluation which inseparably weaves the artistic work into the general canvass of the social life of a given historical epoch and a given social group.

For the formalists, who ignore social evaluation, the work of art breaks down into abstract elements which they study in isolation, only looking at the connection between elements from a narrowly technical standpoint.

If we may conditionally use the term "device," we may say that it in fact does not operate in a neutral linguistic medium, but cuts into the system of social evaluations and thus becomes social activity.

It is precisely this positive aspect of the device, the rearrangements, renewals, and nuances it creates for values, that is important. In this is the meaning and role of the artistic device.

In disregarding this the formalists emasculate the living meaning of the device and trace its secondary and purely negative features, following, as it were, the dead trace left by the device in an abstract linguistic construct of a language deprived of meaning.

Social evaluation therefore mediates between language as an abstract system of possibilities and the concrete reality of language. Social evaluation determines the living historical phenomenon of the utterance, both from the standpoint of linguistic forms and the standpoint of meaning.

The advocates of "inner form" do not understand the mediating role of social evaluation. They try to make social evaluation into some kind of linguistic attribute of the word itself, of language itself, independent of the concrete utterance. They do not understand its historical nature.

In the final analysis, most of the advocates of inner form see it as some kind of naturalized evaluation, mostly psychological in nature. The evaluation is lifted from the process of generation and given a naturalistic substance. This is the origin of the absurd attempts to show inner form in the word itself, in the sentence, in the period, in the language construction in general, taken independently of the utterance and its historical situation.[5] But the fact is that it is only for the given utterance under its particular historical conditions that the unity of meaning, sign, and reality is realized through social evaluation. If we take the concrete utterance outside of its historical generation, in abstraction, we are turning away from precisely what we are seeking.

The notion that evaluation is an individual act is widespread in the contemporary "*Lebensphilosophie*," and leads to conclusions no less false. Evaluation is social; it organizes intercourse. Within the bounds of the individual organism and psyche it could never have led to the creation of the sign, i.e., the ideological body. Even the inner utterance (interior speech) is social; it is oriented toward a possible audience, toward a possible answer, and it is only in the process of such an orientation that it is able to take shape and form.

Social evaluation and the poetic construction

The theory of social evaluation and its role that has been developed above applies to every utterance as a historical speech performance, not just to the poetic work.

But our aim is to clarify the specificity of the artistic construction.

Although we always had the poetic utterance in mind during our brief analysis, we have not yet tried to be specific.

Social evaluation always establishes an organic tie between the unique presence of the utterance and the generality of its meaning. But it does not always penetrate all aspects of the material, does not always make all aspects equally necessary and irreplaceable. The historical reality of the utterance may be subordinate to the reality of the act or object, and so become a mere preparatory stage for the action. Such an utterance is not complete in itself. Social evaluation leads beyond its borders to another reality. The presence of the word is only an accessory to another presence. Social evaluation is such a preparatory action in the fields of epistemology and ethics. It selects the object of the act or cognition.

Every epoch has its sphere of objects for cognition, its own sphere of epistemological interests. The object enters the epistemological purview and becomes the focus of its social energy only to the extent that the actual needs of the given epoch and the given social group dictate. Social evaluation determines the choice of objects for cognition, just as it determines the poet's choice of a theme. Social evaluation also organizes the scientific utterance on all stages of scientific work. But it does not do so for the sake of the utterance. It organizes the work of cognition itself, and the word only as a necessary but dependent aspect of this work. Here evaluation is not complete in the word.

The poetic work is a different matter.

Here the utterance is detached both from its object and from action. Here social evaluation is complete within the utterance itself. One might say its song is sung to the end. The reality of the utterance serves no other reality. Social evaluation pours out and concludes in pure expression. Therefore, all aspects of the material, meaning, and concrete act of realization without exception become equally important and necessary.

What is more, since the utterance is detached from both the real object and from action, its material presence in the here and now becomes the organizing principle of the whole construction. No matter how deep and wide the semantic perspective of the work might be, this perspective should not destroy or remove the plane of the utterance, just as the ideal space of a painting does not destroy the surface of the picture.[6]

For this reason the formation of the utterance, its development in the real time of performance and perception, is the initial and concluding point in the whole organization. Everything is compactly situated on this real plane of expression. But it does not at all follow that this plane becomes "transrational." It can accommodate any semantic perspective without losing its concreteness and nearness.

Therefore, story is not dispensable (in nonmotivated art) or mere motivation for the development of plot (brakings, digressions, etc.). The story develops together with the plot: the event being narrated and the event of narration itself merge in the single event of the artistic work. Social evaluation organizes how we see and conceptualize the event being communicated, for we only see and conceptualize what interests or affects us in one way or another. Social evaluation also organizes the forms by which the event is communicated: the arrangement of the material into digressions, returns, repetitions, etc., is permeated with the single logic of social evaluation.

In the same way, the plane of *skaz* contains the full depth of the narrative. Eikhenbaum is wrong in asserting that "humaneness toward one's inferior fellow man" and Akakii Akakievich's "insignificance" are only motivation for the device of grotesque change from punning intonation to that of sentimental melodrama.[7]

The same principle organizes the way the author sees and conceptualizes the life of someone like Akakii Akakievich and the intonation of the *skaz* about him. The fictional event in life of Akakii Akakievich and the event of the actual *skaz* about it merge in the historical event of Gogol's story. In this way, *The Overcoat* entered the historical life of Russia and became an active factor in it.

Thus, the reality of the artistic representation, its development in the real time of social intercourse, and the ideological significance of the event being represented interpenetrate each other in the unity of the poetic construction.

But this construction cannot be completely understood at a remove from the conditions of its social realization. For the actual development of the work, of the plot or *skaz*, for example, is constantly oriented toward an audience and cannot be understood outside of the interrelationship between speaker and listener or author and reader.

Even the superficial phenomena of plot development that Shklovskii analyzes – digressions, brakings, hints, riddles, etc. – express the unique interaction between author and reader, the play of two consciousnesses, one of which knows while the other does not, one of which waits while the other destroys the expectation, and so on.

Similarly, *skaz* is constantly oriented toward a corresponding audience reaction, on its support as a chorus, or on its opposition. Every *skaz* sharply and profoundly reacts to the atmosphere of social values.

The curve of the *skaz* is the graph of the fluctuations of the value atmosphere of the social collective within which the *skaz* is oriented, or which it stylizes.

Such is the role of social evaluation in the poetic construction.

In the next chapter we will consider in more detail the constructive significance of the various separate elements of the poetic work.

7

M. M. Bakhtin

'The hero's monologic discourse and narrational discourse in Dostoevsky's short novels'

From *Problems of Dostoevsky's Poetics*, edited and translated by
Caryl Emerson (Manchester University Press, 1984, pp. 204–37).

The third extract in this reader is the second section of chapter 5 of *Problems of Dostoevsky's Poetics*, entitled 'Discourse in Dostoevsky'. It contains analyses of passages from two of Dostoevsky's early novels, *Poor Folk* (1846) and *The Double* (1846), and from the later *Notes from Underground* (1864). In addition Bakhtin alludes to *The Adolescent* (1875), and to Dostoevsky's last novel, *The Brothers Karamazov* (1880).

As I explained in chapter 2 of Part I the central claim that Bakhtin makes for Dostoevsky is that he invents the 'polyphonic' novel, in which the voices of the characters are dialogically engaged by the voice of the narrator without the narrator seeking the final word, or seeking to place and explain the characters. 'Discourse in Dostoevsky' describes the textual manifestation of that dialogic engagement: how, that is, that engagement makes itself apparent at the minutest textual level. The chapter begins with an argument that a stylistics based solely on linguistics is inadequate, since linguistics cannot deal with dialogic relationships. This is Bakhtin's classic statement of the necessity of a 'metalinguistics' (see chapter 1 of Part I). He goes on from there to describe the various ways in which discourse can enter the novel, culminating in the typology described in chapter 2 of Part I. It will be recalled that this typology had three broad divisions:

I Direct, unmediated discourse directed exclusively towards its referential object, as an expression of the speaker's ultimate semantic authority

II Objectified discourse (discourse of a represented person)

III Discourse with an orientation towards someone else's discourse (double-voiced discourse)

(PDP 199)

The second and especially the third divisions are minutely subdivided to yield an exhaustive typology of discursive forms; it is into this third division that Dostoevsky's novels fall. But the point of this typology is not to encourage pigeon-holing of novelistic language; rather it is a way of capturing the varieties of dialogic relationships which novels embody.

Poor Folk is the first novel that Dostoevsky wrote, and is an epistolary novel (written in letters). As such Bakhtin argues that it is a variety of *Ich-Erzählung*, or first-person narration, one of his subcategories of 'double-voiced' discourse because the language of both narrator and character can be heard in it. In his analysis of *The Double*, by contrast, Bakhtin takes issue with the formalist Vinogradov's description of *skaz* in the novel, arguing that the peculiar features of the mode of oral narration in the novel cannot be captured by a linguistic stylistics but have to take account of the dialogic relation of the narration to the hero. The extract, in addition to some fine analyses of individual passages, makes use of two important Bakhtinian notions, the word 'with a sideward glance' and the word 'with a loophole'. In both cases these are ideas which allow you to make the transition from precise stylistic analysis to the widest social and ethical questions.

The translator has provided references to the standard Russian edition of Dostoevsky's novels, *Sobranie sochinenii* (Moscow, 1956–8), reference ss, volume number, and page. In addition, she has used the following standard translations:

Poor Folk or *Poor People*, translated by Constance Garnett, in *Three Short Novels by Fyodor Dostoyevsky: Notes from Underground, Poor People, The Friend of the Family* (Dell, New York, 1960).

The Double, translated by Jessie Coulson, in *Dostoyevsky: Notes from Underground and the Double* (London, Penguin Classics, 1972).

The Adolescent, translated by Andrew MacAndrew (Norton, New York, 1981).

The Brothers Karamazov, the Garnett translation revised by Ralph E. Matlaw (Norton Critical Edition, New York, 1976).

Notes from Underground, the Garnett translation revised by Ralph E. Matlaw, in *Fyodor Dostoyevsky: Notes from Underground and the Grand Inquisitor* (Dutton, New York, 1960).

The hero's monologic discourse and narrational discourse in Dostoevsky's short novels

Dostoevsky began with the *refracting word*: with the epistolary form. Apropos of *Poor Folk* he wrote his brother: "They [the public and the critics – M. B.] have grown used to seeing in everything the author's mug; I didn't show mine. And it doesn't even occur to them that Devushkin is speaking and not I, and that Devushkin cannot speak in any other way. They find the novel long-winded, but there is not a superfluous word in it."[1]

It is Makar Devushkin and Varenka Dobroselova who speak in the work, and the author merely distributes their words: his concepts and aspirations are refracted through the words of the hero and heroine. The epistolary form is a variety of *Ich Erzählung*. Discourse here is double-voiced, and in most cases unidirectional. As such it functions as a compositional surrogate of the author's discourse, which is absent. We shall see that authorial understanding is very subtly and carefully refracted through the words of the hero-narrators, even though the entire work is filled with overt and hidden parodies, with overt and hidden (authorial) polemic.

But for now we are interested in Makar Devushkin's speech only as the monologic utterance of a character, and not as the speech of a narrator in an *Ich Erzählung* – a function which it in fact fulfils (since, outside the characters, there are no other carriers of discourse here). For after all, the discourse of any narrator employed by the author to realize his artistic plan belongs in its own right to some specific discursive type, quite apart from the type determined by its function as narration. Of what type, then, is Devushkin's monologic utterance?

The epistolary form in and of itself does not predetermine the type of discourse. In general this form permits broad discursive possibilities, but it is best suited to discourse of the final variety of the third type, that is, the reflected discourse of another. A characteristic feature of the letter is an acute awareness of the interlocutor, the addressee to whom it is directed. The letter, like a rejoinder in a dialogue, is addressed to a specific person, and it takes into account the other's possible reactions, the other's possible reply. This reckoning with an absent interlocutor can be more or less intensive. In Dostoevsky it is extremely intense.

In his first work, Dostoevsky develops that speech style so characteristic of his entire creative art, a style defined by the intense anticipation of another's words. The significance of this style in his subsequent work is enormous: his heroes' most important confessional self-utterances are permeated with an intense sensitivity toward the anticipated words of others about them, and with others' reactions to their own words about themselves. Not only the tone and style but also the internal semantic structure of these self-utterances are defined by an anticipation of another person's words, from Golyadkin's tension – filled reservations and loopholes to the ethical and metaphysical loopholes of Ivan Karamazov. In *Poor Folk* Dostoevsky begins to work out the "degraded" variety of this style – discourse that cringes with a timid and ashamed sideward glance at the other's possible response, yet contains a muffled challenge.

This "sideward glance" manifests itself above all in two traits characteristic of the style: a certain halting quality to the speech, and its interruption by reservations.

I live in the kitchen, or rather, to be more accurate, there is a room near the kitchen (and our kitchen, I ought to tell you, is clean, light and very nice), a little room, a modest corner ... or rather the kitchen is a big room of three windows so I have a partition running along the inside wall, so that it makes as it were another room, an extra lodging; it is roomy and comfortable, and there is a window and all – in fact, every convenience. Well, so that is my little corner. So don't you imagine, my darling, there is anything else about it, any mysterious significance in it; "here he is living in the kitchen!" Well, if you like, I really am living in the kitchen, behind the partition, but that is nothing. I am quite private, apart from everyone, quiet and snug. I have put in a bed, a table, a chest of drawers and a couple of chairs, and I have hung up the ikon. It is true there are better lodgings – perhaps there may be much better, but convenience is the great thing; I have arranged it all for my own convenience, you know, and you must not imagine it is for anything else. (ss 1, 82; *Poor Folk*, Letter of April 8)

After almost every word Devushkin casts a sideward glance at his absent interlocutor: he is afraid she will think he is complaining, he tries in advance to destroy the impression that will be created by the news that he lives in the kitchen, he does not want to distress her, and so forth. The repetition of the words results from his trying to intensify their accent or to give them a new nuance in light of his interlocutor's possible reaction.

In the above excerpt, the reflected discourse turns out to be the potential words of the addressee, Varenka Dobroselova. In most cases Makar Devushkin's speech about himself is determined by the reflected discourse of another, "other person," a stranger. Here is how he defines this stranger: "And what will you do out there among strangers?" he asks Varenka Dobroselova.

I expect you don't know what strangers are like ... You had better ask me and I will tell you what strangers are like. I know them, my darling, I know them very well, I've had to eat their bread. They are spiteful, Varenka, spiteful; so spiteful that you would have no heart left, they would torment it so with reproach, upbraiding and ill looks. (ss 1, 240; *Poor Folk*, Letter of July 1)

A poor man, but a man "with ambition" – such is Makar Devushkin according to Dostoevsky's concept; he constantly senses the "ill look" of this other upon him, a glance which is either reproachful or – perhaps even worse in his eyes – mocking (for heroes of the prouder type, the worst glance another could cast is a compassionate one). Under this other's glance even Devushkin's speech cringes. He, like the hero from the underground, is constantly eavesdropping on others' words about him. "The poor man is exacting; he takes a different view of God's world, and looks askance at every passer-by and turns a troubled gaze about him and looks to every word, wondering whether people are not talking about him ..." (ss 1, 153; *Poor Folk*, Letter of August 1).

This sideward glance at a socially alien discourse determines not only the style and tone of Makar Devushkin's speech, but also his very manner of thinking and experiencing, of seeing and understanding himself and the little world that surrounds him. Between the most superficial elements of a character's manner of speech, the form in which he expresses himself, and the ultimate foundations of his world view Dostoevsky always creates a profound organic bond. A person is wholly present in his every gesture. And the orientation of one person to another person's discourse and consciousness is, in essence, the basic theme of all of Dostoevsky's works. The hero's attitude toward himself is inseparably bound up with his attitude toward another, and with the attitude of another toward him. His consciousness of self is constantly perceived against the background of the other's consciousness of him – "I for myself" against the background of "I for another." Thus the hero's words about himself are structured under the continuous influence of someone else's words about him.

This theme is developed in various works through various forms, filled with varying content and on various spiritual levels. In *Poor Folk*, the self-consciousness of a poor man unfolds against the background of a consciousness about him that is socially alien to him. His affirmation of self sounds like a continuous hidden polemic or hidden dialogue with some other person on the theme of himself. In Dostoevsky's early works this is still given rather simple and direct expression – dialogue has not yet gone within, not yet, so to speak, entered the very atoms of thought and experience. The heroes' world is still small, and the heroes are not yet ideologists. Even the very social degradation of the characters makes their internal sideward glance and internal polemic quite direct and clear-cut, without the highly complex internal loopholes that grow into whole ideological constructions in Dostoevsky's final works. But the profound dialogic and polemical nature of self-awareness and self-affirmation is already revealed here with the utmost clarity.

A day or two ago, in private conversation, Yevstafy Ivanovich said that the most important virtue in a citizen was to earn money. He said in jest

(I know it was in jest) that morality consists in not being a burden to anyone. Well, I'm not a burden to anyone. My crust of bread is my own; it is true it is a plain crust of bread, at times a dry one; but there it is, earned by my toil and put to lawful and irreproachable use. Why, what can one do? I know very well, of course, that I don't do much by copying; but all the same I am proud of working and earning my bread in the sweat of my brow. Why, what if I am a copying clerk, after all? What harm is there in copying, after all? "He's a copying clerk," they say, but what is there discreditable in that? ... So I see now that I am necessary, that I am indispensable, and that it's no use to worry a man with nonsense. Well, let me be a rat if you like, since they see a resemblance! But the rat is necessary, but the rat is of service, but the rat is depended upon, but the rat is given a reward, so that's the sort of rat he is!

Enough about that subject though, my own! I did not intend to talk about that at all, but I got a little heated. Besides, it's pleasant from time to time to do oneself justice. (ss I, 125–6; *Poor Folk*, Letter of June 12)

In an even sharper polemic, Makar Devushkin's self-awareness is revealed when he recognizes himself in Gogol's "Overcoat"; he perceives the story as someone else's words about him personally, and he seeks to destroy those words polemically as something not adequate to him.

But let us now take a closer look at the very structure of this "word with a sideward glance."

In the first excerpt cited, where Devushkin is casting an anxious sideward glance at Varenka Dobroselova while he informs her of his new room, we already notice the peculiar interruptions in speech that determine its syntactic and accentual structure. The other's rejoinder wedges its way, as it were, into his speech, and although this rejoinder is in fact absent, its influence brings about a radical accentual and syntactic restructuring of that speech. The rejoinder is not actually present but its shadow, its trace, falls on his speech, and that shadow, that trace is real. But sometimes the other's rejoinder, quite apart from its influence on the accentual and syntactic structure, leaves behind in Makar Devushkin's speech one or two of its own words, and sometimes a whole sentence: "So don't you imagine, my darling, there is anything else about it, any mysterious significance in it: 'here he is living in the *kitchen*!' Well, if you like, I really am living in the kitchen, behind the partition, but that is nothing ..." The word "kitchen" bursts into Devushkin's speech from out of the other's potential speech, which Devushkin anticipates. This word is presented with the other's accent, which Devushkin somewhat exaggerates polemically. He does not accept this accent, although he cannot help recognizing its power, and he tries to evade it by all sorts of reservations, partial concessions and extenuations, all of which distort the structure of his speech. From this other discourse embedded in him, circles fan out, as it were, across the smooth surface of his speech, furrowing it. Apart from this obviously alien discourse with its obviously alien accent, the majority of words in the quoted passage are chosen by the speaker from two points of view simultaneously: as he himself understands them and wants others to understand them, and as another might actually understand them. Here the other's accent is only hinted at, but it already gives rise to a reservation or a hesitation in speech.

The embedding of words and especially of accents from the other's rejoinder in Makar Devushkin's speech is even more marked and obvious in the second of the quoted passages. The words containing the other's polemically exaggerated accent are even enclosed here in quotation marks: "He's a copying clerk ..." In the preceding lines the word "copy" is repeated three times. In each of these three instances the other's potential accent is present in the word "copy," but it is suppressed by Devushkin's own accent: however, it becomes constantly stronger, until it finally breaks through and assumes the form of the other's direct speech. We are presented here, therefore, with gradations of gradual intensi- fication in the other's accent: "I know very well, of course, that I don't do much by *copying* ... [then follows a reservation – M. B.] Why, what if I am a *copying* clerk, after all? What harm is there in *copying*, after all? 'He's a *COPYING* clerk! ...'" We have indicated by italics and underscoring the other's accent and its gradual intensification, which finally dominates utterly the line of discourse enclosed in quotation marks. But even in these final words, obviously belonging to the other, Devushkin's own voice is present too, for he polemically exaggerates the other's accent. As the other person's accent intensifies, so does Devushkin's counter-accent.

We can descriptively define all the above-mentioned phenomena in the following way: the hero's self-awareness was penetrated by someone else's consciousness of him, the hero's own self-utterance was injected with someone else's words about him; the other's consciousness and the other's words then give rise to specific phenomena that determine the thematic development of Devushkin's self-awareness, its breaking points, loopholes and protests on the one hand, and on the other the hero's speech with its accentual interruptions, syntactic breaking points, repeti- tions, reservations, and long-windedness.

We might offer this graphic definition and explanation of the same phenomena: let us imagine two rejoinders of the most intense dialogue – a discourse and a counter-discourse – which, instead of following one after the other and being uttered by two different mouths, are super-imposed one on the other and merge into a *single* utterance issuing from a *single* mouth. These two rejoinders move in opposite directions and clash with one another; therefore their overlapping and merging into a single utterance results in a most intense mutual interruption. This collision of two rejoinders – each integral in itself and single-accented – is now transformed, in the new utterance resulting from their fusion, into the most acute interruption of voices, contradictory in every detail, in every atom of the utterance. The dialogic collision has gone within, into the subtlest structural elements of speech (and correspondingly, of consciousness).

The above-quoted passage could be approximately paraphrased in the following crude dialogue between Makar Devushkin and the "other person":

THE OTHER: One must know how to earn a lot of money. One shouldn't be a burden to anyone. But you are a burden to others.

MAKAR DEVUSHKIN: I'm not a burden to anyone. I've got my own piece of bread.

THE OTHER: But what a piece of bread it is! Today it's there, and tomorrow it's gone. And it's probably a dry one, at that!

MAKAR DEVUSHKIN: It is true it is a plain crust of bread, at times a dry one, but there it is, earned by my toil and put to lawful and ir-reproachable use.

THE OTHER: But what kind of toil! All you do is copy. You're not capable of anything else.

MAKAR DEVUSHKIN: Well, what can one do! I know very well, of course, that I don't do much by copying, but all the same I am proud of it.

THE OTHER: Oh, there's something to be proud of, all right! Copying! It's disgraceful!

MAKAR DEVUSHKIN: Well, in fact really, so what if I am just a copying clerk! ... [etc.]

It is as if the overlapping and merging of these sides of dialogue into a single voice had resulted in Devushkin's self-utterance quoted above.

Of course this imagined dialogue is extremely primitive, just as the content of Devushkin's consciousness is still primitive. For this is ultimately still an Akaky Akakievich, enlightened by self-consciousness, who has acquired speech and is "elaborating a style." But then the formal structure of his self-consciousness and self-utterances is, because of its primitiveness and crudeness, extremely well-marked and clear. For this reason we are examining it in such detail. All the truly essential self-utterances of Dostoevsky's later heroes could also be turned into dialogues, since all of them arose, as it were, out of two merged rejoinders, but the interruption of voices in them goes so deep, into such subtle elements of thought and discourse, that to turn them into a visible and crude dialogue such as we have done with Devushkin's self-utterance is of course utterly impossible.

The phenomena which we have examined here, the result of a second and alien discourse functioning inside the consciousness and speech of the hero, are presented in *Poor Folk* in the stylistic garb of the speech of a petty Petersburg clerk. The structural characteristics we have noted – "the word with a sideward glance," discourse concealing a hidden polemic, internally dialogic discourse – are refracted here in a strictly and skillfully sustained manner that is sociotypical of Devushkin's speech.[2] For this reason all these phenomena of language – reservations, repetitions, diminutives, the diversity of particles and interjections – would not be possible, in the form in which they occur here, in the mouths of other Dostoevskian heroes belonging to another social world. The same phenomena would appear in a different sociotypical and individually characteristic speech profile. But their essence remains the same: the crossing and intersection, in every element of consciousness and discourse, of two consciousnesses, two points of view, two evaluations – two voices interrupting one another intra-atomically.

In the same sociotypical speech environment, but in a different individually characteristic manner, Dostoevsky constructs the discourse of Golyadkin. In *The Double*, the characteristic trait of consciousness and speech that we examined above is expressed with a sharpness and clarity not found in any other work of Dostoevsky's. The tendencies already embedded in Makar Devushkin are developed here with extraordinary boldness and consistency, carried to their conceptual limits, on the basis of the same deliberately primitive, simple, and crude material.

We cite below the semantic structure and speech profile of Golyadkin's discourse in a parodic stylization done by Dostoevsky himself, in a letter written to his brother while working on *The Double*. As in any parodic stylization, there is an obvious and crude emphasis upon the basic characteristics and tendencies of Golyadkin's discourse.

> **"Yakov Petrovich Golyadkin** holds his own completely. He's a terrible scoundrel and there's no approaching him; he refuses to move forward, pretending that he's not ready yet, that for the present he's on his own, he's all right, nothing is the matter, but that if it comes to that, then he can do that too, why not, what's to prevent it? He's just like everyone else, he's nothing special, just like everyone else. What's it to him! A scoundrel, a terrible scoundrel! He'll never agree to end his career before the middle of November. He's just now spoken with his Excellency, and he just may (and why shouldn't he) be ready to announce his retirement."[3]

As we shall see, *The Double* itself is narrated in this same style, parodying the hero. But to that narration we shall return later.

The influence of another person's words on Golyadkin's speech is absolutely obvious. We immediately sense that his speech, like Devushkin's, gravitates neither toward itself nor toward its referential object. Golyadkin's interrelationships with another's speech and another's consciousness are, however, quite different from Devushkin's. And for this reason the traits in Golyadkin's style produced by the other's discourse are of a different sort.

Golyadkin's speech seeks, above all, to simulate total independence from the other's words: "He's on his own, he's all right." This simulation of independence and indifference also leads to endless repetitions, reservations, and long-windedness, but here they are directed not outward, not toward another, but toward Golyadkin's own self: he persuades himself, reassures and comforts himself, plays the role of another person vis-à-vis himself. Golyadkin's comforting dialogues with himself are the most prominent trait of the whole story. Along with a simulation of indifference, however, goes another attitude toward the other's discourse: the desire to hide from it, to avoid attracting attention to himself, to bury himself in the crowd, to go unnoticed. "After all he's just like everyone else, he's nothing special, just like everyone else." But in this he is trying to convince not himself, but another. Finally, there is a third attitude toward the other's discourse: concession, subordination to it, a submissive assimilation of it, as if Golyadkin thought the same way himself and sincerely agreed with it: "If it comes to that, then he can do that too, why not, what's to prevent it?"

Such are Golyadkin's three general lines of orientation, and they are complicated by other secondary but rather important ones. Each of these three lines in itself gives rise to very complex phenomena in Golyadkin's consciousness and discourse.

We shall concentrate primarily on his simulation of independence and composure.

The pages of *The Double* are filled, as we have said, with the hero's dialogues with himself. It could be said that Golyadkin's entire inner life develops dialogically. We quote two examples of such dialogue:

> "Will it be all right, though?" went on our hero, stepping out of his carriage at the porch of a five-story house on Litciny Street, beside which he had ordered the vehicle to stop; "will it be all right? Is it a proper thing to do? Will this be the right time? However, does it really matter?" he continued as he mounted the stairs, breathing hard and trying to control the beating of his heart, which always seemed to beat hard on other people's stairs; "does it matter? I've come about my own business, after all, and there's nothing reprehensible in that. ... It would be stupid to try to keep anything from him. So I'll just make it appear that it's nothing special, I just happened to be driving past. ... He will see that's how it must have been." (ss 1, p. 215: *The Double*, ch.i)

The second example of interior dialogue is considerably more complex and pointed. Golyadkin conducts it after the appearance of the double; that is, after the second voice has already become objectified for him within his own field of vision.

> Thus Mr. Golyadkin's delighted mood expressed itself, but all the time something went on nagging away at the back of his mind, a kind of ache, which sometimes so drained his spirits that Mr. Golyadkin did not know where to turn for consolation. "However, we'll wait a day, and then we can be happy. Still, what does it amount to, after all? Well, we'll think about it, and we'll see. Well, let's think it over, my young friend, let's discuss it. Well, he's a man like you to begin with, exactly the same. Well, what of that? If that's what he is, ought I to weep over it? What's it got to do with me? I'm outside it; I just whistle, that's all! Let him work! Well, it's something strange and queer; just like the Siamese twins, as they call them. ... Well, why them, the Siamese twins? – all right, they're twins, but even the very greatest people have seemed a bit queer sometimes. Why, even in history, it's well known the famous Suvorov crowed like a cock. ... Well, but that was all for political reasons; and great generals ... but why talk about generals? I go my own way, that's all, and I don't want to know anybody, and in my innocence I scorn my enemies. I am no intriguer, and I'm proud to say it. Honest, straightforward, orderly, agreeable, mild ..." (ss 1, pp. 268–9; *The Double*, ch. vi)

The first question that arises concerns the function of this dialogue with the self in Golyadkin's spiritual life. The question can be briefly answered thus: *the dialogue allows him to substitute his own voice for the voice of another person.*

This substituting function of Golyadkin's second voice is felt in everything. Without understanding it we cannot understand his interior dialogues. Golyadkin addresses himself as if addressing another person ("my young friend"), he praises himself as only another person could, and verbally caresses himself with tender familiarity: "Yakov Petrovich, my dear fellow, you little Golyadka you, what a nice little name you have!;* he reassures and encourages himself with the authoritative tone of an older, more self-confident person. But this second voice of Golyadkin's, confident and calmly self-satisfied, cannot possibly merge with his first voice, the uncertain timid one; the dialogue cannot be transformed into the integral and confident monologue of a single Golyadkin. Moreover, that second voice is to such a degree unable to merge with the first, it feels so threateningly independent, that in place of comforting and encouraging tones there begin to appear teasing, mocking, and treacherous ones. With astonishing tact and artistry Dostoevsky transfers – almost imperceptibly to the reader – Golyadkin's second voice from his interior dialogue to the narration itself: it begins to sound like an outside voice, the voice of the narrator. But of the narration we shall speak somewhat later.

Golyadkin's second voice must compensate for the inadequate recognition he receives from the other person. Golyadkin wants to get by without such recognition, wants to get by, so to speak, on his own. But this "on his own" inevitably takes the form of "you and I, my friend Golyadkin"; that is, it takes dialogic form. In actual fact Golyadkin lives only in another, lives by his reflection in another: "Will it be all right? Is it a proper thing to do?" And this question is always answered from the possible and presumed point of view of another person: Golyadkin *will pretend* that nothing is the matter, that he just happened to be driving by, and the other person will see that "that's how it must have been." It is in the reaction of the other person, in his discourse and his response, that the whole matter lies. There is no way that the confidence of Golyadkin's second voice can rule all of him, nor can it actually take the place of another real person. For him, another's words are the most important thing.

Although Mr. Golyadkin had said all this [about his independence – M. B.] with the utmost possible distinctness and clarity, confidently, weighing his words and calculating their probable effect, nevertheless it was now with anxiety, with the utmost anxiety, that he gazed at Christian Ivanovich. Now he had become all eyes, and awaited Christian Ivanovich's answer with sad and melancholy impatience. (ss 1, pp. 220–21; *The Double*, ch. ii)

In this second excerpt of interior dialogue, the substituting functions of the second voice are absolutely clear. But here there appears in addition a third voice, the direct voice of the other, interrupting the second merely substitute voice. Thus elements appear here that are completely analogous to those we analyzed in Devushkin's speech – words of the other, words partially belonging to the other, and the corresponding accentual interruptions:

Well, it's something strange and queer; just like the Siamese twins, as they call them.... Well, why them, the Siamese twins? – all right, they're twins, but even the very greatest people have seemed a bit queer sometimes. Why, even in history, it's well known the famous Suvorov crowed like a cock.... Well, but that was all for political reasons; and great generals ... but why talk about generals?

Everywhere here, but especially where ellipses appear, the anticipated responses of others wedge themselves in. This passage too could be unfolded in the form of a dialogue. But here it is more complex. While in Devushkin's speech a single integrated voice polemicized with the "other person," here there are two voices: one confident, even too confident, and the other too timid, giving in to everything, capitulating totally.[4]

Golyadkin's second voice (the voice substituting for another person), his first voice hiding away from the other's word ("I'm like everyone else," "I'm all right") and then finally giving in to that other word ("In that case, I'm ready") and, finally, that genuinely other voice forever resounding in him – these three voices are so complexly interrelated that the material provided by them is adequate for the entire intrigue and permits the whole novel to be constructed on them alone. The actual

---

*The name in Russian suggests *golyada*, "tramp" or "beggar," derived from the adjective *golyi*, "naked, bare." The Coulson translation incorrectly reflects the intonation here (ch. 4, p. 158) by rendering the line "You ... you – Golyadkin! (What a name!)." The tone is in fact the opposite: it is tender and protective, as Bakhtin points out, and as the narrator confirms in the subsequent sentence: "However, these flattering remarks addressed to himself at this moment did not mean anything..."

event, namely the unsuccessful courting of Klara Olsufievna, and all the circumstances accompanying it are in fact not represented in the novel at all: they serve only as the stimulus setting inner voices in motion, they make immediate and intensify that inner conflict that is the real object of representation in the novel.

Except for Golyadkin and his double, no other characters take any real part whatsoever in the intrigue, which unfolds entirely within the bounds of Golyadkin's self-consciousness; the other characters merely provide raw material, add, as it were, the fuel necessary for the intense work of that self-consciousness. The external, intentionally obscure intrigue (everything of importance has already taken place before the novel begins) serves also as a firm, barely discernible frame for Golyadkin's inner intrigue. The novel tells the story of Golyadkin's desire to do without the other's consciousness, to do without recognition by another, his desire to avoid the other and assert his own self, and what resulted from this. Dostoevsky intended *The Double* as a "confession"[5] (not in the personal sense, of course), that is, as the representation of an event that takes place within the bounds of self-consciousness. *The Double* is the *first dramatized confession* in Dostoevsky's work.

At the base of the intrigue, therefore, lies Golyadkin's attempt – in view of the total nonrecognition of his personality on the part of others – to find for himself a substitute for the other. Golyadkin plays at being an independent person; his consciousness plays at confidence and self-sufficiency. At the dinner party where Golyadkin is publicly humiliated, this new and acute experience of collision with another person intensifies the split in his personality. Golyadkin's second voice overexerts itself in a desperate simulation of self-sufficiency, in order to save Golyadkin's face. It is impossible for this second voice to merge with Golyadkin; on the contrary, treacherous tones of ridicule grow louder and louder in it. It provokes and teases Golyadkin, it casts off its mask. The double appears. The inner conflict is dramatized; Golyadkin's intrigue with the double begins.

The double speaks in Golyadkin's own words, bringing with him no new words or tones. At first he pretends to be a cringing Golyadkin, Golyadkin surrendering. When Golyadkin brings the double home with him, the latter looks and behaves like the first and uncertain voice in Golyadkin's internal dialogue ("Will it be all right, is it a proper thing to do," etc.)

The visitor [the double – M. B.] evidently felt highly embarrassed and extremely shy; he humbly followed his host's every movement and caught his every look, apparently trying to guess his thoughts from them. All his gestures expressed something meek, downtrodden, and cowed, so that at that moment he was, if the comparison is permissible, like a man who for want of his own clothes is wearing somebody else's; the sleeves have crept half-way up his arms, the waist is almost round his neck, and he is either constantly tugging at the too-short waistcoat, or sliding away somewhere out of the way, or striving to find somewhere to hide, or looking into everybody's eyes and straining to hear whether people are talking about his plight and laughing at him or ashamed of him, and the poor man blushes, he loses his presence of mind, his pride suffers.... (ss i, 270–71; *The Double*, ch. vii)

This is a characterization of the cringing and self-effacing Golyadkin. The double speaks, too, in the tones and style of Golyadkin's first voice. The part of the second voice – confident and tenderly reassuring in its relation to the double – is played by Golyadkin himself, who this time seems to have merged totally with that voice:

"Well, you know, Yakov Petrovich, you and I are going to get on well together," said our hero; "you and I, Yakov Petrovich, will get on like a house on fire, we'll live together like brothers; the two of us will be very clever, old chap, very clever we're going to be; we'll be the ones to intrigue against them ... intrigue against them, that's what we'll do. After all, I know you, Yakov Petrovich, I understand what you're like; you blurt out everything straight away, like the honest soul that you are. You just keep away from all of them, old man" (ss i, 276; *The Double*, ch. vii)[6]

But later on the roles change: the treacherous double takes over the tone of Golyadkin's second voice, parodically exaggerating its affectionate familiarity. At their very next meeting in the office the double has already assumed this tone, and he sustains it until the end of the story, now and then himself emphasizing the identity between expressions from his own speech and Golyadkin's words (the words spoken by him during their first conversation). During one of their meetings at the office, the double, familiarly poking Golyadkin, said to him:

with a smile full of the most venomous and far-reaching implications: "Oh no, you don't, Yakov Petrovich, my little friend, oh no, you don't. We'll dodge you, Yakov Petrovich, we'll dodge you." (ss i, 289; *The Double*, ch. viii)

Or a little later, before their eye-to-eye confrontation in the coffee-house:

"... You've talked me over, my dear boy," said Mr. Golyadkin junior, climbing down from the cab and shamelessly clapping him on the shoulder, "you're such a good sort; for you, Yakov Petrovich, I'm willing to take a side-street (as you so rightly remarked that time, Yakov Petrovich). You're a sly one, you know, you do whatever you like with a man." (ss 1, 337; *The Double*, ch. xi)

This transferral of words from one mouth to another, where the content remains the same although the tone and ultimate meaning are changed, is a fundamental device of Dostoevsky's. He forces his heroes to recognize themselves, their idea, their own words, their orientation, their gesture in another person, in whom all these phenomena change their integrated and ultimate meaning and take on a different sound, the sound of parody or ridicule.[7]

Almost all of Dostoevsky's major heroes, as we have said elsewhere, have their partial double in another person or even in several other people (Stavrogin and Ivan Karamazov). In his last work Dostoevsky again returned to the device of fully embodying the second voice, this time, to be sure, on deep and more subtle grounds. In its externally formal plan Ivan Karamazov's dialogue with the devil is analogous to those interior dialogues that Golyadkin conducts with himself and with his double; for all the dissimilarity in situation and in ideological content, essentially one and the same artistic task is being solved here.

Thus does Golyadkin's intrigue with his double unfold, and it unfolds as the dramatized crisis of his self-consciousness, as a dramatized confession. The action cannot go beyond the bounds of self-consciousness, since the *dramatis personae* are no more than isolated elements of that self-consciousness. The actors here are the three voices into which Golyadkin's voice and consciousness have been dismantled: his "I for myself," which cannot manage without another person and without that person's recognition; his fictitious "I for the other" (reflections in the other), that is, Golyadkin's second substituting voice; and finally the genuinely other voice which does not recognize Golyadkin and yet is not depicted as actually existing outside Golyadkin, since there are no other autonomous characters in the work.[8] What results is a peculiar sort of mystery play, or rather morality play, in which the actors are not whole people but rather the spiritual forces battling within them, a morality play, however, stripped of any formalism or abstract allegorizing.

But who tells the story in *The Double?* What is the positioning of the narrator and what sort of voice does he have?

In the narration too we do not find a single element that exceeds the bounds of Golyadkin's self-consciousness, not a single word or a single tone that could not have been part of his interior dialogue with himself or his dialogue with his double. The narrator picks up on Golyadkin's words and thoughts, intensifies the teasing, mocking tones embedded in them, and in these tones portrays Golyadkin's every act, every gesture, every movement. We have already said that Golyadkin's second voice, through imperceptible transitions, merges with the voice of the narrator; one gets the impression that *the narration is dialogically addressed to Golyadkin himself*, it rings in Golyadkin's own ears as another's voice taunting him, as the voice of his double, although formally the narration is addressed to the reader.

This is how the narrator describes Golyadkin's behavior at the most fateful moment in his escapades, when he tries, uninvited, to gain entrance to the ball at Olsufy Ivanovich's:

> Let us rather turn to Mr. Golyadkin, the real and sole hero of our true to life story.
>
> The fact is that he is now in a position that is, to say the least, extremely strange. He is here too, ladies and gentlemen, that is to say not at the ball, but almost at the ball; he is all right, ladies and gentlemen; he may be on his own, yet at this moment he stands upon a path that is not altogether straight; he stands now – it is strange even to say it – he stands now in the passage from the back entrance of Olsufy Ivanovich's flat. But that he is standing there means nothing; he is all right. He is standing, though, ladies and gentlemen, in a corner, lurking in a much darker, if no warmer, place, half concealed by an enormous cupboard and an old screen, among every kind of dusty rubbish, trash, and lumber, hiding until the proper time and meanwhile only watching the progress of the general business in the capacity of casual looker-on. He is only watching now, ladies and gentlemen; but, you know, he may also go in, ladies and gentlemen ... why not? He has only to take a step, and he is in, and in very neatly. (ss I, 239–40; *The Double*, ch. iv)

In the structure of this narration we observe two voices interrupting each other, and the same merging of two rejoinders that we had earlier observed in the utterances of Makar Devushkin. But here the roles have changed: here it is as if the other person's rejoinder has swallowed up the rejoinder of the hero. The narration glitters with Golyadkin's own words:

"he is all right," "he's on his own," etc. But these words are uttered by the narrator with ridicule, with ridicule and somewhat with reproach, directed at Golyadkin himself and constructed in a form meant to touch his sore spots and provoke him. The mocking narration imperceptibly passes over into the speech of Golyadkin himself. The question "Why not?" belongs to Golyadkin himself, but is given in the teasing, aggressive intonation of the narrator. Even this intonation, however, is not in essence alien to the consciousness of Golyadkin himself. All this could ring in his own head, as his second voice. In fact the author could at any point insert quotation marks without changing the tone, voice, or construction of the sentence.

Somewhat further he does exactly that:

> So there he is now, ladies and gentlemen, waiting for the chance to do things quietly, and he has been waiting for exactly two and a half hours. Why not wait? Villèle himself used to wait. "But what's Villèle got to do with this?" thought Mr. Golyadkin. "Who's Villèle, anyhow? And what if I were to … just go through …? Oh you, bit player, you!" (ss 1, 241; *The Double*, ch. iv)

But why not insert quotation marks two sentences earlier, before the words "Why not wait?", or even earlier, changing the words "So there he is now, ladies and gentlemen…." to "Golyadka, old boy," or some other form of address by Golyadkin to his own self? Of course the quotation marks are not inserted at random. They are inserted in such a way as to make the transition especially subtle and imperceptible. Villèle's name appears in the narrator's last sentence and in the hero's first. Golyadkin's words seem to continue the narration uninterruptedly and answer it in an interior dialogue. "Villèle himself used to wait." '"But what's Villèle got to do with this!"' These are in fact detached rejoinders in Golyadkin's interior dialogue with himself: one side entered the narration, the other remained with Golyadkin. A phenomenon has occurred that is quite the reverse of what we had observed earlier, when we witnessed the interruption-prone merging of two rejoinders. But the result is the same: a double-voiced, interruption-prone construction with all the accompanying phenomena. The field of action is the same, too: a single self-consciousness. Authority in that consciousness, however, has been seized by the other's discourse, which has made its home in it.

We shall quote another example with the same vacillating borders between the narration and the hero's discourse. Golyadkin has made up his mind and has at last entered the hall where the ball is going on, and finds himself before Klara Olsufievna:

> There is not the slightest doubt he could most gladly have sunk through the floor at that moment without so much as blinking; but what's done can't be undone ... no, indeed it can't. What was he to do? "If things go wrong, stand your ground; if all goes well, stand firm." Mr. Golyadkin, of course, was "not an intriguer, nor was he good at polishing the parquet with his shoes ..." Well, now the worst had happened. And besides, the Jesuits were mixed up in it somehow.... However, Mr. Golyadkin had no time for them now! (ss I, 242–43; *The Double*, ch. iv)

The passage is interesting because it contains no grammatically direct discourse belonging to Golyadkin himself, and thus there is no justification for setting off words in quotation marks. The portion of the narration in quotation marks here was set that way, apparently, through a mistake of the editor. Dostoevsky probably set off only the proverb: "If things go wrong, stand your ground; if all goes well, stand firm." The next sentence is given in the third person, although, of course, it belongs to Golyadkin himself. Further on, the pauses marked by ellipses also belong to Golyadkin's inner speech. The sentences preceding and following these ellipses, judging by their accents, relate to one another as do rejoinders in an interior dialogue. The two adjacent sentences with the Jesuits are completely analogous to the above-quoted sentences on Villèle, set off from one another by quotation marks.

Finally, one more excerpt, where perhaps the opposite mistake was committed, quotation marks were not inserted where grammatically they should have been. Golyadkin, driven from the ball, rushes home through a snowstorm and meets a passer-by who later turns out to be his double:

> It was not that he feared this might be some bad character, it was simply perhaps ... "And besides, who knows?" – the thought came unbidden into Mr. Golyadkin's mind – "perhaps this passer-by is – **he**, himself, perhaps he is here and, what matters most, he is not here for nothing, he has a purpose, he is crossing my path, he will brush against me." (ss I, 252; *The Double*, ch. v)

Here the ellipsis serves as a dividing line between the narration and Golyadkin's direct inner speech, which is structured in the first person ("*my* path" "brush against *me*"). But they are merged so closely here that one really does not want to insert quotation marks. For this sentence, after all, must be read with a single voice, albeit an internally dialogized one. Stunningly successful here is the transition from the narration to the hero's speech: we feel, as it were, the wave of a single speech current, one that carries us without dams or barriers from the narration into the hero's soul and out again into the narration; we feel that we are moving essentially within the circle of a single consciousness.

One could cite many more examples proving that the narration is a direct continuation and development of Golyadkin's second voice and that it is addressed dialogically to the hero, but even the above examples are sufficient. The whole work is constructed, therefore, entirely as an interior dialogue of three voices within the limits of a single dismantled consciousness. Every essential aspect of it lies at a point of intersection of these three voices, at a point where they abruptly, agonizingly interrupt one another. Invoking our image, we could say that this is not yet polyphony, but no longer homophony. One and the same word, idea, phenomenon is passed through three voices and in each voice sounds differently. The same set of words, tones, inner orientations is passed through the outer speech of Golyadkin, through the speech of the narrator and through the speech of the double, and these three voices are turned to face one another, they speak not about each other but with each other. Three voices sing the same line, but not in unison; rather, each carries its own part.

But these voices have not yet become fully independent real voices, they are not yet three autonomous consciousness. This occurs only in Dostoevsky's longer novels. In *The Double* there is no monologic discourse gravitating solely toward itself and its referential object. Each word is dismantled dialogically, each word contains an interruption of voices, but there is not yet an authentic dialogue of unmerged consciousnesses such as will later appear in the novels. Already the rudiments of counterpoint are here: it is implied in the very structure of the discourse. The analyses of the sort we have offered here are already, as it were, contrapuntal analyses (speaking figuratively, of course). But these new connections have not yet gone beyond the bounds of monologic material.

Relentlessly ringing in Golyadkin's ears are the provocative and mocking voice of the narrator and the voice of the double. The narrator shouts into Golyadkin's ear Golyadkin's own words and thoughts, but in another, hopelessly alien, hopelessly censuring and mocking tone. This second voice is present in every one of Dostoevsky's heroes, and in his final novel, as we have said, it again takes on an independent existence. The devil shouts into Ivan Karamazov's ear Ivan's very own words, commenting mockingly on his decision to confess in court and repeating in an alien tone his most intimate thoughts. We shall not take up here the actual dialogue between Ivan and the devil, since the principles of authentic dialogue will concern us further on. But we shall quote the passage immediately following this dialogue, Ivan's agitated story to Alyosha. Its structure is analogous to the previously analyzed structure of *The Double*. The same principle obtains for combining voices, although to be sure everything here is deeper and more complex. In this story Ivan passes his own personal thoughts and decisions simultaneously through two voices, he transmits them in two different tonalities. In the quoted excerpt we omit Alyosha's side of the dialogue, for his real voice does not yet fit into our scheme. What interests us now is only the intra-atomic counterpoint of voices, their combination solely within the bounds of a single dismantled consciousness (that is, a microdialogue).

> "He's been teasing me. And you know he does it so cleverly, so cleverly. 'Conscience! What is conscience? I make it up for myself. Why am I tormented by it? From habit. From the universal habit of mankind for seven thousand years. So let us give it up, and we shall be gods.' It was he who said that, it was he who said that!" ...
>
> "Yes, but he is spiteful. He laughed at me. He was impudent, Alyosha," Ivan said, with a shudder of offense. "But he was unfair to me, unfair to me about lots of things. He told lies about me to my face. 'Oh, you are going to perform an act of heroic virtue: to confess you murdered your father, that the lackey murdered him at your instigation.'" ...
>
> "That's what he says, he, and he knows, it. 'You are going to perform an act of heroic virtue, and you don't believe in virtue; that's what tortures you and makes you angry, that's why you are so vindictive.' He said that to me about me and he knows what he says." ...
>
> "Yes, he knows how to torment one. He's cruel," Ivan went on, unheeding. "I had an inkling from the first what he came for. 'Granting that you go through pride, still you had a hope that Smerdyakov might be convicted and sent to Siberia, and Mitya would be acquitted, while you would only be punished with *moral* condemnation' ('Do you hear?' he laughed then – 'and some people will praise you. But now Smerdyakov's dead, he has hanged himself, and who'll believe you alone? But yet you are going, you are going, you'll go all the same, you've decided to go. What are you going for now?' That's awful, Alyosha. I can't endure such

questions. Who dare ask me such questions?" (ss x, 184–85; *The Brothers Karamazov*, Part IV, Book II, ch. 10)

All the loopholes in Ivan's thoughts, all his sideward glances at another's words and another's consciousness, all his attempts to get around the other's words and to replace them in his soul with an affirmation of his own self, all the reservations of his conscience that serve to interrupt his every thought, his every word and experience, condense and thicken here into the completed replies of the devil. Ivan's words and the devil's replies do not differ in content but only in tone, only in accent. But this change of accent changes their entire ultimate meaning. The devil, as it were, transfers to the main clause what had been for Ivan merely a subordinate clause, uttered under his breath and without independent accent, and the content of the main clause he makes into an unaccented subordinate clause. Ivan's reservation concerning the main motive for his decision is transformed by the devil into the main motive, and the main motive becomes merely a reservation. What results is a combination of voices that is highly intense and maximally eventful, but which at the same time is not dependent on any opposition in content or plot.

But of course this full dialogization of Ivan's consciousness is – as is always the case with Dostoevsky – prepared for in a leisurely fashion. The other's discourse gradually, stealthily penetrates the consciousness and speech of the hero: now in the form of a pause where one would not be appropriate in monologically confident speech, now in the form of someone else's accent breaking up the sentence, now in the form of an abnormally heightened, exaggerated, or anguished personal tone, and so on. From Ivan's first words and from his entire inner orientation in Zosima's cell, through his conversations with Alyosha, with his father, and especially with Smerdyakov before his departure to Chermashnya, and finally through his three meetings with Smerdyakov after the murder, this process of the gradual dialogic dismantling of Ivan's consciousness stretches out, a process more profound and ideologically complicated than was the case with Golyadkin, but structurally fully analogous to it.

Someone else's voice whispering into the ear of the hero his own words with a displaced accent, and the resulting unrepeatably unique combination of vari-directional words and voices within a single word, a single speech, the intersection of two consciousnesses in a single consciousness

– in one form or another, to one degree or another, in one ideological direction or another – all this is present in every one of Dostoevsky's works. This contrapuntal combination of vari-directional voices within the bounds of a single consciousness also serves him as the basis, the ground, on which he introduces other real voices as well. But we will return to that later. At this point we would like to quote one passage from Dostoevsky where, with stunning artistic power, he offers a musical image for the interrelationship of voices analyzed by us above. This page from *The Adolescent* is all the more interesting because in his works Dostoevsky, with the exception of this passage, almost never speaks of music.

Trishatov is telling the adolescent of his love for music, and explains to him his plan for an opera:

"Tell me, do you like music? I'm crazy about music. I'll play you something when I come to see you. I've studied piano for years seriously, and I can play really well. If I were to compose an opera, I'd choose a theme from *Faust.* I love *Faust.* I keep composing music for that scene in the cathedral – oh, just in my head, of course.... The interior of that Gothic cathedral, the choir, the hymns.... In comes Gretchen ... the choir is medieval – you can hear the fifteenth century at once. Gretchen is in despair. First, a recitative, played very softly, but full of suffering and terror, while the choir thunders grimly, sternly, and impersonally, '*Dies irae, dies illa!' And then, all of a sudden, the devil's voice sings the devil's song. You can't see him, there's only his song mingling with the hymns, almost blending into them, although it's completely different from them – I must manage to convey that somehow.* The devil's song is long, persistent. A tenor – it absolutely must be a tenor. It begins softly and tenderly: 'Do you remember, Gretchen, when, still an innocent chid, you came here with your mother and lisped your prayers from the old prayer book?' But the devil's voice grows louder, more passionate, more intense, it floats on higher notes that contain despair, tears, and infinite, irretrievable hopelessness: 'There's no forgiveness, Gretchen, no forgiveness here for you!' Gretchen wants to pray but only cries of pain come from her breast – you know, the breast shaken by sobs and convulsions.... And all this time the devil's song continues and pierces her soul deeper and deeper like a spear – the notes get higher and higher and then, suddenly, it all breaks off in a shriek: 'Accursed one, this is the end!' ... Gretchen falls on her knees, her hands clasped in front of her. And then comes her prayer. Something very short, a semi-recitative, but completely simple, without ornamentation, again very medieval, only four lines – Stradella has a passage with a score a bit like that.... And then, on the last note, she faints! There's general confusion, they pick her up, and suddenly the choir thunders forth. It must sound like an explosion of voices, an inspirational, triumphant, irresistible outburst, somewhat like 'Borne on high by angels...' So that everything is shaken to its foundations and it all merges into one single overwhelming, exalted 'Hosanna!' – like an outcry from the whole universe.... And they carry Gretchen off, and just at that moment the curtain must fall..." (ss VII, 482–83; *The Adolescent*, Part III, ch. 5, iii)

A part of that musical plan – although in the form of literary works – was indisputably realized by Dostoevsky, and realized quite frequently and with the most varied material.[9]

But let us return to Golyadkin, we have not yet finished with him; or rather, we have not yet finished with the narrator's discourse. From an utterly different point of view – namely the point of view of linguistic stylistics – a definition of narration in *The Double* analogous to ours has been provided by V. Vinogradov in his article "The Style of the Petersburg Poem *The Double*."[10]

Here is Vinogradov's basic claim:

> The introduction of "interjections" and expressions from Golyadkin's speech into the narrational *skaz* achieves an effect whereby it seems, from time to time, that hidden behind the narrator's mask Golyadkin himself begins to appear, narrating his own adventures. In *The Double* this convergence of Mr. Golyadkin's controversial speech with the narrational *skaz* of the storyteller is further intensified, because in indirect speech Golyadkin's style remains unchanged, falling, therefore, to the author's responsibility. And since Golyadkin says the same thing over and over not only with his language but also with his glance, his appearance, his gestures and movements, it is fully understandable why almost all the descriptions (significantly making reference to the 'perpetual habits' of Mr. Golyadkin) glitter with unmarked citations from his speech.

After citing a series of examples where the narrator's speech coincides with Golyadkin's speech, Vinogradov continues:

> This number of excerpts could be considerably increased, but even the ones we have cited, illustrating this combination of Golyadkin's self-definitions and the minor verbal brush-stokes of a detached observer, stress clearly enough the idea that the 'Petersburg poem,' at least in many parts, expresses itself as a story about Golyadkin told by his 'double,' that is, by 'a person with his language and concepts.' The use of this innovative device explains the failure of *The Double*.[11]

Vinogradov's analysis is subtle and well-substantiated and his conclusions are correct, but he remains, of course, within the bounds of his chosen method, and what is most important and fundamental simply cannot be fitted within those bounds.

Vinogradov, it seems to us, could not perceive the real uniqueness of syntax in *The Double*, because syntactic structure here is not determined by the *skaz* in and of itself, nor by a clerk's conversational dialect, nor by official bureaucratese, but first and foremost by the collision and interruption of various accents within the bounds of a single syntactic whole, that is, precisely by the fact that this whole, while being one, accommodates in itself the accents of two voices. Furthermore, there is no understanding or indication of the fact that the narration is *dialogically addressed* to Golyadkin, in fact manifest in very clear external features: for example, in the fact that the first line Golyadkin speaks is quite often an obvious response to the sentence preceding it in the narration. There is no understanding, finally, of the fundamental connection between the narration and Golyadkin's interior dialogue: the narration, after all, makes no attempt to reproduce Golyadkin's speech in general, but directly continues only the speech of his second voice.

On the whole it is impossible, while remaining within the limits of linguistic stylistics, to tackle the proper artistic problem of style. No single formal linguistic definition of a word can cover all its artistic functions in the work. The authentic style-generating factors remain outside the field of vision available to linguistic stylistics.

The style of the narration in *The Double* contains yet another very fundamental feature, also correctly noted by Vinogradov but not explained by him. "In the narrational *skaz*," he says, "there is a predominance of motor images, and its basic stylistic device is the registering of movements independent of their repetitiveness."[12]

In fact the narration does, with the most tedious precision, register all the minutest movements of the hero, not sparing endless repetitions. The narrator is literally fettered to his hero; he cannot back off from him sufficiently to give a summarizing and integrated image of his deeds and actions. Such a generalizing image would already lie outside the hero's own field of vision, and on the whole such images presume some stable position on the outside. The narrator does not have access to such a position, he has none of the perspective necessary for an artistically finalizing summation of the hero's image or of his acts as a whole.[13]

This peculiar feature of narration in *The Double* is, with certain modifications, preserved throughout all of Dostoevsky's subsequent work. Narration in Dostoevsky is always narration without perspective. Employing a term from art criticism, we could say that Dostoevsky had no "distance perspective" on the hero and the event. The narrator finds himself in immediate proximity to the hero and to the ongoing event, and it is from this maximally close, aperspectival point of view that he structures their representation. It is true that Dostoevsky's chroniclers write their notes after events have already come to a close and as if from a certain temporal perspective. The narrator of *The Possessed*, for example, quite often says: "now, after everything is over," "now, when we remember all this," etc., but in fact he structures his narration without any significant perspective at all.

However, in contrast to narration in *The Double*, Dostoevsky's later narrations make no effort to register all the minutest movements of the hero, they are not at all long-winded, and are completely devoid of any repetitions. Narration in Dostoevsky's later period is brief, dry, and even somewhat abstract (especially in those places where information is provided about earlier events). But this brevity and dryness of narration, "sometimes bordering on Gil Blas," results not from perspective, but on the contrary, from a lack of perspective. Such deliberate lack of perspective is preordained by Dostoevsky's entire artistic plan, for, as we know, a firm and finalized image of the hero and the event is excluded in advance from that plan.

But let us return again to narration in *The Double*. In addition to its above-mentioned relationship to the hero's speech, we notice in it yet another parodic intention. In the narration of *The Double*, as in Devushkin's letters, there are clear elements of literary parody.

As early as *Poor Folk* the author was already using the voice of his hero to refract parodic intentions. This he achieved by various means: the parodies were either simply introduced into Devushkin's letters and motivated by the plot (the excerpts from Ratazyaev's compositions: parodies on the high society novel, on the historical novel of the time, and finally on the Naturalist School,) or parodic brush strokes were made part of the very structure of the story (for example, "Teresa and Faldoni"). And he introduced into the story, finally, a polemic with Gogol directly refracted through the hero's voice, a polemic parodically colored (Devushkin's reading of "The Overcoat" and his indignant reaction to it. In the subsequent episode, where the general helps the hero, there is a hidden juxtaposition to the episode with the "important personage" in Gogol's "Overcoat").[14]

In *The Double*, a parodic stylization of the "high style" from *Dead Souls* is refracted through the narrator's voice; in general, *The Double* is sprinkled with parodic and semiparodic allusions to various works of Gogol. It should be noted that these parodic tones in the narration are directly interwoven with a mimicry of Golyadkin.

To introduce a parodic and polemical element into the narration is to make it more multi-voiced, more interruption-prone, no longer gravitating toward itself or its referential object. But literary parody on the other hand, strengthens the element of literary conventionality in the narrator's discourse, depriving it even more of its independence and finalizing power in relation to the hero. In subsequent works as well, this element of literary conventionality, and the various forms used to expose it, always served to intensify greatly the direct and autonomous signifying power of the hero and the independence of the hero's position. In this sense literary conventionality, in Dostoevsky's overall plan, not only did not reduce the signifying- and idea-content of his novels, but on the contrary could only increase it (as was also the case, incidentally, with Jean Paul and even with Sterne). Dostoevsky's destruction in his works of the usual monologic orientation led him to exclude altogether from his construction certain elements of this monologic orientation, and conscientiously to neutralize others. One means of neutralization was literary conventionality, that is, introducing into the narration or into the principles of construction a conventionalized discourse, stylized or parodic.[15]

As concerns a dialogic addressing of the narration to the hero, this feature did of course remain in Dostoevsky's subsequent works, but it changed shape and became deeper and more complex. No longer is every word of the narrator addressed to the hero, but rather the narration as a whole, the very orientation of the narration. Within the narration, speech in most cases is dry and colorless: the best definition for it is "documentary style." But this documentation taken as a whole functions basically to expose and to provoke; it is addressed to the hero, speaking as it were to him and not about him, speaking however with its entire mass and not with its individual elements. To be sure, even in the latest works individual heroes are illuminated by a style that directly parodies and taunts them, a style that sounds like an exaggerated rejoinder from their own interior dialogue. Thus, for example, is the narrative of *The Possessed* constructed in relation to Stepan Trofimovich, but only in relation to him. Isolated notes of this taunting style are scattered throughout the other novels as well. They are present even in *The Brothers Karamazov.* But on the whole they are considerably weakened. A basic tendency of Dostoevsky in his later period is to make his style and tone dry and precise, to neutralize it. But wherever this predominating, documentarily dry and neutralized narration is replaced by sharply accented tones colored with value judgments, those tones are invariably addressed to the hero and are born out of a rejoinder in his potential interior dialogue with himself.

From *The Double* we move immediately to "Notes from Underground," passing over a whole series of intervening works.

"Notes from Underground" is a confessional *Ich Erzählung.* Originally the work was entitled "A Confession."[16] And it is in fact an authentic confession. Of course, "confession" is understood here not in the personal sense. The author's intention is refracted here, as in any *Ich Erzählung*; this is not a personal document but a work of art.

In the confession of the Underground Man what strikes us first of all is its extreme and acute dialogization: there is literally not a single monologically firm, undissociated word. From the very first sentence the hero's speech has already begun to cringe and break under the influence of the anticipated words of another, with whom the hero, from the very first step, enters into the most intense internal polemic.

"I am a sick man ... I am a spiteful man. I am an unpleasant man." Thus begins the confession. The ellipsis and the abrupt change of tone after it are significant. The hero began in a somewhat plaintive tone "I am a sick man," but was immediately enraged by that tone: it looked as if he were complaining and needed sympathy, as if he were seeking that sympathy in another person, as if he needed another person! And then there occurs an abrupt dialogic turnaround, one of those typical breaks in accent so characteristic of the whole style of the "Notes," as if the hero wants to say: you, perhaps, were led to believe from my first word that I am seeking your sympathy, so take this: I am a spiteful man. I am an unpleasant man!

Characteristic here is a gradual increase in negative tone (to spite the other) under the influence of the other's anticipated reaction. Such breaks in accent always lead to an accumulation of ever-intensifying abusive words or words that are, in any case, unflattering to the other person, as in this example:

To live longer than forty years is bad manners; it is vulgar, immoral. Who does live beyond forty? Answer that, sincerely and honestly. I will tell you who: fools and worthless people do. I tell all old men that to their face, all those respectable old men, all those silver-haired and reverend old men! I tell the whole world that to its face. I have a right to say so, for I'll go on living to sixty myself. I'll live till seventy! Till eighty! Wait, let me catch my breath. (ss IV, 135; "Notes," Part One, 1)

In the opening words of the confession, this internal polemic with the other is concealed. But the other's words are present invisibly, determining the style of speech from within. Midway into the first paragraph, however, the polemic has already broken out into the open: the anticipated response of the other takes root in the narration, although, to be sure, still in a weakened form. "No, I refuse to treat it out of spite. You probably will not understand that. Well, but *I* understand it."

At the end of the third paragraph there is already a very characteristic anticipation of the other's reaction:

Well, are you not imagining, gentlemen, that I am repenting for something now, that I am asking your forgiveness for something? I am sure you are imagining that. However, I assure you it does not matter to me if you are.

At the end of the next paragraph comes the above-quoted polemical attack against the "reverend old men." The following paragraph begins directly with the anticipation of a response to the preceding paragraph:

No doubt you think, gentlemen, that I want to amuse you. You are mistaken in that too. I am not at all such a merry person as you imagine, or as you may imagine; however, if irritated by all this babble (and I can feel that you are irritated) you decide to ask me just who I am – then my answer is, I am a certain low-ranked civil servant.

The next paragraph again ends with an anticipated response:

… I'll bet you think I am writing all this to show off, to be witty at the expense of men of action; and what is more, that out of ill-bred showing-off, I am clanking a sword, like my officer.

Later on such endings to paragraphs become more rare, but it remains true that all basic semantic sections of the work become sharper and more shrill near the end, in open anticipation of someone else's response.

Thus the entire style of the "Notes" is subject to the most powerful and all-determining influence of other people's words, which either act on speech covertly from within as in the beginning of the work, or which, as the anticipated response of another person, take root in the very fabric of speech, as in those above-quoted ending passages. The work does not contain a single word gravitating exclusively toward itself and its referential object; that is, there is not a single monologic word. We shall see that this intense relationship to another's consciousness in the Underground Man is complicated by an equally intense relationship to his own self. But first we shall make a brief structural analysis of this act of anticipating another's response.

Such anticipation is marked by one peculiar structural trait: it tends toward a vicious circle. The tendency of these anticipations can be reduced to a necessity to retain for oneself the final word. This final word must express the hero's full independence from the views and words of the other person, his complete indifference to the other's opinion and the other's evaluation. What he fears most of all is that people might think he is repenting before someone, that he is asking someone's forgiveness, that he is reconciling himself to someone else's judgment or evaluation, that his self-affirmation is somehow in need of affirmation and recognition by another. And it is in this direction that he anticipates the other's response. But precisely in this act of anticipating the other's response and in responding to it he again demonstrates to the other (and to himself) his own dependence on this other. He *fears* that the other might think he *fears* that other's opinion. But through this fear he immediately demonstrates his own dependence on the other's consciousness, his own inability to be at peace with his own definition of self. With his refutation, he confirms precisely what he wishes to refute, and he knows it. Hence the inescapable circle in which the hero's self-consciousness and discourse are trapped: "Well, are you not imagining, gentlemen, that I am repenting for something now? ... I am sure you are imagining that. However, I assure you it does not matter to me if you are...."

During that night out on the town, the Underground Man, insulted by his companions, wants to show them that he pays them no attention:

> I smiled contemptuously and walked up and down the other side of the room, opposite the sofa, along the wall, from the table to the stove and back again. I tried my very utmost to show them that I could do without them, and yet I purposely stomped with my boots, thumping with my heels. But it was all in vain. They paid no attention at all. (ss IV, 199; "Notes," Part Two, ch. IV)

Meanwhile our underground hero recognizes all this perfectly well himself, and understands perfectly well the impossibility of escaping from that circle in which his attitude toward the other moves. Thanks to this attitude toward the other's consciousness, a peculiar *perpetuum mobile* is achieved, made up of his internal polemic with another and with himself, an endless dialogue where one reply begets another, which begets a third, and so on to infinity, and all of this without any forward motion.

Here is an example of that inescapable *perpetuum mobile* of the dialogized self-consciousness:

> You will say that it is vulgar and base to drag all this [the hero's dreaming – M. B.] into public after all the tears and raptures I have myself admitted. But why is it base? Can you imagine that I am ashamed of it all, and that it was stupider than anything in your life, gentlemen? And I can assure you that some of these fancies were by no means badly composed. Not everything took place on the shores of Lake Como. And yet you are right – it really is vulgar and base. And what is most base of all is that I have now started to justify myself to you. And even more base than that is my making this remark now. But that's enough, or, after all, there will be no end to it; each step will be more base than the last. (ss IV, 181; "Notes," Part Two, ch. II)

Before us is an example of a vicious circle of dialogue which can neither be finished nor finalized. The formal significance of such inescapable dialogic oppositions in Dostoevsky's work is very great. But nowhere in his subsequent works does this opposition appear in such naked, abstractly precise, one could even say directly mathematical, form.[17]

As a result of the Underground Man's attitude toward the other's consciousness and its discourse – extraordinary dependence upon it and at the same time extreme hostility toward it and nonacceptance of its judgments – his narration takes on one highly essential artistic characteristic. This is a deliberate clumsiness of style, albeit subject to a certain artistic logic. His discourse does not flaunt itself and cannot flaunt itself, for there is no one before whom it can flaunt. It does not, after all, gravitate naively toward itself and its referential object. It is addressed to another person and to the speaker himself (in his internal dialogue with himself). And in both of these directions it wants least of all to flaunt itself and be "artistic" in the usual sense of the word. In its attitude toward the other person it strives to be deliberately inelegant, to "spite" him and his tastes in all respects. But this discourse takes the same position even in regard to the speaker himself, for one's attitude toward oneself is inseparably interwoven with one's attitude toward another. Thus discourse is pointedly cynical, calculatedly cynical, yet also anguished. It strives to play the holy fool, for holy-foolishness is indeed a sort of form, a sort of aestheticism – but, as it were, in reverse.

As a result, the prosaic triteness of the portrayal of his inner life is carried to extreme limits. In its material, in its theme, the first part of "Notes from Underground" is lyrical. From a formal point of view, this is the same prose lyric of spiritual and emotional quest, of spiritual unfulfillment that we find, for example, in Turgenev's "Phantoms" or "Enough,"* or in any lyrical page from a confessional *Ich Erzählung* or a page from *Werther*. But this is a peculiar sort of lyric, analogous to the lyrical expression of a toothache.

This expression of a toothache, oriented in an internally polemical way toward the listener and toward the sufferer, is spoken by the Underground Hero himself, and he speaks of it, of course, not by chance. He suggests eavesdropping on the groans of an "educated man of the nineteenth century" who suffers from a toothache, on the second or third day of his illness. He tries to expose the peculiar sensuality behind this whole cynical expression of pain, an expression intended for the "public":

> His moans become nasty, disgustingly spiteful, and go on for whole days and nights. And, after all, he himself knows that he does not benefit at all from his moans; he knows better than anyone that he is only lacerating and irritating himself and others in vain; he knows that even the audience for whom he is exerting himself and his whole family now listen to him with loathing, do not believe him for a second, and that deep down they understand that he could moan differently, more simply, without trills and flourishes, and that he is only indulging himself like that out of spite, out of malice. Well, sensuality exists precisely in all these consciousnesses and infamies. "It seems I am troubling you, I am lacerating your hearts. I am keeping everyone in the house awake. Well, stay awake then, you, too, feel every minute that I have a toothache. I am no longer the hero to you now that I tried to appear before, but simply a nasty person, a scoundrel. Well, let it be that way, then! I am very glad that you see through me. Is it nasty for you to hear my foul moans? Well, let it be

---

*"Phantoms," the least successful of Turgenev's several stories on the supernatural; "Enough" (1865) is one of Turgenev's periodic gestures of withdrawal, a sort of prose poem announcing to his public his disillusionment with life and art. Both pieces, and their author, are vigorously parodied by Dostoevsky in the character of Karmazinov in *The Possessed*.

nasty. Here I will let you have an even nastier flourish in a minute...."
(ss IV, 144; "Notes," Part One, ch. IV)

Of course any implied comparison here between the structure of the Underground Man's confession and the expression of a toothache is on the level of parodic exaggeration, and in this sense is cynical. But the orientation of this expression of a toothache, with all its "trills and flourishes," nevertheless does, in its relation to the listener and to the speaker himself, reflect very accurately the orientation of discourse in a confession – although, we repeat, it reflects not objectively but in a taunting, parodically exaggerating style, just as *The Double* reflected the internal speech of Golyadkin.

The destruction of one's own image in another's eyes, the sullying of that image in another's eyes as an ultimate desperate effort to free oneself from the power of the other's consciousness and to break through to one's self for the self alone – this, in fact, is the orientation of the Underground Man's entire confession. For this reason he makes his discourse about himself deliberately ugly. He wants to kill in himself any desire to appear the hero in others' eyes (and in his own): "I am no longer the hero to you now that I tried to appear before, but simply a nasty person, a scoundrel...."

To accomplish this he must banish from his discourse all epic and lyrical tones, all "heroizing" tones; he must make his discourse *cynically* objective. A soberly objective definition of himself, without exaggeration or mockery, is impossible for a hero from the underground, because such a soberly prosaic definition would presuppose a word without a sideward glance, a word without a loophole; neither the one nor the other exist on his verbal palette. True, he is continually trying to break through to such a word, to break through to spiritual sobriety, but for him the path lies through cynicism and holy-foolishness. He has neither freed himself from the power of the other's consciousness nor admitted its power over him,[18] he is for now merely struggling with it, polemicizing with it maliciously, not able to accept it but also not able to reject it. In this striving to trample down his own image and his own discourse as they exist in and for the other person, one can hear not only the desire for sober self-definition, but also a desire to annoy the other person; and this forces him to overdo his sobriety, mockingly exaggerating it to the point of cynicism and holy-foolishness: "Is it nasty for you to hear my foul moans? Well, let it be nasty. Here I will let you have an even nastier flourish in a minute...."

But the underground hero's word about himself is not only a word with a sideward glance; it is also, as we have said, a word with a loophole. The influence of the loophole on the style of his confession is so great that his style cannot be understood without a consideration of its formal activity. The word with a loophole has enormous significance in Dostoevsky's works in general, especially in the later works. And here we pass on to another aspect of the structure of "Notes from Underground": the hero's attitude toward his own self, which throughout the course of the entire work is interwoven and combined with his dialogue with another.

What, then, is this loophole of consciousness and of the word?

A loophole is the retention for oneself of the possibility for altering the ultimate, final meaning of one's own words. If a word retains such a loophole this must inevitably be reflected in its structure. This potential other meaning, that is, the loophole left open, accompanies the word like a shadow. Judged by its meaning alone, the word with a loophole should be an ultimate word and does present itself as such, but in fact it is only the penultimate word and places after itself only a conditional, not a final, period.

For example, the confessional self-definition with a loophole (the most widespread form in Dostoevsky) is, judging by its meaning, an ultimate word about oneself, a final definition of oneself, but in fact it is forever taking into account internally the responsive, contrary evaluation of oneself made by another. The hero who repents and condemns himself actually wants only to provoke praise and acceptance by another. Condemning himself, he wants and demands that the other person dispute this self-definition, and he leaves himself a loophole in case the other person should suddenly in fact agree with him, with his self-condemnation, and not make use of his privilege as the other.

Here is how the hero from the underground tells of his "literary" dreams:

> I, for instance, was triumphant over everyone; everyone, of course, lay in the dust and was *forced* to recognize my superiority *spontaneously*, and I forgave them all. I, a famous poet, and a courtier, fell in love; I inherited countless millions and immediately devoted them to humanity, and *at the same time I confessed before all the people my shameful deeds, which, of course, were not merely shameful, but contained an enormous amount of "the sublime and the beautiful," something in the Manfred style. Everyone would weep and kiss me (what idiots they would be if they did not)*, while I would go barefoot and hungry preaching new ideas and fighting a victorious Austerlitz against the reactionaries. (ss IV, 181; "Notes," Part Two, ch. II)

[190]

Here he ironically relates dreams of heroic deeds with a loophole, dreams of confession with a loophole. He casts a parodic light on these dreams. But his very next words betray the fact that his repentant confession of his dreams has its own loophole, too, and that he himself is prepared to find in these dreams and in his very confessing of them something, if not in the Manfred style, then at least in the realm of "the sublime and the beautiful," if anyone should happen to agree with him that the dreams are indeed base and vulgar: "You will say that it is vulgar and base to drag all this into public after all the tears and raptures I have myself admitted. But why is it base? Can you imagine that I am ashamed of it all, and that it was stupider that anything in your life, gentlemen? And I can assure you that some of these fancies were by no means badly composed...."

And this passage, already cited by us above, is caught up in the vicious circle of self-consciousness with a sideward glance.

The loophole creates a special type of fictive ultimate word about oneself with an unclosed tone to it, obtrusively peering into the other's eyes and demanding from the other a sincere refutation. We shall see that the word with a loophole achieves especially sharp expression in Ippolit's confession, but it is to one degree or another inherent in all the confessional self-utterances of Dostoevsky's heroes.[19] The loophole makes all the heroes' self-definitions unstable, the word in them has no hard and fast meaning, and at any moment, like a chameleon, it is ready to change its tone and its ultimate meaning.

The loophole makes the hero ambiguous and elusive even for himself. In order to break through to his self the hero must travel a very long road. The loophole profoundly distorts his attitude toward himself. The hero does not know whose opinion, whose statement is ultimately the final judgement on him: is it his own repentant and censuring judgment, or on the contrary is it another person's opinion that he desires and has compelled into being, an opinion that accepts and vindicates him? The image of Nastasya Filippovna, for example, is built almost entirely on this motif alone. Considering herself guilty, a fallen woman, she simultaneously assumes that the other person, precisely as the other, is obliged to vindicate her and cannot consider her guilty. She genuinely quarrels with Myshkin, who vindicates her in everything, but she equally genuinely despises and rejects all those who agree with her self-condemnation and consider her a fallen woman. Ultimately Nastasya Filippovna does not know even her own final word on herself; does she really consider herself a fallen woman, or does she vindicate herself? Self-condemnation and self-vindication, divided between two voices – I condemn myself, another vindicates me – but anticipated by a single voice, create in that voice interruptions and an internal duality. An anticipated and obligatory vindication by the other merges with self-condemnation, and both tones begin to sound simultaneously in that voice, resulting in abrupt interruptions and sudden transitions. Such is the voice of Nastasya Filippovna, such is the style of her discourse. Her entire inner life (and, as we shall see, her outward life as well) is reduced to a search for herself and for her own undivided voice beneath the two voices that have made their home in her.

The Underground Man conducts the same sort of inescapable dialogue with himself that he conducts with the other person. He cannot merge completely with himself in a unified monologic voice simply by leaving the other's voice entirely outside himself (whatever that voice might be, without a loophole), for, as is the case with Golyadkin, his voice must also perform the function of surrogate for the other person. He cannot reach an agreement with himself, but neither can he stop talking with himself. The style of his discourse about himself is organically alien to the period, alien to finalization, both in its separate aspects and as a whole. This is the style of internally endless speech which can be mechanically cut off but cannot be organically completed.

But precisely for that reason is Dostoevsky able to conclude his work in a way so organic and appropriate for the hero; he concludes it on precisely that which would foreground the tendency toward eternal endlessness embedded in his hero's notes.

> But enough; I don't want to write more from "underground" …
>
> The "notes" of this paradoxalist do not end here, however. He could not resist and continued them. But it also seems to me that we may stop here. (ss IV, 224; "Notes," Part Two, ch.X)

In conclusion we will comment upon two additional characteristics of the Underground Man. Not only his discourse but his face too has its sideward glance, its loophole, and all the phenomena resulting from these. It is as if interference, voices interrupting one another, penetrate his entire body, depriving him of self-sufficiency and unambiguousness. The Underground Man hates his own face, because in it he senses the power of another person over him, the power of that other's evaluations and opinions. He himself looks on his own face with another's eyes, with the eyes of the other. And this alien glance interruptedly merges with his own glance and creates in him a peculiar hatred toward his own face:

> For instance, I hated my face; I thought it disgusting, and even suspected that there was something base in its expression and therefore every time I turned up at the office I painfully tried to behave as independently as possible so that I might not be suspected of being base, and to give my face as noble an expression as possible. "Let my face even be ugly," I thought, "but let it be noble, expressive, and above all, extremely intelligent." But I was absolutely and painfully certain that my face could never express those perfections; but what was worst of all, I thought it positively stupid-looking. And I would have been quite satisfied if I could have looked intelligent. In fact, I would even have put up with looking base if, at the same time, my face could have been thought terribly intelligent (ss IV, 168; "Notes," Part Two, ch.I)

Just as he deliberately makes his discourse about himself unattractive, so is he made happy by the unattractiveness of his face:

> I happened to look at myself in the mirror. My harassed face struck me as extremely revolting, pale, spiteful, nasty, with dishevelled hair. "No matter, I am glad of it," I thought; "I am glad that I shall seem revolting to her; I like that." (ss IV, 206; "Notes," Part Two, ch.V)

This polemic with the other on the subject of himself is complicated in "Notes from Underground" by his polemic with the other on the subject of the world and society. The underground hero, in contrast to Devushkin and Golyadkin, is an ideologist.

In his ideological discourse we can easily uncover the same phenomena that are present in his discourse about himself. His discourse about the world is both overtly and covertly polemical; it polemicizes not only with other people, with other ideologies, but also with the very subject of its thinking – with the world and its order. And in this discourse on the world there are two voices, as it were, sounding for him, among which he cannot find himself and his own world, because even the world he defines with a loophole. Just as his body had become an "interrupted" thing in his own eyes, so is the world, nature, society perceived by him as "interrupted." In each of his thoughts about them there is a battle of choices, evaluations, points of view. In everything he senses above all *someone else's will* predetermining him. It is within the framework of this alien will that he perceives the world order, nature with its mechanical necessity, the social order. His own thought is developed and structured as *the thought of someone personally insulted by the world order*, personally humiliated by its blind necessity. This imparts a profoundly intimate and passionate character to his ideological discourse, and permits it to become tightly interwoven with his discourse about himself. It seems (and such indeed was Dostoevsky's intent) that we are dealing here with a single discourse, and only by arriving at himself will the hero arrive at his world. Discourse about the world, just like discourse about oneself, is profoundly dialogic: the hero casts an energetic reproach at the world order, even at the mechanical necessity of nature, as if he were talking not about the world but with the world. Of these peculiarities of ideological discourse we will speak below, when we take up the general issue of hero-ideologists and Ivan Karamazov in particular; in him these features are especially acute and clear-cut.

The discourse of the Underground Man is entirely a discourse-address. To speak, for him, means to address someone; to speak about himself means to address his own self with his own discourse; to speak about another person means to address that other person; to speak about the world means to address the world. But while speaking with himself, with another, with the world, he simultaneously addresses a third party as well: he squints his eyes to the side, toward the listener, the witness, the judge.[20] This simultaneous triple-directedness of his discourse and the fact that he does not acknowledge any object without addressing it is also responsible for the extraordinarily vivid, restless, agitated, and one might say, obtrusive nature of this discourse. It cannot be seen as a lyrical or epic discourse, calmly gravitating toward itself and its referential object; no, first and foremost one reacts to it, responds to it, is drawn into its game; it is capable of agitating and irritating, almost like the personal address of a living person. It destroys footlights, but not because of its concern for topical issues or for reasons that have any direct philosophical significance, but precisely because of that formal structure analyzed by us above.

The element of *address* is essential to every discourse in Dostoevsky, narrative discourse as well as the discourse of the hero. In Dostoevsky's world generally there is nothing merely thing-like, no mere matter, no object – there are only subjects. Therefore there is no word-judgment, no word about an object, no secondhand referential word – there is only the word as address, the word dialogically contacting another word, a word about a word addressed to a word.

8

M. M. Bakhtin
'Heteroglossia in the novel'

From 'Discourse in the novel', in *The Dialogic Imagination: Four Essays*,
edited by Michael Holquist; translated by Caryl Emerson and
Michael Holquist (University of Texas Press, 1981, pp. 301–31).

'Discourse in the novel', written in the mid-1930s, is one of Bakhtin's richest and
fullest statements of the interrelationship between linguistic diversity and the
aesthetics of the novel. It contains a luminous account of the notion of
'heteroglossia' (see chapter 1 of Part I), as well as a fine positive statement of a
socially informed pragmatics – that is, of the way that any utterance, in
negotiating its relation both to its object and the interlocutor, encounters a
myriad socially and historically formed other words which it has to measure
itself against. In addition, after the section that I have extracted, the essay goes
on to provide another of Bakhtin's histories of the novel, suggestions about the
way that the externally authoritative word becomes the internally persuasive
word, and a notion of 're-accentuation' as a way of describing the historical life
of novels. These ideas are discussed in chapters 2 and 4 of Part I.

The essay then is a dense and ambitious one; in fact it is really a misnomer to
call it an essay, since it is the length of a short book and develops a range of
connected ideas in a way characteristic of a book rather than an essay. The section
that I have included bears the subtitle 'Heteroglossia in the novel'; I have chosen
it because it is especially rich in analyses of novelistic discourse with which an
English-speaking reader is likely to be familiar. It is preceded by two sections
which address the inadequacy of traditional stylistics for the novel, and which
seek to draw a fundamental distinction between the way the novel draws upon
linguistic diversity, and the way that poetry's task is essentially to ignore or
overcome it. These two questions are intimately related in Bakhtin's account
because the inadequacy of traditional stylistics is precisely due to its basis in
poetry; poetry in this account has a radically different relation to the unifying and
diversifying forces of language, as compared to the novel. Therefore any attempt
to found a stylistics of the novel upon poetry is bound to be misguided, for what
the novel essentially does is to exploit those diversifying forces. The novel
reproduces within itself the heteroglossia on which it draws and in which it lives.

This may be compared with the kind of analysis which Bakhtin makes of

Dostoevsky's short novels in the previous extract. The analysis here is no less 'dialogic'; that is, it insists, no less than in the analysis of Dostoevsky, that novelistic prose has built into it more than one consciousness, so that the forms of dialogue are internal to it – it is 'internally dialogized'. But by comparison with *Problems of Dostoevsky's Poetics*, this dialogism has become more fully social and historical; what are now engaged in the novel are diverse forms of life that are realized in competing and conflicting words. The novel is the form which draws upon those historical energies; to that extent the analysis here is epochal. But it is also and more narrowly historical, for in the actual analyses – of *Little Dorrit* for example – Bakhtin locates the novel in the conflicting to and fro of the diverse language forms of mid-nineteenth century England. And in this respect also the analysis is a profoundly intertextual one, since it sees the very texture of novels as transforming, parodying, reproducing and undermining other socially located languages within a heteroglossia.

Heteroglossia in the novel

The compositional forms for appropriating and organizing heteroglossia in the novel, worked out during the long course of the genre's historical development, are extremely heterogeneous in their variety of generic types. Each such compositional form is connected with particular stylistic possibilities, and demands particular forms for the artistic treatment of the heteroglot "languages" introduced into it. We will pause here only on the most basic forms that are typical for the majority of novel types.

The so-called comic novel makes available a form for appropriating and organizing heteroglossia that is both externally very vivid and at the same time historically profound; its classic representatives in England were Fielding, Smollett, Sterne, Dickens, Thackeray and others, and in Germany Hippel and Jean Paul.

In the English comic novel we find a comic-parodic re-processing of almost all the levels of literary language, both conversational and written, that were current at the time. Almost every novel we mentioned above as being a classic representative of this generic type is an encyclopedia of all strata and forms of literary language: depending on the subject being represented, the storyline parodically reproduces first the forms of parliamentary eloquence, then the eloquence of the court, or particular forms of parliamentary protocol, or court protocol, or forms used by reporters in newspaper articles, or the dry business language of the City, or the dealings of speculators, or the pedantic speech of scholars, or the high epic style, or Biblical style, or the style of the hypocritical moral sermon or finally the way one or another concrete and socially determined personality, the subject of the story, happens to speak.

This usually parodic stylization of generic, professional and other strata of language is sometimes interrupted by the direct authorial word (usually as an expression of pathos, of sentimental or idyllic sensibility), which directly embodies (without any refracting) semantic and axiological intentions of the author. But the primary source of language usage in the comic novel is a highly specific treatment of "common language." This "common language" – usually the average norm of spoken and written language for a given social group – is taken by the author precisely as the *common view,* as the verbal approach to people and things normal for a given sphere of society, as the *going point of view* and the going *value.* To one degree or another, the author distances himself from this common language, he steps back and objectifies it, forcing his own intentions to refract and diffuse themselves through the medium of this common view that has become embodied in language (a view that is always superficial and frequently hypocritical).

The relationship of the author to a language conceived as the common view is not static – it is always found in a state of movement and oscillation that is more or less alive (this sometimes is a rhythmic oscillation): the author exaggerates, now strongly, now weakly, one or another aspect of the "common language," sometimes abruptly exposing its inadequacy to its object and sometimes, on the contrary, becoming one with it, maintaining an almost imperceptible distance, sometimes even directly forcing it to reverberate with his own "truth," which occurs when the author completely merges his own voice with the common view. As a consequence of such a merger, the aspects of common language, which in the given situation had been parodically exaggerated or had been treated as mere things, undergo change. The comic style demands of the author a lively to-and-fro movement in his relation to language, it demands a continual shifting of the distance between author and language, so that first some, then other aspects of language are thrown into relief. If such were not the case, the style would be monotonous or would require a greater individualization of the narrator – would, in any case, require a quite different means for introducing and organizing heteroglossia.

Against this same backdrop of the "common language," of the impersonal, going opinion, one can also isolate in the comic novel those parodic stylizations of generic, professional and other languages we have mentioned, as well as compact masses of direct authorial discourse – pathos-filled, moral-didactic, sentimental-elegiac or idyllic. In the comic novel the direct authorial word is thus realized in direct, unqualified stylizations of poetic genres (idyllic, elegiac, etc.) or stylizations of rhetorical genres (the pathetic, the moral-didactic). Shifts from common language to parodying of generic and other languages and shifts to the direct authorial word may be gradual, or may be on the contrary quite abrupt. Thus does the system of language work in the comic novel.

We will pause for analysis on several examples from Dickens, from his novel *Little Dorrit*.

(1) The conference was held at four or five o'clock in the afternoon, when all the region of Harley Street, Cavendish Square, was resonant of carriage wheels and double-knocks. It had reached this point when Mr. Merdle came home *from his daily occupation of causing the British name to be more and more respected in all parts of the civilized globe capable of appreciation of world-wide commercial enterprise and gigantic combinations of skill and capital.* For, though nobody knew with the least precision what Mr. Merdle's business was, except that it was to coin money, these were the terms in which everybody defined it on all ceremonious occasions, and which it was the last new polite reading of the parable of the camel and the needle's eye to accept without inquiry. (book I, ch. 33)

The italicized portion represents a parodic stylization of the language of ceremonial speeches (in parliaments and at banquets). The shift into this style is prepared for by the sentence's construction, which from the very beginning is kept within bounds by a somewhat ceremonious epic tone. Further on – and already in the language of the author (and consequently in a different style) – the parodic meaning of the ceremoniousness of Merdle's labours becomes apparent: such a characterization turns out to be "another's speech," to be taken only in quotation marks ("these were the terms in which everybody defined it on all ceremonious occasions").

Thus the speech of another is introduced into the author's discourse (the story) in *concealed form*, that is, without any of the *formal* markers usually accompanying such speech, whether direct or indirect. But this is not just another's speech in the same "language" – it is another's utterance in a language that is itself "other" to the author as well, in the archaicized language of oratorical genres associated with hypocritical official celebrations.

(2) In a day or two it was announced to all the town, that Edmund Sparkler, Esquire, son-in-law of the eminent Mr. Merdle of worldwide renown, was

made one of the Lords of the Circumlocution Office; and proclamation was issued, to all true believers, that this admirable *appointment was to be hailed as a graceful and gracious mark of homage, rendered by the graceful and gracious Decimus, to that commercial interest which must ever in a great commercial country – and all the rest of it, with blast of trumpet.* So, bolstered by this mark of Government homage, the *wonderful* Bank and all the other *wonderful* undertakings went on and went up; and gapers came to Harley Street, Cavendish Square, only to look at the house where the golden wonder lived. (book 2, ch. 12)

Here, in the italicized portion, another's speech in another's (official-ceremonial) language is openly introduced as indirect discourse. But it is surrounded by the hidden, diffused speech of another (in the same official-ceremonial language) that clears the way for the introduction of a form more easily perceived *as* another's speech and that can reverberate more fully as such. The clearing of the way comes with the word "Esquire," characteristic of official speech, added to Sparkler's name; the final confirmation that this is another's speech comes with the epithet "wonderful." This epithet does not of course belong to the author but to that same "general opinion" that had created the commotion around Merdle's inflated enterprises.

(3) It was a dinner to provoke an appetite, though he had not had one. The rarest dishes, sumptuously cooked and sumptuously served; the choicest fruits, the most exquisite wines; marvels of workmanship in gold and silver, china and glass; innumerable things delicious to the senses of taste, smell, and sight, were insinuated into its composition. *O, what a wonderful man this Merdle, what a great man, what a master man, how blessedly and enviably endowed* – in one word, what a rich man! (book 2, ch. 12)

The beginning is a parodic stylization of high epic style. What follows is an enthusiastic glorification of Merdle, a chorus of his admirers in the form of the concealed speech of another (the italicized portion). The whole point here is to expose the real basis for such glorification, which is to unmask the chorus' hypocrisy: "wonderful," "great," "master," "endowed" can all be replaced by the single word "rich." This act of authorial unmasking, which is openly accomplished within the boundaries of a single simple sentence, merges with the unmasking of another's speech. The ceremonial emphasis on glorification is complicated by a second emphasis that is indignant, ironic, and this is the one that ultimately predominates in the final unmasking words of the sentence.

We have before us a typical double-accented, double-styled *hybrid construction.*

What we are calling a hybrid construction is an utterance that belongs, by its grammatical (syntactic) and compositional markers, to a single speaker, but that actually contains mixed within it two utterances, two speech manners, two styles, two "languages," two semantic and axiological belief systems. We repeat, there is no formal – compositional and syntactic – boundary between these utterances, styles, languages, belief systems; the division of voices and languages takes place within the limits of a single syntactic whole, often within the limits of a simple sentence. It frequently happens that even one and the same word will belong simultaneously to two languages, two belief systems that intersect in a hybrid construction – and, consequently, the word has two contradictory meanings, two accents (examples below). As we shall see, hybrid constructions are of enormous significance in novel style.[1]

(4) But Mr. Tite Barnacle was a buttoned-up man, and *consequently* a weighty one. (book 2, ch. 12)

The above sentence is an example of *pseudo-objective motivation*, one of the forms for concealing another's speech – in this example, the speech of "current opinion." If judged by the formal markers above, the logic motivating the sentence seems to belong to the author, i.e., he is formally at one with it; but in actual fact, the motivation lies within the subjective belief system of his characters, or of general opinion.

Pseudo-objective motivation is generally characteristic of novel style,[2] since it is one of the manifold forms for concealing another's speech in hybrid constructions. Subordinate conjunctions and link words ("thus," "because," "for the reason that," "in spite of" and so forth), as well as words used to maintain a logical sequence ("therefore," "consequently," etc.) lose their direct authorial intention, take on the flavour of someone else's language, become refracted or even completely reified.

Such motivation is especially characteristic of comic style, in which someone else's speech is dominant (the speech of concrete persons, or, more often, a collective voice).[3]

(5) As a vast fire will fill the air to a great distance with its roar, so the sacred flame which the mighty Barnacles had fanned caused the air to resound more and more with the name of Merdle. It was deposited on every lip, and carried into every ear. There never was, there never had been, there never again should be, such a man as Mr. Merdle. Nobody, as aforesaid, knew what he had done; but *everybody knew him to be the greatest that had appeared*. (book 2, ch. 13)

Here we have an epic, "Homeric" introduction (parodic, of course) into whose frame the crowd's glorification of Merdle has been inserted (concealed speech of another in another's language). We then get direct authorial discourse; however, the author gives an objective tone to this "aside" by suggesting that "everybody knew" (the italicized portion). It is as if even the author himself did not doubt the fact.

(6) That illustrious man and great national ornament, Mr. Merdle, continued his shining course. It began to be widely understood that one who had done society the admirable service *of making so much money out of it*, could not be suffered to remain a commoner. A baronetcy was spoken of with confidence; a peerage was frequently mentioned (book 2, ch. 24)

We have here the same fictive solidarity with the hypocritically ceremonial general opinion of Merdle. All the epithets referring to Merdle in the first sentences derive from general opinion, that is, they are the concealed speech of another. The second sentence – "it began to be widely understood," etc. – is kept within the bounds of an emphatically objective style, representing not subjective opinion but the admission of an objective and completely indisputable fact. The epithet "who had done society the admirable service" is completely at the level of common opinion, repeating its official glorification, but the subordinate clause attached to that glorification ("of making so much money out of it") are the words of the author himself (as if put in parentheses in the quotation). The main sentence then picks up again at the level of common opinion. We have here a typical hybrid construction, where the subordinate clause is in direct authorial speech and the main clause in someone else's speech. The main and subordinate clauses are constructed in different semantic and axiological conceptual systems.

The whole of this portion of the novel's action, which centers around Merdle and the persons associated with him, is depicted in the language (or more accurately, the languages) of hypocritically ceremonial common opinion about Merdle, and at the same time there is a parodic stylization of that everyday language of banal society gossip, or of the ceremonial language of official pronouncements and banquet speeches, or the high epic style or Biblical style. This atmosphere around Merdle, the common opinion about him and his enterprises, infects the positive heroes of the novel as well, in particular the sober Pancks, and forces him to invest his entire estate – his own, and Little Dorrit's – in Merdle's hollow enterprises.

(7) Physician had engaged to break the intelligence in Harley Street. Bar could not at once return to his inveiglements of the most enlightened and remarkable jury he had ever seen in that box, with whom, he could tell his learned friend, no shallow sophistry would go down, and no unhappily abused professional tact and skill prevail (this was the way he meant to begin with them); so he said he would go too, and would loiter to and fro near the house while his friend was inside. (book 2, ch. 25, mistakenly given as ch. 15 in Russian text, tr.)

Here we have a clear example of hybrid construction where within the frame of authorial speech (informative speech) – the beginning of a speech prepared by the lawyer has been inserted, "The Bar could not at once return to his inveiglements ... of the jury ... so he said he would go too.... " etc. – while this speech is simultaneously a fully developed epithet attached to the subject of the author's speech, that is, "jury." The word "jury" enters into the context of informative authorial speech (in the capacity of a necessary object to the word "inveiglements") as well as into the context of the parodic-stylized speech of the lawyer. The author's word "inveiglement" itself emphasizes the parodic nature of the re-processing of the lawyer's speech, the hypocritical meaning of which consists precisely in the fact that it would be impossible to inveigle such a remarkable jury.

(8) It followed that Mrs. Merdle, as a woman of fashion and good breeding *who had been sacrificed to wiles of a vulgar barbarian* (for Mr. Merdle was found out from the crown of his head to the sole of his foot, the moment he was found out in his pocket), must be actively championed by her order for her order's sake. (book 2, ch. 33)

This is an analogous hybrid construction, in which the definition provided by the general opinion of society – "a sacrifice to the wiles of a vulgar barbarian" – merges with authorial speech, exposing the hypocrisy and greed of common opinion.

So it is throughout Dickens' whole novel. His entire text is, in fact, everywhere dotted with quotation marks that serve to separate out little islands of scattered direct speech and purely authorial speech, washed by heteroglot waves from all sides. But it would have been impossible actually to insert such marks, since, as we have seen, one and the same word often figures both as the speech of the author and as the speech of another – and at the same time.

Another's speech – whether as storytelling, as mimicking, as the display of a thing in light of a particular point of view, as a speech that is in most cases impersonal ("common opinion," professional and generic languages) – is at none of these points clearly separated from authorial speech: the boundaries are deliberately flexible and ambiguous, often passing through a single syntactic whole, often through a simple sentence, and sometimes even dividing up the main parts of a sentence. This varied *play with the boundaries of speech types*, languages and belief systems is one of the most fundamental aspects of comic style.

Comic style (of the English sort) is based, therefore, on the stratification of common language and on the possibilities available for isolating from these strata, to one degree or another, one's own intentions, without ever completely merging with them. *It is precisely the diversity of speech, and not the unity of a normative shared language, that is the ground of style.* It is true that such speech diversity does not exceed the boundaries of literary language conceived as a linguistic whole (that is, language defined by abstract linguistic markers), does not pass into an authentic heteroglossia and is based on an abstract notion of language as unitary (that is, it does not require knowledge of various dialects or languages). However a mere concern for language is but the abstract side of the concrete and active (i.e., dialogically engaged) understanding of the living heteroglossia that has been introduced into the novel and artistically organized within it.

In Dickens' predecessors, Fielding, Smollett and Sterne, the men who founded the English comic novel, we find the same parodic stylization of various levels and genres of literary language, but the distance between these levels and genres is greater than it is in Dickens and the exaggeration is stronger (especially in Sterne). The parodic and objectivized incorporation into their work of various types of literary language (especially in Sterne) penetrates the deepest levels of literary and ideological thought itself, resulting in a parody of the logical and expressive structure of any ideological discourse as such (scholarly, moral and rhetorical, poetic) that is almost as radical as the parody we find in Rabelais.

Literary parody understood in the narrow sense plays a fundamental role in the way language is structured in Fielding, Smollett and Sterne (the Richardsonian novel is parodied by the first two, and almost all contemporary novel-types are parodied by Sterne). Literary parody serves to distance the author still further from language, to complicate still further his relationship to the literary language of his time, especially in the novel's own territory. The novelistic discourse dominating a given epoch is itself turned into an object and itself becomes a means for refracting new authorial intentions.

Literary parody of dominant novel-types plays a large role in the history of the European novel. One could even say that the most important novelistic models and novel-types arose precisely during this parodic destruction of preceding novelistic worlds. This is true of the work of Cervantes, Mendoza, Grimmelshausen, Rabelais, Lesage and many others.

In Rabelais, whose influence on all novelistic prose (and in particular the comic novel) was very great, a parodic attitude toward almost all forms of ideological discourse – philosophical, moral, scholarly, rhetorical, poetic and in particular the pathos-charged forms of discourse (in Rabelais, pathos almost always is equivalent to lie) – was intensified to the point where it became a parody of the very act of conceptualizing anything in language. We might add that Rabelais taunts the deceptive human word by a parodic destruction of syntactic structures, thereby reducing to absurdity some of the logical and expressively accented aspects of words (for example, predication, explanations and so forth). Turning away from language (by means of language, of course), discrediting any direct or unmediated intentionality and expressive excess (any "weighty" seriousness) that might adhere in ideological discourse, presuming that all language is conventional and false, maliciously inadequate to reality – all this achieves in Rabelais almost the maximum purity possible in prose. But the truth that might oppose such falsity receives almost no direct intentional and verbal expression in Rabelais, it does not receive its *own* word – it reverberates only in the parodic and unmasking accents in which the lie is present. Truth is restored by reducing the lie to an absurdity, but truth itself does not seek words; she is afraid to entangle herself in the word, to soil herself in verbal pathos.

Rabelais' "philosophy of the word" – a philosophy expressed not as much in direct utterances as in stylistic practice – has had enormous influence on all consequent novel prose and in particular of the great representative forms of the comic novel; with that in mind we bring forward the purely Rabelaisian formulation of Sterne's Yorick, which might serve as an epigraph to the history of the most important stylistic lines of development in the European novel:

> For aught I know there might be some mixture of unlucky wit at the bottom of such Fracas: – For, to speak the truth, Yorick had an invincible

dislike and opposition in his nature to gravity; – not to gravity as such; – for where gravity was wanted, he would be the most grave or serious of mortal men for days and weeks together; – but he was an enemy to the affectation of it, and declared open war against it only as it appeared a cloak for ignorance, or for folly; and then, whenever it fell his way, however sheltered and protected, he seldom gave it much quarter.

Sometimes, in his wild way of talking, he would say, That gravity was an errant scoundrel; and he would add, – of the most dangerous kind too, – because a sly one; and that, he verily believed, more honest, well-meaning people were bubbled out of their goods and money by it in one twelve-month, than by pocket-picking and shop-lifting in seven. In the naked temper which a merry heart discovered, he would say, There was no danger, – but to itself: – whereas the very essence of gravity was design, and consequently deceit; – 'twas a taught trick to gain credit of the world for more sense and knowledge than a man was worth; and that, with all its pretensions, – it was no better, but often worse, than what a French wit had long ago defined it, – viz. A mysterious carriage of the body to cover the defects of the mind; – which definition of gravity, Yorick, with great imprudence, would say, deserved to be wrote in letters of gold. (Bakhtin does not locate citation; it is from *Tristram Shandy*, vol. I, ch. II, tr.)

Close to Rabelais, but in certain respects even exceeding him in the decisive influence he had on all of novelistic prose, is Cervantes. The English comic novel is permeated through and through with the spirit of Cervantes. It is no accident that this same Yorick, on his deathbed, quotes the words of Sancho Panza.

While the attitude toward language and toward its stratification (generic, professional and otherwise) among the German comic writers, in Hippel and especially in Jean Paul, is basically of the Sternean type, it is raised – as it is in Sterne himself – to the level of a purely philosophical problem, the very possibility of literary and ideological speech as such. The philosophical and ideological element in an author's attitude toward his own language forces into the background the play between intention and the concrete, primarily generic and ideological levels of literary language (cf. the reflection of just this in the aesthetic theories of Jean Paul).[4]

Thus the stratification of literary language, its speech diversity, is an indispensable prerequisite for comic style, whose elements are projected onto different linguistic planes while at the same time the intention of the author, refracted as it passes through these planes, does not wholly give itself up to any of them. It is as if the author has no language of his own, but does possess his own style, his own organic and unitary law of governing the way he plays with languages and the way his own real semantic and expressive intentions are refracted within them. Of course this play with languages (and frequently the complete absence of a direct discourse of his own) in no sense degrades the general, deep-seated intentionality, the overarching ideological conceptualization of the work as a whole.

In the comic novel, the incorporation of heteroglossia and its stylistic utilization is characterized by the two distinctive features:

(1) Incorporated into the novel are a multiplicity of "language" and verbal-ideological belief systems – generic, professional, class-and-interest-group (the language of the nobleman, the farmer, the merchant, the peasant); tendentious, everyday (the languages of rumour, of society chatter, servants' language) and so forth, but these languages are, it is true, kept primarily within the limits of the literary written and conversational language; at the same time these languages are not, in most cases, consolidated into fixed persons (heroes, storytellers) but rather are incorporated in an impersonal form "from the author," alternating (while ignoring precise formal boundaries) with direct authorial discourse.

(2) The incorporated languages and socio-ideological belief systems, while of course utilized to refract the author's intentions, are unmasked and destroyed as something false, hypocritical, greedy, limited, narrowly rationalistic, inadequate to reality. In most cases these languages – already fully formed, officially recognized, reigning languages that are authoritative and reactionary – are (in real life) doomed to death and displacement. Therefore what predominates in the novel are various forms and degrees of *parodic stylization* of incorporated languages, a stylization that, in the most radical, most Rabelaisian[5] representatives of this novel-type (Sterne and Jean Paul), verges on a rejection of any straightforward and unmediated seriousness (true seriousness is the destruction of all false seriousness, not only in its pathos-charged expression but in its sentimental one as well);[6] that is, it limits itself to a principled criticism of the word as such.

There is a fundamental difference between this comic form for incorporating and organizing heteroglossia in the novel and other forms that are defined by their use of a personified and concretely posited author (written speech) or teller (oral speech).

Play with a posited author is also characteristic of the comic novel (Sterne, Hippel, Jean Paul), a heritage from *Don Quixote*. But in these examples such play is purely a compositional device, which strengthens the general trend toward relativity, objectification and the parodying of literary forms and genres.

The posited author and teller assume a completely difference signific-ance where they are incorporated as carriers of a particular verbal-ideological linguistic belief system, with a particular point of view on the world and its events, with particular value judgments and intonations – "particular" both as regards the author, his real direct discourse, and also as regards "normal" literary narrative and language.

This particularity, this distancing of the posited author or teller from the real author and from conventional literary expectations, may occur in differing degrees and may vary in its nature. But in every case a particular belief system belonging to someone else, a particular point of view on the world belonging to someone else, is used by the author because it is highly productive, that is, it is able on the one hand to show the object of representation in a new light (to reveal new sides or dimensions in it) and on the other hand to illuminate in a new way the "expected" literary horizon, that horizon against which the particularities of the teller's tale are perceivable.

For example: Belkin was chosen (or better, created) by Pushkin because of his particular "unpoetic" point of view on objects and plots that are traditionally poetic (the highly characteristic and calculated use of the *Romeo and Juliet* plot in "Mistress into Maid" or the romantic "Dances of Death" in "The Coffinmaker"). Belkin, who is on the same level with those narrators-at-third-remove out of whose mouths he has taken his stories, is a "prosaic" man, a man without a drop of poetic pathos. The successful "prosaic" resolutions of the plots and the very means of the story's telling destroy any expectation of traditional poetic effects. The fruitfulness of the prosaic quality in Belkin's point of view consists in just this failure to understand poetic pathos.

Maxim Maximych in *A Hero of Our Time*, Rudy Panko, the narrators of "Nose" and "Overcoat," Dostoevsky's chroniclers, folkloric narrators and storytellers who are themselves characters in Melnikov-Pechersky and Mamin-Sibiryak, the folkloric and down-to-earth storytellers in Leskov, the character-narrators in populist literature and finally the narrators in Symbolist and post Symbolist prose (in Remizov, Zamyatin and others) – with all their widely differing forms of narration (oral and written), with all their differing narrative languages (literary, profes-sional, social-and-special-interest-group language, everyday, slang, dialects and others) – everywhere, they recommend themselves as specific and limited verbal ideological points of view, belief systems opposed to the literary expectations and points of view that constitute the background needed to perceive them; but these narrators are productive precisely *because* of this very limitedness and specificity.

The speech of such narrators is always *another's speech* (as regards the real or potential direct discourse of the author) and in *another's language* (i.e., insofar as it is a particular variant of the literary language that clashes with the language of the narrator).

Thus we have in this case "nondirect speaking" – not *in* language but *through* language, through the linguistic medium of another – and consequently through a refraction of authorial intentions.

The author manifests himself and his point of view not only in his effect on the narrator, on his speech and his language (which are to one or another extent objectivized, objects of display) but also in his effect on the subject of the story – as a point of view that differs from the point of view of the narrator. Behind the narrator's story we read a second story, the author's story; he is the one who tells us how the narrator tells stories, and also tells us about the narrator himself. We acutely sense two levels at each moment in the story; one, the level of the narrator, a belief system filled with his objects, meanings and emotional expressions, and the other, the level of the author, who speaks (albeit in a refracted way) by means of this story and through this story. The narrator himself, with *his* own discourse, enters into this authorial belief system along with what is actually being told. We puzzle out the author's emphases that overlie the subject of the story, while we puzzle out the story itself and the figure of the narrator as he is revealed in the process of telling his tale. If one fails to sense this second level, the intentions and accents of the author himself, then one has failed to understand the work.

As we have said above, the narrator's story or the story of the posited author is structured against the background of normal literary language, the expected literary horizon. Every moment of the story has a conscious relationship with this normal language and its belief system, is in fact set against them, and set against them *dialogically*: one point of view opposed to another, one evaluation opposed to another, one accent opposed to another (i.e., they are not contrasted as two abstractly linguistic phenomena). This interaction, this dialogic tension between two languages and two belief systems, permits authorial intentions to be realized in such a way that we can acutely sense their presence at every point in the work.

The author is not to be found in the language of the narrator, not in the normal literary language to which the story opposes itself (although a given story may be closer to a given language) – but rather, the author utilizes now one langauge, now another, in order to avoid giving himself up wholly to either of them; he makes use of this verbal give-and-take, this dialogue of languages at every point in his work, in order that he himself might remain as it were neutral with regard to language, a third party in a quarrel between two people (although he might be a *biased* third party).

All forms involving a narrator or a posited author signify to one degree or another by their presence the author's freedom from a unitary and singular language, a freedom connected with the relativity of literary and language systems; such forms open up the possibility of never having to define oneself in language, the possibility of translating one's own intentions from one linguistic system to another, of fusing "the language of truth" with "the language of everyday," of saying "I am me" in someone else's language, and in my own language, "I am other."

Such a refracting of authorial intentions takes place in all these forms (the narrator's tale, the tale of a posited author or that of one of the characters); it is therefore possible to have in them, as in the comic novel, a variety of different distances between distinct aspects of the narrator's language and the author's language: the refraction may be at times greater, at times lesser, and in some aspects of language there may be an almost complete fusion of voices.

The next form for incorporating and organizing heteroglossia in the novel – a form that every novel without exception utilizes – is the language used by characters.

The language used by characters in the novel, how they speak, is verbally and semantically autonomous; each character's speech possesses its own belief system, since each is the speech of another in another's language; thus is may also refract authorial intentions and consequently may to a certain degree constitute a second language for the author. Moreover, the character speech almost always influences authorial speech (and sometimes powerfully so), sprinkling it with another's words (that is, the speech of a character perceived as the concealed speech of another) and in this way introducing into it stratification and speech diversity.

Thus even where there is no comic element, no parody, no irony and so forth, where there is no narrator, no posited author or narrating character, speech diversity and language stratification still serve as the basis for style in the novel. Even in those places where the author's voice seems at first glance to be unitary and consistent, direct and unmediatedly intentional, beneath that smooth single-languaged surface we can nevertheless uncover prose's three-dimensionality, its profound speech diversity, which enters the project of style and is its determining factor.

Thus the language and style of Turgenev's novels have the appearance of being single-languaged and pure. Even in Turgenev, however, this unitary language is very far from poetic absolutism. Substantial masses of this language are drawn into the battle between points of view, value judgments and emphases that the characters introduce into it; they are infected by mutually contradictory intentions and stratifications; words, sayings, expressions, definitions and epithets are scattered throughout it, infected with others' intentions with which the author is to some extent at odds, and through which his own personal intentions are refracted. We sense acutely the various distances between the author and various aspects of his language, which smack of the social universes and belief systems of others. We acutely sense in various aspects of his language varying degrees of the presence of the author and of his *most recent semantic instantiation*. In Turgenev, heteroglossia and language stratification serve as the most fundamental factors of style, and orchestrate an authorial truth of their own; the author's linguistic consciousness, his consciousness as a writer of prose, is thereby relativized.

In Turgenev, social heteroglossia enters the novel primarily in the direct speeches of his characters, in dialogues. But this heteroglossia, as we have said, is also diffused throughout the authorial speech that surrounds the characters, creating highly particularized *character zones* [*zony geroev*]. These zones are formed from the fragments of character speech [*polureč'*], from various forms for hidden transmission of someone else's word, from scattered words and sayings belonging to someone else's speech, from those invasions into authorial speech of others' expressive indicators (ellipsis, questions, exclamations). Such a character zone is the field of action for a character's voice, encroaching in one way or another upon the author's voice.

However – we repeat – in Turgenev, the novelistic orchestration of the theme is concentrated in direct dialogues; the characters do not create around themselves their own extensive or densely saturated zones, and in Turgenev fully developed, complex stylistic hybrids are relatively rare.

We pause here on several examples of diffuse heteroglossia in Turgenev.*

(1) His name is Nikolai Petrovich Kirsanov. Some ten miles from the coaching-inn stands a respectable little property of his consisting of a couple of hundred serfs – or five thousand acres, as he expresses it now that he has divided up his land and let it to the peasants, and started a "farm." (*Fathers and Sons*, ch. 1)

Here the new expressions, characteristic of the era and in the style of the liberals, are put in quotation marks or otherwise "qualified."

(2) He was secretly beginning to feel irritated. Bazarov's complete indifference exasperated his aristocratic nature. *This son of a medico was not only self-assured: he actually returned abrupt and reluctant answers, and there was a churlish, almost insolent note in his voice.* (*Fathers and Sons*, ch. 6)

The third sentence of this paragraph, while being a part of the author's speech if judged by its formal syntactic markers, is at the same time in its choice of expressions ("this son of a medico") and in its emotional and expressive structure the hidden speech of someone else (Pavel Petrovich).

(3) Pavel Petrovich sat down at the table. He was wearing an elegant suit cut in the English fashion, and a gay little fez graced his head. The fez and the carelessly knotted cravat carried a suggestion of the more free life in the country but the stiff collar of his shirt – not white, it is true, but striped *as is correct for morning wear* – stood up as inexorably as ever against his well-shaven chin. (*Fathers and Sons*, ch. 5)

This ironic characterization of Pavel Petrovich's morning attire is consistent with the tone of a gentleman, precisely in the style of Pavel Petrovich. The statement "as is correct for morning wear" is not, of course, a simple authorial statement, but rather the norm of Pavel Petrovich's gentlemanly circle, conveyed ironically. One might with some justice put it in quotation marks. This is an example of a pseudo-objective underpinning.

(4) *Matvei Ilyich's suavity of demeanour was equalled only by his stately manner.* He had a gracious word for everyone – with an added shade of disgust in some cases and deference in others; he was gallant, "un vrai chevalier français," to all the ladies, and was continually bursting into hearty resounding laughter, in which no one else took part, as befits a high official. (*Fathers and Sons*, ch. 14)

---

*Citations from *Fathers and Sons* are from: Ivan Turgenev, *Fathers and Sons*, tr. Rosemary Edmonds (London: Penguin, 1965).

Here we have an analogous case of an ironic characterization given from the point of view of the high official himself. Such is the nature of this form of pseudo-objective underpinning: "as befits a high official."

(5) The following morning Nezhdanov betook himself to Sipyagin's town residence, and there, in a magnificent study, filled with furniture of a severe style, *in full harmony with the dignity of a liberal politician and modern gentleman....* (*Virgin Soil*, ch. 4)

This is an analogous pseudo-objective construction.

(6) Semyon Petrovich was in the ministry of the Court, he had the title of a *kammeryunker. He was prevented by his patriotism from joining the diplomatic service,* for which he seemed destined by everything, his education, his knowledge of the world, his popularity with women, and his very appearance.... (*Virgin Soil*, ch. 5)*

The motivation for refusing a diplomatic career is pseudo-objective. The entire characterization is consistent in tone and given from the point of view of Kallomyetsev himself, fused with his direct speech, being – at least judging by its syntactic markers – a subordinate clause attached to authorial speech ("for which he seemed destined by everything ... mais quitter la Russie!" and so forth).

(7) Kallomyetsev had come to S——— Province on a two months' leave to look after his property, that is to say, "to scare some and squeeze others." *Of course, there's no doing anything without that.* (*Virgin Soil*, ch. 5)

The conclusion of the paragraph is a characteristic example of a pseudo-objective statement. Precisely in order to give it the appearance of an objective authorial judgment, it is not put in quotation marks, as are the preceding words of Kallomyetsev himself; it is incorporated into authorial speech and deliberately placed directly after Kallomyetsev's own words.

(8) But Kallomyetsev deliberately stuck his round eyeglass between his nose and his eyebrow, and stared at the [snit of a] *student who dared not share* his "apprehensions." (*Virgin Soil*, ch. 7)

This is a typical hybrid construction. Not only the subordinate clause but also the direct object ("the [snit of a] student") of the main authorial

---

* Citations from *Virgin Soil* are from: Ivan Turgenev, *Virgin Soil*, tr. Constance Garnett (New York: Grove Press, n.d.).

sentence is rendered in Kallomyetsev's tone. The choice of words ("snit of a student," "dared not share") are determined by Kallomyetsev's irritated intonation, and at the same time, in the context of authorial speech, these words are permeated with the ironic intonation of the author; therefore the construction has two accents (the author's ironic transmission, and a mimicking of the irritation of the character).

Finally, we adduce examples of an intrusion of the emotional aspects of someone else's speech into the syntactic system of authorial speech (ellipsis, questions, exclamations).

(9) Strange was the state of his mind. In the last two days so many new sensations, new faces.... For the first time in his life he had come close to a girl, whom, in all probability, he loved; he was present at the beginning of the thing to which, in all probability, all his energies were consecrated.... Well? was he rejoicing? No. Was he wavering, afraid, confused? Oh, certainly not. Was he at least, feeling that tension of his whole being, that impulse forward into the front ranks of the battle, to be expected as the struggle grew near? No again. Did he believe, then, in this cause? Did he believe in his own love? "Oh, damned artistic temperament! sceptic!" his lips murmured inaudibly. Why this weariness, this disinclination to speak even, without shrieking and raving? What inner voice did he want to stifle with those ravings? (*Virgin Soil*, ch. 18)

Here we have, in essence, a form of a character's quasi-direct discourse [*nesobstvenno-prjamaja reč'*]. Judging by its syntactic markers, it is authorial speech, but its entire emotional structure belongs to Nezhdanov. This is his inner speech, but transmitted in a way regulated by the author, *with provocative questions from the author and with ironically debunking reservations* ("in all probability"), although Nezhdanov's emotional overtones are preserved.

Such a form for transmitting inner speech is common in Turgenev (and is generally one of the most widespread forms for transmitting inner speech in the novel). This form introduces order and stylistic symmetry into the disorderly and impetuous flow of a character's internal speech (a disorder and impetuosity which would otherwise have to be re-processed into direct speech) and, moreover, through its syntactic (third-person) and basic stylistic markers (lexicological and other), such a form permits another's inner speech to merge, in an organic and structured way, with a context belonging to the author. But at the same time it is precisely this form that permits us to preserve the expressive structure of the character's inner speech, its inability to exhaust itself in words, its flexibility, which would be absolutely impossible within the dry and logical form of indirect discourse [*kosvennaja reč'*]. Precisely these features make this form the most convenient for transmitting the inner speech of characters. It is of course a hybrid form, for the author's voice may be present in varying degrees of activity and may introduce into the transmitted speech a second accent of its own (ironic, irritated and so on).

The same hybridization, mixing of accents and erasing of boundaries between authorial speech and the speech of others is also present in other forms for transmitting characters' speech. With only three templates for speech transcription (direct speech [*prjamaja reč'*], indirect speech [*kosvennaja reč'*] and quasi-direct speech [*nesobstvenno-prjamaja reč'*]) a great diversity is nevertheless made possible in the treatment of character speech – i.e., the way characters overlap and infect each other – the main thing being how the authorial context succeeds in exploiting the various means for replicating frames and re-stratifying them.

The examples we have offered from Turgenev provide a typical picture of the character's role in stratifying the language of the novel and incorporating heteroglossia into it. A character in a novel always has, as we have said, a zone of his own, his own sphere of influence on the authorial context surrounding him, a sphere that extends – and often quite far – beyond the boundaries of the direct discourse allotted to him. The area occupied by an important character's voice must in any event be broader than his direct and "actual" words. This zone surrounding the important characters of the novel is stylistically profoundly idiosyncratic: the most varied hybrid constructions hold sway in it, and it is always, to one degree or another, dialogized; inside this area a dialogue is played out between the author and his characters – not a dramatic dialogue broken up into statement-and-response, but that special type of novelistic dialogue that realizes itself within the boundaries of constructions that externally resemble monologues. The potential for such dialogue is one of the most fundamental privileges of novelistic prose, a privilege available neither to dramatic nor to purely poetic genres.

Character zones are a most interesting object of study for stylistic and linguistic analysis: in them one encounters constructions that cast a completely new light on problems of syntax and stylistics.

Let us pause finally on one of the most basic and fundamental forms for incorporating and organizing heteroglossia in the novel – "incorporated genres."

The novel permits the incorporation of various genres, both artistic (inserted short stories, lyrical songs, poems, dramatic scenes, etc.) and extra-artistic (everyday, rhetorical, scholarly, religious genres and others). In principle, any genre could be included in the construction of the novel, and in fact it is difficult to find any genres that have not at some point been incorporated into a novel by someone. Such incorporated genres usually preserve within the novel their own structural integrity and independence, as well as their own linguistic and stylistic peculiarities.

There exists in addition a special group of genres that play an especially significant role in structuring novels, sometimes by themselves even directly determining the structure of a novel as a whole – thus creating novel-types named after such genres. Examples of such genres would be the confession, the diary, travel notes, biography, the personal letter and several others. All these genres may not only enter the novel as one of its essential structural components, but may also determine the form of the novel as a whole (the novel-confession, the novel-diary, the novel-in-letters, etc.). Each of these genres possesses its own verbal and semantic forms for assimilating various aspects of reality. The novel, indeed, utilizes these genres precisely because of their capacity, as well-worked-out forms, to assimilate reality in words.

So great is the role played by these genres that are incorporated into novels that it might seem as if the novel is denied any primary means for verbally appropriating reality, that it has no approach of its own, and therefore requires the help of other genres to re-process reality; the novel itself has the appearance of being merely a secondary syncretic unification of other seemingly primary verbal genres.

All these genres, as they enter the novel, bring into it their own languages, and therefore stratify the linguistic unity of the novel and further intensify its speech diversity in fresh ways. It often happens that the language of a nonartistic genre (say, the epistolary), when introduced into the novel, takes on a significance that creates a chapter not only in the history of the novel, but in the history of literary language as well.

The languages thus introduced into a novel may be either directly intentional or treated completely as objects, that is, deprived of any authorial intentions – not as a word that has been spoken, but as a word to be displayed, like a thing. But more often than not, these languages do refract, to one degree or another, authorial intentions – although separate aspects of them may in various ways *not* coincide with the semantic operation of the work that immediately precedes their appearance.

Thus poetic genres of verse (the lyrical genres, for example) when introduced into the novel may have the direct intentionality, the full semantic charge, of poetry. Such, for example, are the verses Goethe introduced into *Wilhelm Meister.* In such a way did the Romantics incorporate their own verses into their prose – and, as is well known, the Romantics considered the presence of verses in the novel (verses taken as directly intentional expressions of the author) one of its constitutive features. In other examples, incorporated verses refract authorial intentions; for example, Lensky's poem in *Evgenij Onegin*, "Where, o where have you gone...." Although the verses from *Wilhelm Meister* may be directly attributed to Goethe (which is actually done), then "Where, o where have you gone...." can in no way be attributed to Pushkin, or if so, only as a poem belonging to a special group comprising "parodic stylizations" (where we must also locate Grinev's poem in *The Captain's Daughter*). Finally, poems incorporated into a novel can also be completely objectified, as are, for example, Captain Lebyadkin's verses in Dostoevsky's *The Possessed.*

A similar situation is the novel's incorporation of every possible kind of maxim and aphorism; they too may oscillate between the purely objective (the "word on display") and the directly intentional, that is, the fully conceptualized philosophical dicta of the author himself (unconditional discourse spoken with no qualifications or distancing). Thus we find, in the novels of Jean Paul – which are so rich in aphorisms – a broad scale of gradations between the various aphorisms, from purely objective to directly intentional, withe the author's intentions refracted in varying degrees in each case.

In *Evgenij Onegin* aphorisms and maxims are present either on the plane of parody or of irony – that is, authorial intentions in these dicta are to a greater or lesser extent refracted. For example, the maxim

> He who has lived and thought can never
> Look on mankind without disdain;
> He who has felt is haunted ever
> By days that will not come again;
> No more for him enchantments semblance,
> On him the serpent of remembrance
> Feeds, and remorse corrodes his heart*

is given us on a lighthearted, parodic plane, although one can still feel

---

* Citations from *Eugene Onegin* are from the Walter Arndt translation (New York: Dutton, 1963), slightly modified to correspond with Bakhtin's remarks about particulars.

throughout a close proximity, almost a fusion with authorial intentions. And yet the lines that immediately follow:

> All this is likely to impart
> An added charm to conversation

(a conversation of the posited author with Onegin) strengthen the parodic-ironic emphasis, make the maxim more of an inert thing. We sense that the maxim is constructed in a field of activity dominated by Onegin's voice, in his – Onegin's – belief system, with his – Onegin's – emphases.

But this refraction of authorial intentions, in the field that resounds with Onegin's voice, in Onegin's zone – is different than the refraction in, say, Lensky's zone (cf. the almost objective parody on his poems).

This example may also serve to illustrate the influence of a character's language on authorial speech, something discussed by us above: the aphorism in question here is permeated with Onegin's (fashionably Byronic) intentions, therefore the author maintains a certain distance and does not completely merge with him.

The question of incorporating those genres fundamental to the novel's development (the confession, the diary and others) is much more complicated. Such genres also introduce into the novel their own languages, of course, but these languages are primarily significant for making available points of view that are generative in a material sense, since they exist outside literary conventionality and thus have the capacity to broaden the horizon of language available to literature, helping to win for literature new worlds of verbal perception, worlds that had been already sought and partially subdued in other – extraliterary – spheres of linguistic life.

A comic playing with languages, a story "not from the author" (but from a narrator, posited author or character), character speech, character zones and lastly various introductory or framing genres are the basic forms for incorporating and organizing heteroglossia in the novel. All these forms permit languages to be used in ways that are indirect, conditional, distanced. They all signify a relativizing of linguistic consciousness in the perception of language borders – borders created by history and society, and even the most fundamental borders (i.e., those between languages as such) – and permit expression of a feeling for the materiality of language that defines such a relativized consciousness. This relativizing of linguistic consciousness in no way requires a corresponding relativizing in the semantic intentions themselves: even within a prose linguistic consciousness, intentions themselves can be un-conditional. But because the idea of a singular language (a sacrosanct, unconditional language) is foreign to prose, prosaic consciousness must orchestrate its *own* – even though unconditional – semantic intentions. Prose consciousness feels cramped when it is confined to only *one* out of a multitude of heteroglot languages, for one linguistic timbre is in-adequate to it.

We have touched upon only those major forms typical of the most important variants of the European novel, but in themselves they do not, of course, exhaust all the possible means for incorporating and organizing heteroglossia in the novel. A combination of all these forms in separate given novels, and consequently in various generic types generated by these novels, is also possible. Of such a sort is the classic and purest model of the novel as genre – Cervantes' *Don Quixote*, which realizes in itself, in extraordinary depth and breadth, all the artistic possibilities of heteroglot and internally dialogized novelistic discourse.

Heteroglossia, once incorporated into the novel (whatever the forms for its incorporation), is *another's speech in another's language*, serving to express authorial intentions but in a refracted way. Such speech constitutes a special type of *double-voiced discourse*. It serves two speakers at the same time and expresses simultaneously two different intentions: the direct intention of the character who is speaking, and the refracted intention of the author. In such discourse there are two voices, two meanings and two expressions. And all the while these two voices are dialogically inter-related, they – as it were – know about each other (just as two exchanges in a dialogue know of each other and are structured in this mutual knowledge of each other); it is as if they actually hold a conversation with each other. Double-voiced discourse is always internally dialogized. Examples of this would be comic, ironic or parodic discourse, the refracting discourse of a narrator, refracting discourse in the language of a character and finally the discourse of a whole incorporated genre – all these discourses are double-voiced and internally dialogized. A potential dialogue is embedded in them, one as yet unfolded, a concentrated dialogue of two voices, two world views, two languages.

Double-voiced, internally dialogized discourse is also possible, of course, in a language system that is hermetic, pure and unitary, a system alien to the linguistic relativism of prose consciousness; it follows that such discourse is also possible in the purely poetic genres. But in those systems there is no soil to nourish the development of such discourse in the slightest meaningful or essential way. Double-voiced discourse is very widespread in rhetorical genres, but even there – remaining as it does within the boundaries of a single language system – it is not fertilized by a deep rooted connection with the forces of historical becoming that serve to stratify language, and therefore rhetorical genres are at best merely a distanced echo of this becoming, narrowed down to an individual polemic.

Such poetic and rhetorical double-voicedness, cut off from any process of linguistic stratification, may be adequately unfolded into an individual dialogue, into individual argument and conversation between two persons, even while the exchanges in the dialogue are immanent to a single unitary langauge: they may not be in agreement, they may even be opposed, but they are diverse neither in their speech nor in their language. Such double-voicing, remaining within the boundaries of a single hermetic and unitary language system, without any underlying fundamental socio-linguistic orchestration, may be only a stylistically secondary accompaniment to the dialogue and forms of polemic.[7] The internal bifurcation (double-voicing) of discourse, sufficient to a single and unitary language and to a consistently monologic style, can never be a fundamental form of discourse: it is merely a game, a tempest in a teapot.

The double-voicedness one finds in prose is of another sort altogether. There – on the rich soil of novelistic prose – double-voicedness draws its energy, its dialogized ambiguity, not from *individual* dissonances, misunderstandings or contradictions (however tragic, however firmly grounded in individual destinies);[8] in the novel, this double-voicedness sinks its roots deep into a fundamental, socio-linguistic speech diversity and multi-languagedness. True, even in the novel heteroglossia is by and large always personified, incarnated in individual human figures, with disagreements and oppositions individualized. But such oppositions of individual wills and minds are submerged in *social* heteroglossia, they are reconceptualized through it. Oppositions between individuals are only surface upheavals of the untamed elements in social heteroglossia, surface manifestations of those elements that play *on* such individual oppositions, make them contradictory, saturate their consciousness and discourses with a more fundamental speech diversity.

Therefore the internal dialogism of double-voiced prose discourse can never be exhausted thematically (just as the metaphoric energy of language can never be exhausted thematically); it can never be developed into the motivation or subject for a manifest dialogue, such as might fully embody, with no residue, the internally dialogic potential embedded in linguistic heteroglossia. The internal dialogism of authentic prose discourse, which grows organically out of a stratified and heteroglot language, cannot fundamentally be dramatized or dramatically resolved (brought to an authentic end); it cannot ultimately be fitted into the frame of any manifest dialogue, into the frame of a mere conversation between persons; it is not ultimately divisible into verbal exchanges possessing precisely marked boundaries.[9] This double-voicedness in prose is prefigured in language itself (in authentic metaphors, as well as in myth), in language as a social phenomenon that is becoming in history, socially stratified and weathered in this process of becoming.

The relativizing of linguistic consciousness, its crucial participation in the social multi- and vari-languagedness of evolving languages, the various wanderings of semantic and expressive intentions and the trajectory of this consciousness through various languages (languages that are all equally well conceptualized and equally objective), the inevitable necessity for such a consciousness to speak indirectly, conditionally, in a refracted way – these are all indispensable prerequisites for an authentic double-voiced prose discourse. This double-voicedness makes its presence felt by the novelist in the living heteroglossia of language, and in the multi-languagedness surrounding and nourishing his own consciousness; it is not invented in superficial, isolated rhetorical polemics with another person.

If the novelist loses touch with this linguistic ground of prose style, if he is unable to attain the heights of a relativized, Galilean linguistic consciousness, if he is deaf to organic double-voicedness and to the internal dialogization of living and evolving discourse, then he will never comprehend, or even realize, the actual possibilities and tasks of the novel as a genre. He may, of course, create an artistic work that compositionally and thematically will be similar to a novel, will be "made" exactly as a novel is made, but he will not thereby have created a novel. The style will always give him away. We will recognize the naively self-confident or obtusely stubborn unity of a smooth, pure single-voiced language (perhaps accompanied by a primitive, artificial, worked up double-voicedness). We quickly sense that such an author finds it easy to purge his work of speech diversity: he simply does not listen to the fundamental heteroglossia inherent in actual language; he mistakes social overtones, which create the timbres of words, for irritating noises that it is his task to eliminate. The novel, when torn out of authentic linguistic speech diversity, emerges in most cases as a "closet drama," with detailed, fully developed and "artistically worked out" stage directions (it is, of course, bad drama). In such a novel, divested of its language diversity, authorial language inevitably ends up in the awkward and absurd position of the language of stage directions in plays.[10]

The double-voiced prose word has a double meaning. But the poetic word, in the narrow sense, also has a double, even a multiple, meaning. It is this that basically distinguishes it from the word as concept, or the word as term. The poetic word is a trope, requiring a precise feeling for the two meanings contained in it.

But no matter how one understands the interrelationship of meanings in a poetic symbol (a trope), this interrelationship is never of the dialogic sort; it is impossible under any conditions or at any time to imagine a trope (say, a metaphor) being unfolded into the two exchanges of a dialogue, that is, two meanings parceled out between two separate voices. For this reason the dual meaning (or multiple meaning) of the symbol never brings in its wake dual accents. On the contrary, one voice, a single-accent system, is fully sufficient to express poetic ambiguity. It is possible to interpret the interrelationships of different meanings in a symbol logically (as the relationship of a part or an individual to the whole, as for example a proper noun that has become a symbol, or the relationship of the concrete to the abstract and so on); one may grasp this relationship philosophically and ontologically, as a special kind of representational relationship, or as a relationship between essence and appearance and so forth, or one may shift into the foreground the emotional and evaluative dimension of such relationship – but all these types of relationships between various meanings do not and cannot go beyond the boundaries of the relationship between a word and its object, or the boundaries of various aspects in the object. The entire event is played out between the word and its object; all of the play of the poetic symbol is in that space. A symbol cannot presuppose any fundamental relationship to another's word, to another's voice. The polysemy of the poetic symbol presupposes the unity of a voice with which it is identical, and it presupposes that such a voice is completely alone within its own discourse. As soon as another's voice, another's accent, the possibility of another's point of view breaks through this play of the symbol, the poetic plane is destroyed and the symbol is translated onto the plane of prose.

[221]

To understand the difference between ambiguity in poetry and double-voicedness in prose, it is sufficient to take any symbol and give it an ironic accent (in a correspondingly appropriate context, of course), that is, to introduce into it one's own voice, to refract within it one's own fresh intention.[11] In this process the poetic symbol – while remaining, of course, a symbol – is at one and the same time translated onto the plane of prose and becomes a double-voiced word: in the space between the word and its object another's word, another's accent intrudes, a mantle of materiality is cast over the symbol (an operation of this sort would naturally result in a rather simple and primitive double-voiced structure).

An example of this simplest type of prosification of the poetic symbol in *Evgenij Onegin* is the stanza on Lensky:

> Of love he [Lensky] sang, love's service choosing,
> And timid was his simple tune
> As ever artless maiden's musing,
> As babes aslumber, as the moon....[12]

The poetic symbols of this stanza are organized simultaneously at two levels: the level of Lensky's lyrics themselves – in the semantic and expressive system of the "Göttigen Geist" – and on the level of Pushkin's speech, for whom the "Göttigen Geist" with its language and its poetics is merely an instantiation of the literary heteroglossia of the epoch, but one that is already becoming typical: a fresh tone, a fresh voice amid the multiple voices of literary language, literary world views and the life these world views regulate. Some other voices in this heteroglossia – of literature and of the real life contemporaneous with it – would be Onegin's Byronic-Chateaubriandesque language, the Richardsonian language and world of the provincial Tatiana, the down-to-earth rustic language spoken at the Larins' estate, the language and the world of Tatiana in Petersburg and other languages as well – including the indirect languages of the author – which undergo change in the course of the work. The whole of this heteroglossia (*Evgenij Onegin* is an encyclopedia of the styles and languages of the epoch) orchestrates the intentions of the author and is responsible for the authentically novelistic style of this work.

Thus the images in the above-cited stanza, being ambiguous (metaphorical) poetic symbols serving Lensky's intentions in Lensky's belief system, become double-voiced prose symbols in the system of Pushkin's speech. These are, of course, authentic prose symbols, arising from the heteroglossia inherent in the epoch's evolving literary language, not a superficial, rhetorical parody or irony.

Such is the distinction between true double-voicedness in fictive practice, and the *single-voiced* double or multiple meaning that finds expression in the purely poetic symbol. The ambiguity of double-voiced discourse is internally dialogized, fraught with dialogue, and may in fact even give birth to dialogues comprised of truly separate voices (but such dialogues are not dramatic; they are, rather, interminable prose dialogues). What is more, double-voicedness is never exhausted in these dialogues, it cannot be extracted fully from the discourse – not by a rational, logical counting of the individual parts, nor by drawing distinctions between the various parts of a monologic unit of discourse (as happens in rhetoric), nor by a definite cut-off between the verbal exchanges of a finite dialogue, such as occurs in the theater. Authentic double-voicedness, although it generates novelistic prose dialogues, is not exhausted in these dialogues and remains in the discourse, in language, like a spring of dialogism that never runs dry – for the internal dialogism of discourse is something that inevitably accompanies the social, contradictory historical becoming of language.

If the central problem in poetic theory is the problem of the poetic symbol, then the central problem in prose theory is the problem of the double-voiced, internally dialogized word, in all its diverse types and variants.

For the novelist working in prose, the object is always entangled in someone else's discourse about it, it is already present with qualifications, an object of dispute that is conceptualized and evaluated variously, inseparable from the heteroglot social apperception of it. The novelist speaks of this "already qualified world" in a language that is heteroglot and internally dialogized. Thus both object and language are revealed to the novelist in their historical dimension, in the process of social and heteroglot becoming. For the novelist, there is no world outside his socioheteroglot perception – and there is no language outside the heteroglot intentions that stratify that world. Therefore it is possible to have, even in the novel, that profound but unique unity of a language (or more precisely, of languages) with its own object, with its own world, unity of the sort one finds in poetry. Just as the poetic image seems to have been born out of language itself, to have sprung organically from it, to have been pre-formed in it, so also novelistic images seem to be grafted organically on to their own double-voiced language, pre-formed, as it were, within it, in the innards of the distinctive multi-speechedness organic to that language. In the novel, the "already bespoke quality" [*ogovorennost'*] of the world is woven together with the "already uttered" quality [*peregovorennost'*] of language, into the unitary event of the world's heteroglot becoming, in both social consciousness and language.

Even the poetic word (in the narrow sense) must break through to its object, penetrate the alien word in which the object is entangled; it also encounters heteroglot language and must break through in order to create a unity and a pure intentionality (which is neither given nor ready-made). But the trajectory of the poetic word toward its own object and toward the unity of language is a path along which the poetic word is continually encountering someone else's word, and each takes new bearings from the other; the records of the passage remain in the slag of the creative process, which is then cleared away (as scaffolding is cleared away once construction is finished), so that the finished work may rise as unitary speech, one co-extensive with its object, as if it were speech about an "Edenic" world. This single-voiced purity and unqualified directness that intentions possess in poetic discourse so crafted is purchased at the price of a certain conventionality in poetic language.

If the art of poetry, as a utopian philosophy of genres, gives rise to the conception of a purely poetic, extrahistorical language, a language far removed from the petty rounds of everyday life, a language of the gods – then it must be said that the art of prose is close to a conception of languages as historically concrete and living things. The prose art presumes a deliberate feeling for the historical and social concreteness of living discourse, as well as its relativity, a feeling for its participation in historical becoming and in social struggle; it deals with discourse that is still warm from that struggle and hostility, as yet unresolved and still fraught with hostile intentions and accents; prose art finds discourse in this state and subjects it to the dynamic-unity of its own style.

9

M. M. Bakhtin
From 'The grotesque image of the body and its sources'

From *Rabelais and His World*, translated by Helene Iswolsky
(Indiana University Press, 1984, pp. 316–44, 362–7).

The following extract makes up the majority of chapter 5 of *Rabelais and His World*, 'The grotesque image of the body and its sources'. As I explained in chapter 4 of Part I, grotesque realism is the central aesthetic concept of the Rabelais book; this chapter describes the grotesque body on which this concept is focused, and seeks to place it in a variety of different sources in folkloric, medieval and Renaissance culture. But this is not 'source-study' of a traditional kind; in the following analyses the surface unity of Rabelais' writing is dissolved to reveal the epochally and historically prepared ground on which it rests.

I have cut two substantial sections of the chapter. The first fifteen or so pages are taken up with Bakhtin's critique of a late nineteenth-century scholar's account of the grotesque. Bakhtin criticizes him for considering the grotesque solely in a negative or satirical manner, and corrects his analyses by insisting on the positive, regenerative forces that are also present in Rabelais' images. The second excision concerns a mass of source material for the grotesque image of the body that Bakhtin adduces from classical and medieval culture – from mystery plays, relics, oaths and curses, comic performers of the market-place, and ancient medicine. Rabelais' text emerges from these pages as intersected by the most diverse and profound popular and learned generic forms.

The two substantial sections that remain provide evidence of two poles among these forms. On the one hand the analyses point to the ancient, epochally prepared folkloric roots upon which the grotesque image of the body draws. But in the second section, Bakhtin equally points to analogies with contemporary Renaissance philosophy, in order to distinguish Rabelais from a simple celebration of the biological body. In this argument, the biological body becomes the means by which the vertical hierarchies of medieval culture are subverted, and replaced by a new, historic and potentially scientific conception of human life.

The passages from Rabelais' novel are from the translation by Jacques LeClercq (Heritage Press, 1936).

From 'The grotesque image of the body and its sources'

Of all the features of the human face, the nose and mouth play the most important part in the grotesque image of the body; the head, ears, and nose also acquire a grotesque character when they adopt the animal form or that of inanimate objects. The eyes have no part in these comic images; they express an individual, so to speak, self-sufficient human life, which is not essential to the grotesque. The grotesque is interested only in protruding eyes, like the eyes of the stutterer in the scene described earlier. It is looking for that which protrudes from the body, all that seeks to go out beyond the body's confines. Special attention is given to the shoots and branches, to all that prolongs the body and links it to other bodies or to the world outside. Moreover, the bulging eyes manifest a purely bodily tension. But the most important of all human features for the grotesque is the mouth. It dominates all else. The grotesque face is actually reduced to the gaping mouth; the other features are only a frame encasing this wide-open bodily abyss.

The grotesque body, as we have often stressed, is a body in the act of becoming. It is never finished, never completed; it is continually built, created, and builds and creates another body. Moreover, the body swallows the world and is itself swallowed by the world (let us recall the grotesque image in the episode of Gargantua's birth on the feast of cattle-slaughtering). This is why the essential role belongs to those parts of the grotesque body in which it outgrows its own self, transgressing its own body, in which it conceives a new, second body: the bowels and the phallus. These two areas play the leading role in the grotesque image, and it is precisely for this reason that they are predominantly subject to positive exaggeration, to hyperbolization; they can even detach them-selves from the body and lead an independent life, for they hide the rest of the body, as something secondary (the nose can also in a way detach itself from the body). Next to the bowels and the genital organs is the mouth, through which enters the world to be swallowed up. And next is the anus. All these convexities and orifices have a common characteristic; it is within them that the confines between bodies and between the body and the world are overcome: there is an interchange and an inter-orientation. This is why the main events in the life of the grotesque body, the acts of the bodily drama, take place in this sphere. Eating, drinking, defecation and other elimination (sweating, blowing of the nose, sneez-ing), as well as copulation, pregnancy, dismemberment, swallowing up by another body – all these acts are performed on the confines of the body and outer world, or on the confines of the old and new body. In all these events the beginning and end of life are closely linked and interwoven.

Thus the artistic logic of the grotesque image ignores the closed, smooth, and impenetrable surface of the body and retains only its excrescences (sprouts, buds) and orifices, only that which leads beyond the body's limited space or into the body's depths.[1] Mountains and abysses, such is the relief of the grotesque body; or speaking in architectural terms, towers and subterranean passages.

Grotesque images may, of course, present other members, organs and parts of the body (especially dismembered parts), but they play a minor role in the drama. They are never stressed unless they replace a leading image.

Actually, if we consider the grotesque image in its extreme aspect, it never presents an individual body; the image consists of orifices and convexities that present another, newly conceived body. It is a point of transition in a life eternally renewed, the inexhaustible vessel of death and conception.

As we have said, the grotesque ignores the impenetrable surface that closes and limits the body as a separate and completed phenomenon. The grotesque image displays not only the outward but also the inner features of the body: blood, bowels, heart and other organs. The outward and inward features are often merged into one.

We have already sufficiently stressed the fact that grotesque imagery constructs what we might call a double body. In the endless chain of bodily life it retains the parts in which one link joins the other, in which the life of one body is born from the death of the preceding, older one.

Finally, let us point out that the grotesque body is cosmic and universal. It stresses elements common to the entire cosmos: earth, water, fire, air; it is directly related to the sun, to the stars. It contains the signs of the zodiac. It reflects the cosmic hierarchy. This body can merge with various natural phenomena, with mountains, rivers, seas, islands, and continents. It can fill the entire universe.

The grotesque mode of representing the body and bodily life prevailed in art and creative forms of speech over thousands of years. From the point of view of extensive use, this mode of representation still exists today; grotesque forms of the body not only predominate in the art of European peoples but also in their folklore, especially in the comic genre. Moreover, these images predominate in the extra-official life of the people. For example, the theme of mockery and abuse is almost entirely bodily and grotesque. The body that figures in all the expressions of the unofficial speech of the people is the body that fecundates and is fecundated, that gives birth and is born, devours and is devoured, drinks, defecates, is sick and dying. In all languages there is a great number of expressions related to the genital organs, the anus and buttocks, the belly, the mouth and nose. But there are few expressions for the other parts of the body: arms and legs, face, and eyes. Even these comparatively few forms of speech have, in most cases, a narrow, practical character, they are related to the nearby area, determine distance, dimensions, or number. They have no broader, symbolic meaning, nor are they especially expressive. They do not participate in abuse and mockery.

Wherever men laugh and curse, particularly in a familiar environment, their speech is filled with bodily images. The body copulates, defecates, overeats, and men's speech is flooded with genitals, bellies, defecations, urine, disease, noses, mouths, and dismembered parts. Even when the flood is contained by norms of speech, there is still an eruption of these images into literature, especially if the literature is gay or abusive in character. The common human fund of familiar and abusive gesticulations is also based on these sharply defined images.

This boundless ocean of grotesque bodily imagery within time and space extends to all languages, all literatures, and the entire system of gesticulation; in the midst of it the bodily canon of art, belles lettres, and polite conversation of modern times is a tiny island. This limited canon never prevailed in antique literature. In the official literature of European peoples it has existed only for the last four hundred years.

We shall give a brief characterization of the new canon, concerning ourselves less with the pictorial arts than with literature. We shall build this characterization by comparing it to the grotesque conception and bringing out the differences.

The new bodily canon, in all its historic variations and different genres, presents an entirely finished, completed, strictly limited body, which is shown from the outside as something individual. That which protrudes, bulges, sprouts, or branches off (when a body transgresses its limits and a new one begins) is eliminated, hidden, or moderated. All orifices of the body are closed. The basis of the image is the individual, strictly limited mass, the impenetrable façade. The opaque surface and the body's "valleys" acquire an essential meaning as the border of a closed individuality that does not merge with other bodies and with the world.

All attributes of the unfinished world are carefully removed, as well as all the signs of its inner life. The verbal norms of official and literary language, determined by the canon, prohibit all that is linked with fecundation, pregnancy, childbirth. There is a sharp line of division between familiar speech and "correct" language.

The fifteenth century was an age of considerable freedom in France. In the sixteenth century the norms of language become more strict, and the borderline between the different norms grew more evident. This process intensified at the end of the century, when the canon of polite speech that was to prevail in the seventeenth century was definitely formed. At the end of the century Montaigne protested in his "Essays" against these prohibitions.

> What harm has the genital act, so natural, so necessary, and so lawful, done to humanity, that we dare not speak of it without shame, and exclude it from serious and orderly conversation? We boldly utter the words, *kill*, *rob*, *betray*: and the other we only dare utter under our breath. Does this mean that the less of it we breathe in words, the more are we at liberty to swell our thoughts with it? For it is amusing that the words which are least used, least written, and most hushed up should be the best known and the most generally understood. There is no person of any age or morals but knows them as well as he knows the word *bread*. They are impressed upon each of us, without being expressed, without voice and without form. (And the sex that does it most is charged to hush it up.) (Montaigne, "Essays," III, Chapter 5. Translated by George B. Ivez, copyright Harvard University Press, 1925. Reproduced by permission.)

In the new canon, such parts of the body as the genital organs, the buttocks, belly, nose and mouth cease to play the leading role. Moreover, instead of their original meaning they acquire an exclusiveness: in other words, they convey a merely individual meaning of the life of one single, limited body. The belly, nose, and mouth, are of course retained in the image and cannot be hidden, but in an individual, completed body they either fulfil purely expressive functions (this is true of the mouth only) or the functions of characterization and individualization. There is no symbolic, broad meaning whatever in the organs of this body. If they are not interpreted as a characterization and an expressive feature, they are referred to on the merely practical level in brief explanatory comments. Generally speaking, all that does not contain an element of characterization in the literary image is reduced to a simple bodily remark added to speech or action.

In the modern image of the individual body, sexual life, eating, drinking, and defecation have radically changed their meaning: they have been transferred to the private and psychological level where their connotation becomes narrow and specific, torn away from the direct relation to the life of society and to the cosmic whole. In this new connotation they can no longer carry on their former philosophical functions.

In the new bodily canon the leading role is attributed to the individually characteristic and expressive parts of the body: the head, face, eyes, lips, to the muscular system, and to the place of the body in the external world. The exact position and movements of this finished body in the finished outside world are brought out, so that the limits between them are not weakened.

The body of the new canon is merely one body: no signs of duality have been left. It is self-sufficient and speaks in its name alone. All that happens within it concerns it alone, that is, only the individual, closed sphere. Therefore, all the events taking place within it acquire one single meaning: death is only death, it never coincides with birth; old age is torn away from youth; blows merely hurt, without assisting an act of birth. All actions and events are interpreted on the level of a single, individual life. They are enclosed within the limits of the same body, limits that are the absolute beginning and end and can never meet.

In the grotesque body, on the contrary, death brings nothing to an end, for it does not concern the ancestral body, which is renewed in the next generation. The events of the grotesque sphere are always developed on the boundary dividing one body from the other and, as it were, at their points of intersection. One body offers its death, the other its birth, but they are merged in a two-bodied image.

In the new canon the duality of the body is preserved only in one theme, a pale reflection of its former dual nature. This is the theme of nursing a child.[2] But the image of the mother and the child is strictly individualized and closed, the line of demarcation cannot be removed. This is a completely new phase of the artistic conception of bodily interaction.

Finally, the new canon is completely alien to hyperbolization. The individualized image has no place for it. All that is permitted is a certain accentuation of expressive and characterized features. The severance of the organs from the body or their independent existence is no longer permitted.

We have roughly sketched the basic outlines of the modern canon, as they generally appear in the norms of literature and speech.[3]

The comic conception, inherited from folk culture of humor, from grotesque realism and from elements of familiar speech, culminates in Rabelais' novel. In all the episodes that we have analyzed, and in their separate images, we have seen the grotesque body. Its mighty torrent flows through the entire novel: the dismembered parts, the separate organs (as in Panurge's wall), the gaping mouths devouring, swallowing, drinking, the defecation, urine, death, birth, childhood, and old age. The bodies are merged with each other or with objects (as in the image of *carême-prenant*) and with the world. A tendency toward duality can be glimpsed everywhere. Everywhere the cosmic, ancestral element of the body is stressed.

The tendency to duality can be found to a greater or smaller extent in the episodes we have examined. Let us offer an example of a more external and uncouth projection of duality.

> The emblem in his (Gargantua's) hat? Against a base of gold weighing over forty pounds was an enamel figure very much in keeping. It portrayed a man's body with two heads facing one another, four arms, four feet, a pair of arses and a brace of sexual organs, male and female. Such according to Plato's *Symposium*, was human nature in its mystical origins. (Book I, Chapter 8)

The androgyne theme was popular in Rabelais' time. In the sphere of pictorial art I will recall a similar presentation in Leonardo da Vinci's "Coitus," showing this act in its inner bodily aspect.

Rabelais not only represents the grotesque image of the body in its essential forms. He also offers the theory of the body in its ancestral aspect. Panurge's arguments quoted previously are typical in this respect. In another passage he says that in the realm of Salmagundi:

> ... no malefactor would be put to death by law, without friggling like a pelican (as lustily as belly can), until his spermatic vessels were drained of the few drops required to trace a Greek Y, the letter sacred to Priapus. After all, here was a wealth too rich to waste. Your criminal, begetting a male, would die content, forfeiting his life, he would have left the world another. (Book 3, Chapter 26)

In his famous speech about debtors and creditors, describing the utopian world where all lend money and receive loans, Panurge also develops the theory of the ancestral body:

> The interdependent universe was so beautifully organized that, the

problem of nutrition perfected, it went on to lend to those unborn – a loan, by means of which it sought to perpetuate and multiply itself in its own image: children.

"To this end, each particular elects and pares off the most precious elements of its food to dispatch them downward into vessels and receptacles most suitably contrived by nature. These elements flow down long circuits and flexuosities into the genitories; receive a competent form: find chambers designed, in both male and female, for the preservation and perpetuation of humankind. And all of it is done by loans and debts, a fact proved by the phrase 'the obligations of wedlock.'" (Book 3, Chapter 4)

Again, in the Third Book, there is an explanation of why newly married men are not forced to go to war. Here the ancestral theory is developed once more. This is one of the leading themes of the entire Third Book.

We shall resume this theme in our next chapter, examining it in its historic aspect as the growth and immorality of the human race, as expressed in Gargantua's famous letter to Pantagruel. The relative immorality of the semen is seen here in its intimate relation to mankind's historic progress. The human race is not merely renewed with each new generation, it rises to a new level of development. This theme, as we shall see, is also found in the praise of "Pantagruelion."

Thus, in Rabelais' book the image of the ancestral body is merged with the people's vivid awareness of historic immorality. We have seen that this awareness forms the very nucleus of the entire system of popular-festive imagery. The grotesque conception of the body is interwoven not only with the cosmic but also with the social, utopian, and historic theme, and above all with the theme of the change of epochs and the renewal of culture.

In all the episodes and images discussed in the preceding chapters, the material bodily lower stratum was most often represented in the narrow sense of the word. But in these images a leading role is also played, as we have said, by the gaping mouth. This is of course, related to the lower stratum; it is the open gate leading downward into the bodily underworld. The gaping mouth is related to the image of swallowing, this most ancient symbol of death and destruction. At the same time, a series of banquet images are also linked to the mouth (to the teeth and the gullet).

These are some of the central images of the popular-festive system. The exaggeration of the mouth is the fundamental traditional method of rendering external comic features, as pictured by comic masks, various "gay monsters" (Mâchecroûte of the Lyon carnival), devils in diableries, and Lucifer himself.

It is obvious why the gaping mouth, the teeth, the swallowing have an essential meaning in the Rabelaisian system of images. The gaping mouth plays a specially important part in *Pantagruel*. One may say that it is the hero of this book.

Neither Pantagruel's name nor the nucleus of his image was created by Rabelais. The name existed before him in literature as that of a character of the diableries; it also existed in spoken language as a colloquial term for a hoarseness caused by excessive drinking. The colloquialism referred to the mouth, throat, to overindulgence and disease, in other words, to the characteristic grotesque complex. Pantagruel's character is also linked to the broader, cosmic complex of the diableries.

We already know that the diableries were part of the mysteries and that their images had a popular-festive character. The body they presented had a distinctly grotesque form. It was in this grotesque atmosphere that the figure of Pantagruel appeared on the scene.

We first encounter him in a mystery of the second part of the fifteenth century, "The Acts of the Apostles," by Simon Gréban. In the diablerie of this play Proserpina, mother of the devils, brings four of her sons (*petits dyables*) to Lucifer. Each little devil represents one of the four elements: earth, water, air, and fire, and each exercises his specific activity in his own sphere. A broad picture of the elements is thus unfolded. One of the four devils, whose name is Pantagruel and who represents water, says: "I fly over the seas, more sprightly than a bird of prey." During his flights he becomes saturated with sea salt and is therefore related to the substance that causes thirst. In this mystery Lucifer says that at night, awaiting other activities, he throws salt into the mouths of drunkards.

The devil Pantagruel appears in a similar role in another play, *Saint Louis*. He delivers a monologue, relating in great detail that he spent the night among some young men who had been reveling all evening; with great precaution not to awaken them he threw salt into their mouths, and so "Glory be to God, when they awoke they were more thirsty than before!"

This image of Pantagruel as a mystery-play devil is linked on one hand with the cosmic elements water and sea salt and on the other hand with the grotesque image of the body (open mouth, thirst, drunkenness).

Finally, he is linked with a purely carnivalesque gesture of throwing salt into an open mouth. All these features, which are the basis of the image of Pantagruel, are closely related to one another. This traditional nucleus was fully retained by Rabelais.

We must specially point out that *Pantagruel* was conceived and written by Rabelais during the unusual heat wave and drought of 1532. Men actually walked with their mouths wide open. Abel Lefranc is right in surmising that the little devil's name and his tricks of causing thirst were often mentioned in Rabelais' entourage, provoking jokes and curses. The weather conditions rendered this image popular. It is quite possible that Rabelais made use of Pantagruel's character because of the drought.

Pantagruel's first chapter immediately introduces the grotesque body with all its characteristic traits. It describes the origin of the giant race to which Pantagruel belongs. After the killing of Abel, the earth, saturated with his blood, became exceptionally fertile.

Here is the beginning of this first chapter:

> You must therefore remember that I speak of the beginning of the world, of long ages since, of more than forty times forty nights ago, to reckon as the Druids did.
>
> A little while after Cain slew his brother Abel, the earth, imbued with the blood of the just, was one year extremely fertile in all fruits. Medlars were particularly plentiful and large, just three to the bushel. So that year was recorded in the memory of men as the year of the great medlars. (Book 2, Chapter 1)

Such is the first bodily theme of this chapter. Its grossly carnivalesque traits are obvious. The first death (according to the Bible, Abel was the first man to die) renewed the earth's fertility. Here we have the combination of killing and birth with which we are familiar. Death, the dead body, blood as a seed buried in the earth, rising for another life – this is one of the oldest and most widespread themes. A variant is death inseminating mother earth and making her bear fruit once more. This variant often produces a flowering of erotic images (of course, not in the narrow, specific sense of the word). Rabelais speaks elsewhere of the "sweet, much desired embrace of ... Mother Earth, which we call burial." (Book Three, Chapter 48). This image of a burial is probably inspired by Pliny, who gives a detailed picture of the earth's motherhood and of burial as a return to her womb. ("Natural History," II, 63.) Rabelais is inclined to conceive this image in all its variations and nuances, not in the high style of the antique mysteries but in the carnivalesque, popular-festive spirit: a gay and sober belief in the relative historic immortality of the people and of himself within the people.

Thus, the theme of death-renewal-fertility was Rabelais' initial theme, the opening of his immortal novel (since *Pantagruel* was the first book to be written). We stress this fact.

The earth became especially rich in medlars (*en mesl*). But men who ate these medlars began to develop abnormally; one part of the body would grow to monstrous dimensions. Rabelais presents a number of typical grotesque forms of exaggerated body parts that completely hide the normal members of the body. This is actually a picture of dismemberment, of separate areas of the body enlarged to gigantic dimensions. First of all, we see men with monstrous bellies (a typical grotesque hyperbola); Saint Pansard (St. Paunchman) and Mardi Gras belong to this gay race. Saint Pansard's ironic name was associated with carnival, and King Carnival, himself, is related to the family of fat paunches. Next, Rabelais depicts hunchbacks with humps of huge proportions, or monstrous noses, abnormally long legs, gigantic ears. There are men with disproportionate phalli (wound six times around their waists) and others with unusually large testes. We have a picture of a giant grotesque body and at the same time an array of carnival figures.

Directly preceding this gallery of grotesque human members, Rabelais pictures cosmic perturbations in the skies, which also have a carnivalesque nature: the star Spica is transferred from Virgo to Libra. But these phenomena are so difficult to understand that the astrologers would merely break their teeth on them. The grotesque image of teeth reaching up to the skies was inspired by the common expression "to chew" a difficult astrological problem.

Further, Rabelais gives a long enumeration of the giants who were Pantagruel's ancestors. We find here a great number of Biblical, antique, medieval, and imaginary names. Rabelais was a connoisseur, possessing a wealth of information on this subject, for the ancient giants had already been listed by the scholar Ravisius Textor, whose works were used by Rabelais. The giants and their legends are closely related to the grotesque conception of the body. We have already pointed out the role of giants in antique satyric drama (which was precisely a drama of the body). Most local legends connect such natural phenomena as mountains, rivers, rocks, and islands with the bodies of giants or with their different organs; these bodies are, therefore, not separated from the world or from nature.

[235]

We have also pointed out that giants were an indispensable part of popular-festive carnival images.

Such is the content of *Pantagruel*'s first chapter. Grotesque figures are interwoven with cosmic phenomena. The entire array of the novel's images starts with the theme of death-renewal-fertility.

This theme also opens the second chapter:

> At the age of four hundred fourscore and forty-four years, Gargantua begat his son Pantagruel upon his wife named Badebec, daughter to the king of the dimly-seen Amaurotes in Utopia. She died in the throes of childbirth. Alas! Pantagruel was so extraordinarily large and heavy that he could not have possibly come to light without suffocating his mother. (Book 2, Chapter 2)

This is the theme already familiar to us from the Roman carnival of combined killing and childbirth. Here, the killing is done by the newborn himself, in the very act of his birth.

Birth and death are the gaping jaws of the earth and the mother's open womb. Further on, gaping human and animal mouths will enter into the picture.

The terrible drought which occurred at the time of Pantagruel's birth is described in the novel:

> ... beasts were found dead in the fields, their mouths agape.
>
> As for the men, their state was very piteous. You should have seen them with their tongues dangling like a hound's after a run of six hours. Not a few threw themselves into the wells. Others lay under a cow's belly to enjoy the shade.... It was hard enough, God knows, to save the holy water in the churches ... scores of parched, unhappy wretches followed the priest who distributed it, their jaws yawning for one tiny driblet.... Ah! thrice happy that year the man who had a cool, well-plenished wine cellar underground. (*Ibid*).

We must point out that the images of the "well," the "cow's belly," and the "cellar" are equivalent to the "gaping mouth." The latter corresponds in grotesque topography to the belly and to the uterus. Thus, side by side with the erotic image of the *trou* (the "hole") the entrance to the underworld is represented: the gaping mouth of Satan, the "jaws of hell." The "well" is a current medieval image of the fruit-bearing womb. The cellar has a similar connotation, with the theme of death, of swallowing down, more strongly accentuated. Thus, the earth and its orifice acquire here an additional grotesque element. This picture prepares the further assimilation of earth and sea as a bodily category.

Rabelais goes on to recall the ancient myth of Phaeton who, driving the sun's chariot, came too near to earth and almost set it on fire; the earth was covered with sweat so that the seas became salty. (Plutarch attributes this explanation to Empidocles.) Rabelais transfers these images from the high mythical level to the gay level of popular-festive degradation:

> Earth at that time was so excessively heated that it broke into an enormous sweat which ran over the sea, making the latter salty, since all sweat is salt. If you do not admit this last statement, then taste of your own sweat. Or savor the perspiration of your pox-stricken friends when they are put in sweat-boxes for treatment. It is all one to me. (*Ibid.*)

The entire complex of images composing this passage is extremely characteristic. The typical grotesque image of sweating (similar to other elimination) plays a leading role, and even a cosmic role, since the earth itself sweats and pours its sweat into the sea. Further, we have the image of the merry disease, syphilis, related to the bodily lower stratum. Finally, sweat is related to eating (the taste of sweat); this weakened form of scatophagy is characteristic of medical grotesque (as early as Aristophanes). This passage implicitly contains the traditional nucleus of the little devil Pantagruel, related to the sea element and causing thirst. At the same time, the hero of this passage is the earth. In the first chapter the earth, saturated with the blood of Abel, became fertile and gave birth; in the second chapter it sweats and thirsts.

Rabelais goes on to give a bold parody of a religious procession. During a ceremony organized by the Church, the faithful who were praying for rain suddenly saw drops of heavy sweat appearing on the ground as on the brow of a human being. They thought it was dew sent by heaven in answer to their prayers. But they were mistaken, for when they tried to quench their thirst, they found the liquid was a pickled solution even saltier than sea water. Thus, the miracle deceived the pious people. Here once more, the material bodily element appears in its role of uncrowning.

Precisely on that day and at that hour Pantagruel was born. His name in Rabelais' burlesque etymology means "the all-thirsting one." The hero's birth itself occurs in a grotesque atmosphere; before he emerges from his mother's womb, he is preceded by a caravan of wagons loaded with salted (thirst-arousing) food. Only then does the child Pantagruel appear, "shaggy as a bear." The third chapter develops the ambivalent death-birth theme. Gargantua does not know whether to weep over his wife's death or to laugh with joy at the birth of his son. He now laughs "like a calf" (a newborn animal), or moos "like a cow" (birth-giving and dying).

The fourth chapter tells of Pantagruel's early feats when he was still in his cradle; all of these exploits are acts of devouring and swallowing. At each feeding he sucked the milk of 4,600 cows. He was served his gruel in a gigantic bell. His teeth were already so strong and solid that he chewed off a big portion of his bowl. One morning, wishing to suck one of the cows, he freed one hand from his swaddling clothes and seizing the cow by the legs, chewed off the udder and half the stomach, as well as the liver and kidneys. The cow was taken away from him, but he held onto one of the legs and swallowed it like a sausage. Another time Gargantua's pet bear came near Pantagruel; he seized it, tore it to pieces and devoured it as if it were a chicken. He was so strong that he had to be chained to his cradle, but one day he appeared carrying the cradle on his back in the hall where Gargantua was presiding over a huge banquet; the child's hands were tied, so he put out his tongue and licked the food off the table.

All these feats are related to sucking, devouring, swallowing, tearing to pieces. We see the gaping mouth, the protruding tongue, the teeth, the gullet, the udder, and the stomach.

We shall continue to analyze some of the more typical banquet images.

In the episode of the Limousin student, Pantagruel seizes him by the throat, which a few years later causes the man to "die the death of Roland," that is, death of thirst. The traditional character of the little devil Pantagruel appears in this episode.

In Chapter 14 we find the following image: during a feast, offered at the end of the lawsuit of My Lords Kissarse and Bumfondle, the drunken Panurge declares:

"God help me, mate, if I could rise up as fast as I swallow down, I would long ago have been above the sphere of the moon with My Lord Empedocles, who was hoisted thither by an eruption of Aetna. But I can't tell what's the matter. This wine is strong and delicious, yet the more I drink, the thirstier I get. I think the mere shadow of My Lord Pantagruel engenders thirst even as the moon produces catarrhs." (Book 2, Chapter 14)

Let us here point out the topographic content: the highest sphere of the sky and the lower part of the stomach. Once more we also find the traditional nucleus of Pantagruel's image, the arousing of thirst. But in this passage the leading role is played by Pantagruel's shadow (note the similarity to the shadow of the belfry). The grotesque element also appears in the ancient, traditional idea of the influence of the moon (or other heavenly bodies) on diseases.

During the banquet Panurge relates the story we already know, how he was almost roasted alive in Turkey but instead roasted a Turk on a spit, and how he was almost torn to pieces by dogs. He was cured from "toothache" (caused by the dog's teeth) by throwing to the animals the lard in which he had been wrapped. We also find here the image of fire that burned down the Turkish town and an image of a cure by fire: roasting on a spit cured Panurge of rheumatism. This purely carnivalesque scene ends by Panurge's eulogy of the spit and of the roast.

Pantagruel's traditional image reappears in the Thaumastes episode. After his first interview with Pantagruel, Thaumastes was so thirsty that he had to drink wine all night long and rinse his throat with water. During the dispute, when the public began to applaud, Pantagruel shouted at them to hold their peace:

> At which they sat there, struck of a heap and blinking like owls. Had they swallowed fifteen pounds of feathers, they would not have dared cough. The mere sound of his voice so parched their throats that their tongues hung a half-foot out of their mugs. It was as though Pantagruel had salted their throats. (Book 2, Chapter 18)

In the burning of the knights episode and in the banquet with which we are already familiar we see Pantagruel's gaping mouth. The knight whom he captured was afraid that Pantagruel was going to swallow him up. The giant's gullet was so large that he could have swallowed his prisoner like "a sugared almond," and the knight would appear in his captor's mouth no bigger than a grain of millet in the mouth of an ass.

The war against King Anarchus clearly presents all the leading images of the first chapter: the gaping mouth, the gullet, salt, thirst, and urine (instead of sweat). Pantagruel sends to King Anarchus a captured knight with a casket of euphorbium syrup and red pepper in order to make him thirsty:

> King Anarchus barely swallowed one spoonful when a terrific burning seared his mouth, ulcerated his uvula and peeled the whole surface of his tongue. No remedy offered him seemed to bring the slightest relief save incessant drinking; the moment he took the cup from his lips, his tongue

scorched. So they kept pouring wine down his throat through a funnel.... Whereupon, the whole host began to booze, guzzle and swill until in the end they fell into a dead sleep, grunting and snoring like hogs. (Book 2, Chapter 28)

At the same time Pantagruel and his companions made their own preparations in view of the battle. He took 237 casks of wine, filled the ship's dinghy with salt, and attached it to his belt. He then took a dose of a diuretic. Finally, King Anarchus' camp was set on fire while the enemy was asleep after a drunken orgy. The further development of this episode is so characteristic that we quote it in full:

> Meanwhile Pantagruel scattered the salt from his dinghy into their gaping mouths in such quantities that the poor wretches barked like foxes.
> "Oh, oh, Pantagruel," they hawked. "Why do you add further heat to the firebrands in our throats?"
> Suddenly Panurge's drugs began to take effect and Pantagruel felt an imperious need of draining his bladder. So he voided on their camp so freely and torrentially as to drown them all and flood the countryside ten leagues around. We know from history that had his father Gargantua's great mare been present and likewise disposed to piss, the resultant deluge would have made Deucalion's flood seem like a drop in a bucket. A mare of the first water, Gargantua's; it could not relieve itself without making another Rhone or Danube.
> The soldiers sallying from the city saw the whole thing.
> "The enemy has been hacked to pieces," they exulted. "See the blood run."
> But they were mistaken. What they believed in the glow from the burning camp and the dim moonlight to be blood of slaughtered enemies was but the wine from our giant's bladder.
> The enemy now awakened thoroughly to see their camp blazing on one hand and Pantagruel's urinal inundation on the other. They were, so to speak, between the fiery devil and the deep Red Sea. Some vowed the end of the world was at hand, bearing out the prophecy that the last judgment would be by fire. Others were certain they were persecuted by the sea-gods Neptune, Proteus, Triton and others. Certainly the waters flowing over them were salty. (Book 2, Chapter 28)

We see once more all the fundamental images of the book's first chapters, but here the salt liquid is not sweat but urine, and it is not eliminated by the earth but by Pantagruel. However, as a giant Pantagruel acquires a cosmic meaning. The traditional nucleus of the Pantagruel image is hyperbolized: an entire army of gaping mouths, a boat full of salt poured into them, the element of water and the gods of the sea, a flood of salted urine. This is a characteristic interplay of images: urine-blood-seawater. All these images are put together to form the picture of a cosmic catastrophe, the destruction of the world by flood and fire.

Medieval eschatology in this episode is degraded and renewed in the absolute material bodily lower stratum. It is turned into carnivalesque fire that causes the world's rebirth. Let us recall Goethe's feast of fire in the "Roman Carnival," with its cry "Death to thee!" Let us also recall the vision of a world catastrophe in the "prophetic riddle": a flood that is actually nothing but sweat and a world conflagration that turns out to be a kitchen hearth. In our episode all the dividing lines between bodies and objects are erased, even the boundaries between a banquet and war. The banquet, salt, and thirst are the means used for war. Blood is substituted by torrents of urine after a drunken orgy.

We must not forget that urine (as well as dung) is gay matter, which degrades and relieves at the same time, transforming fear into laughter. If dung is a link between body and earth (the laughter that unites them), urine is a link between body and sea. Thus is why the little devil Pantagruel, who in the mystery play is the incarnation of the salt sea element, becomes in Rabelais' novel the incarnation of the gay element of urine. (Pantagruel's urine, as we shall later see, possesses certain curative properties.) Dung and urine lend a bodily character to matter, to the world, to the cosmic elements, which become closer, more intimate, more easily grasped, for this is the matter, the elemental force, born from the body itself. It transforms cosmic terror into a gay carnival monster.

We must take into consideration the importance of cosmic terror, the fear of the immeasurable, the infinitely powerful. The starry sky, the gigantic material masses of the mountains, the sea, the cosmic upheavals, elemental catastrophes – these constitute the terror that pervades ancient mythologies, philosophies, the systems of images, and language itself with its semantics. An obscure memory of cosmic perturbations in the distant past and the dim terror of future catastrophes form the very basis of human thought, speech, and images. This cosmic terror is not mystic in the strict sense of the word; rather it is the fear of that which is materially huge and cannot be overcome by force. It is used by all religious systems to oppress man and his consciousness. Even the most ancient images of folklore express the struggle against fear, against the memories of the past, and the apprehension of future calamities, but folk images relating to this struggle helped develop true human fearlessness. The struggle against cosmic terror in all its forms[4] and manifestations did not rely on abstract hope or on the eternal spirit, but on the material principle in man himself. Man assimilated the cosmic elements: earth, water, air, and fire; he discovered them and became vividly conscious of them in his own body. He became aware of the cosmos within himself.

This assimilation of cosmic elements within the body was most acutely felt at the time of the Renaissance. It found its theoretical expression in the idea of the microcosm, which was used by Rabelais in Panurge's comments about creditors and debtors quoted earlier. We shall further discuss these aspects of Renaissance philosophy. We must here stress that it was in the material acts and eliminations of the body – eating, drinking, defecation, sexual life – that man found and retraced within himself the earth, sea, air, fire, and all the cosmic matter and its manifestations, and was thus able to assimilate them. Indeed, the images of the material bodily lower stratum have a prevailingly cosmic connotation.

In the sphere of imagery cosmic fear (as any other fear) is defeated by laughter. Therefore dung and urine, as comic matter that can be interpreted bodily, play an important part in these images. They appear in hyperbolic quantities and cosmic dimensions. Cosmic catastrophe represented in the material bodily lower stratum is degraded, humanized, and transformed into grotesque monsters. Terror is conquered by laughter.

Let us return to the episode of the war against Anarchus. We have a detailed description of Pantagruel's single combat with Werewolf. This is an interplay of similar images. Werewolf advanced with gaping jaws (*la gueule ouverte*), and Pantagruel poured over his enemy some eighteen casks and one tub of salt which stuffed his throat, nose, and eyes. Then Pantagruel hit Werewolf in the groin and spilled some wine; his opponent thought that his bladder was pierced, mistaking the wine for urine.

The next chapter describes the resurrection of Epistemon and his visit to the underworld. If we recall that in bodily topography hell is represented as Lucifer's gaping jaws and that death swallows up and returns the body to the bosom of the earth, it will then become clear that we are still within the sphere of familiar images: the open mouth and womb. The visit to the underworld will be analysed in detail in the next chapter.

The episode of the war against King Anarchus ends in two images of a purely carnivalesque type.

The first image is a grotesque-utopian banquet "for all the world." When the victors arrived in the land of the Amaurotes, bonfires were lighted everywhere, and tables with tasty food were spread in the streets. It seemed, writes Rabelais, that the times of Saturn had returned. The second image is the uncrowning of King Anarchus in which he is made into a green-sauce crier. Thus the war ends in a carnivalesque banquet and degradation.

The chapter that follows (Book Two, Chapter 32) relates how, during a torrential rain, Pantagruel covered a whole army with his tongue. We have next the description of the journey of the author (Alcofribas) into Pantagruel's mouth. Finding himself inside these gaping jaws, Alcofribas discovers an entirely new unknown world: wide fields, woods, fortified cities, and more than twenty-five kingdoms. The citizens living in Pantagruel's mouth are convinced that their world is more ancient than the earth. Alcofribas spends six months in the giant's mouth; he feeds on the morsels of food that enter it and defecates in Pantagruel's throat.

This episode, inspired by Lucian ("True Stories"), is an excellent conclusion to the series of images of the gaping mouth already described. Pantagruel's mouth contains an entire universe, a kind of buccal underworld. Like Epistemon's Hades, this hell is also organized as a world "turned inside out." Here, for instance, men are paid not for working but for sleeping.

The story of a universe older than earth expresses the idea of the relativity of the evaluation of time and space, presented in its grotesque aspect.

Chapter 33 tells about Pantagruel's sickness and recovery. He had stomach trouble, and during his sickness his abundant urine formed hot springs, of therapeutic value, in various parts of France and Italy. Here, once more, Pantagruel symbolizes a gay cosmic element.

The episode further relates the story of the descent into Pantagruel's stomach in order to clean it. Men armed with picks, shovels, and baskets are enclosed in a copper globe that Pantagruel swallows like a pill. (Note the image of swallowing.) Once inside the stomach, the visitors climb out of their glove and do their cleaning operation. Like Pantagruel's mouth in the preceding chapter, his stomach has enormous, almost cosmic dimensions.

In the concluding chapter of the Second Book we find more grotesque images of the body. The chapter contains a plan of the next parts of the novel. Among the projected episodes is the destruction of the underworld by Pantagruel, who tosses Proserpina into the fire and breaks Lucifer's four teeth and one horn. Further, the plan includes Pantagruel's journey to the moon in order to ascertain whether during its decline the three quarters of the moon are hidden in the heads of women.

Thus, from beginning to end this book of the novel presents as its main theme the images of the open mouth, the gullet, the teeth, and the tongue. The gaping jaws belong to the traditional nucleus of the devilkin Pantagruel in the mystery.

This image is organically combined on the one hand with swallowing and devouring, on the other hand with the stomach, the womb, and childbirth. At the same time the banquet images, as well as those of death, destruction, and hell are also related to this system. Finally, the open mouth is linked with another basic element of Pantagruel's traditional image, a composite of thirst, water, wine, and urine.

All the main organs and areas, as well as all the basic acts of the grotesque body, are pictured and developed around the central image of the gaping jaws. This is the most vivid expression of the body as not impenetrable but open. Further, the gaping jaws are a wide entrance leading into the depths of the body, and these characters are accentuated by the fact that an entire inhabited universe is located in Pantagruel's mouth and that people can descend into the stomach as into an underground mine. The same features (gaping jaws and depths) also appear in the open womb of Pantagruel's mother, as well as in the image of the earth that has absorbed the blood of Abel and the image of the underworld. The bodily depths are fertile; the old dies in them, and the new is born in abundance. The entire Second Book is saturated with pictures of procreative force, fertility, abundance. The phallus and the codpiece (as a substitute for the phallus) constantly appear within this open sphere. The grotesque body has no façade, no impenetrable surface, neither has it any expressive features. It represents either the fertile depths or the convexities of procreation and conception. It swallows and generates, gives and takes.

Such a body, composed of fertile depths and procreative convexities is never clearly differentiated from the world but is transferred, merged, and fused with it. It contains, like Pantagruel's mouth, new unknown spheres. It acquires cosmic dimensions, while the cosmos acquires a bodily nature. Cosmic elements are transformed into the gay form of the body that grows, procreates, and is victorious.

Pantagruel was conceived and written during the misfortunes suffered

[244]

by France in 1532. True, these misfortunes were not catastrophic, but they were serious enough to affect the people's consciousness and to awaken their cosmic terror and eschatological expectations. Rabelais' book was a merry answer to these fears and pious moods. Once again we have a remarkable example of a Renaissance piece of journalism based on the popular tradition of the marketplace. It is a militant echo of the events and thoughts of that historic period.

In 1532, as we have said, there was a long and intense spell of hot weather and drought which lasted for six months, until September. The dry weather threatened the crops and especially the vineyards. Because of these conditions, the Church organized many religious ceremonies and processions, reflected in the parodies at the beginning of the novel. In the autumn of the year the plague broke out in various parts of France and lasted throughout the following year. There is an allusion to the plague in *Pantagruel*, where it is explained as the result of lethal vapors arising from Pantagruel's sick stomach.

The unfortunate weather conditions and the plague awakened a cosmic terror, like that of the fourteenth century, a terror related to a system of eschatological images and mystical ideas. But natural catastrophes, like other catastrophes, usually also awaken historical criticism and lead to a revision of all dogmatic positions (as in the case of Boccaccio and Langland in the fourteenth century). Something similar, though in a less drastic form, took place when *Pantagruel* was written. The historic events served as a starting point for Rabelais' novel. It is quite possible that the image of the devilkin Pantagruel, who makes men thirsty, and the very tonality of this figure were born from the free colloquial element of the marketplace and from the familiarity of table talk. For the devilkin was the object of gay curses intended for the world and for nature; he was the hero of the free parodies of eschatology, divine providence, and world catastrophes. But around this central figure Rabelais accumulated an enormous mass of material from the culture of folk humor developed during thousands of years: a culture that reflected the struggle against cosmic terror and created the image of the gay, material bodily cosmos, ever-growing and self-renewing.

The Second Book is the most cosmic. This element is not as strong in the other books in which the historic, social and political themes are emphasized. But the overcoming of cosmic fear and eschatology still remains a leading theme to the end of the novel.

In the development of this theme the grotesque body plays a most

[245]

important part. It is the people's growing and ever-victorious body that is "at home" in the cosmos. It is the cosmos' own flesh and blood, possessing the same elemental force but better organized. The body is the last and best word of the cosmos, its leading force. Therefore it has nothing to fear. Death holds no terror for it. The death of the individual is only one moment in the triumphant life of the people and of mankind, a moment indispensable for their renewal and improvement.

Let us now examine some of the sources of the grotesque body, confining ourselves to Rabelais' immediate source material. The grotesque concept of the body lived especially in the familiar and colloquial forms of the language. The grotesque was the basis of all the abuses, uncrownings, teasing, and impertinent gestures (as pointing at the nose or the buttocks, spitting, and others). Finally, this conception of the body is contained in the most varied types of folklore. These patterns were scattered everywhere and were easily understood and familiar to all Rabelais' contemporaries. The groups of sources we intend to examine are but the separate characteristic expressions of this prevailing form, directly related to the theme of Rabelais' novel.

Let us first look at the legend of the giants. This is an essentially grotesque image of the body, but of course the theme can be more or less developed.

In the *roman de chevalerie*, which was widely known, the giants had almost entirely lost their grotesque character. They symbolized in most cases unusual physical strength and allegiance to the lord who had conquered them.

In the Italian heroic-comic tradition of Pulci (*Il Morgante Maggiore*) and especially of Folengo (*Fracassus*), the grotesque features of the giants, transferred from the genre of chivalry, reappear once more. The Italian tradition of comic giants was well known to Rabelais and must be considered as one of his sources.

But the direct source was, as we know, the chapbook entitled "The Great Chronicles of Gargantua" (1532). This anonymous work contains certain travestied elements reflecting the King Arthur cycle; it does not represent, however, a parody in the modern sense of the word. The giant image has here a strong grotesque bodily character. The chapbook was inspired by the oral folk legend of Gargantua, which lived in folk tradition up to the time of the "Great Chronicles" and continues to live in its oral form even today, not only in France but also in England. The different versions of the "Chronicles" were written down in the nineteenth century and collected in the book of Paul Sébillot, *Gargantua dans les traditions populaires*, 1883. Contemporary *berrichon* legends of Gargantua and other giants are contained in the book of Jean Baffier, *Nos Géants d'autrefois, Récits berrichons*, Paris, 1920. Even in the late oral tradition Gargantua's image preserves a completely grotesque bodily character. The giant's enormous appetite is brought out first of all. Even today we hear the French expression *quel Gargantua!* (what a glutton!).

All the legends of giants are closely related to the relief of the locality where the story is told. The legend always finds a visible, obvious support in the physical setting; the dismembered, scattered, or flattened body of the giant is discovered in the natural landscape. Even in modern France a great number of rocks, stones, megalithic formations, dolmens, and menhirs have been named after Gargantua; we have Gargantua's finger, tooth, cup, armchair, stick, etc. This is actually a Rabelaisian complex of the giant's chopped members, of his kitchen utensils and other paraphernalia. In Rabelais' time this world of rock and stone was, of course, much larger.

The parts of the giants' dismembered bodies and their houseware, scattered throughout France, had an obviously grotesque character; they could not fail to exercise an influence on Rabelais' images. Thus mention is made in *Gargantua* of the gigantic bowl in which the young hero ate his gruel, and the author adds that the bowl can still be seen at Bourges. There is nothing which reminds us of Gargantua in the modern city, but a sixteenth-century document states that there was in Bourges an immense rock scooped out like a bowl which was known as *Scutella gigantis*, the giant's cup. Once a year wine merchants filled it with wine for the poor. Rabelais borrowed his image from true life.[5]

Besides the bodily grotesque of the "Great Chronicles," we must also recall "Pantagruel's Disciple," an anonymous book published in 1537. This work reflected the influence of Rabelais' novel as well as of Lucian's "True Stories." But we also find in it popular-festive elements and the influence of the oral tradition of legendary giants. This work had in its turn an influence on Rabelais.

We must stress the role of popular-festive giants. They were common figures in the shows produced at fairs, in which they still appear in our days together with midgets. The giant was also the protagonist of carnival parades and of the processions of Corpus Christi. At the end of the Middle Ages a number of cities that employed permanent "town jesters" also had permanent "town giants" and even "families of giants," paid by the city and obliged to take part in all the pageantries. This institution of town giants in a number of cities and villages of Northern France and Belgium, for instance, in Lille, Douai, and Kassel, was maintained up to the nineteenth century. In Kassel a celebration was held in 1835 to commemorate the famine of 1638; on that feast a giant distributed free soup to the people. This connection of the giant with food is characteristic. In Belgium there were festive "giants' songs" closely relating the giant to the family hearth and to cooking.

The figure of the giant as part of folk festivals and carnivals was, of course, familiar to Rabelais. He also knew the local legends that have not survived in our time. His novel mentions the names of giants connected with eating and swallowing: Happemousche, Engolevent, Maschefain, and others.

Finally, he was familiar with the giants of antiquity, especially with Euripides' cyclopes, which are twice mentioned in his novel.

Such are Rabelais' sources. We may conjecture that the popular-festive giants were the most important in his eyes. They enjoyed immense vogue, were familiar to everyone, and were saturated with the free atmosphere of the marketplace. They were closely connected with the popular conception of material-bodily wealth and abundance. The image and the atmosphere of the giant appearing at the fairs doubtless contributed to the shaping of the Gargantuan legend of the "Great Chronicles." The influence of popular giants of fairs and marketplaces on the first two books of Rabelais' novel is quite obvious.

As to the "Great Chronicles," its influence was mainly external and was actually reduced to a few topical themes.

[...]

Abel Lefranc links Rabelais' philosophic thought (especially in connection with the immortality of the soul) with the Paduan school of Pomponazzi. In his treatise "Of the Soul's Immortality" (*De immortalitate animi*), Pomponazzi proved the identity of the body and soul. The soul cannot be separated from the body that creates it, individualizes it, directs its activity, lends it content. Outside the body the soul would be completely empty. In Pomponazzi's mind the body is a microcosm that assembles in one single entity all that is scattered and alienated in the rest of the cosmos. Rabelais was familiar with Pomponazzi's school.

Étienne Dolet, Rabelais' intimate friend, was the Italian philosopher's pupil and follower.

The grotesque concept of the body in some of its essential elements represented the humanist and, above all, the Italian philosophy of that period. It had conceived, as we have seen, the idea of the microcosm (based on ancient tradition) as adopted by Rabelais. The human body was the center of a philosophy that contributed to the destruction of the medieval hierarchic picture of the world and to the creation of a new concept. We shall now examine this new picture.

The medieval cosmos was built according to Aristotle. It was based on the precept of the four elements (earth, water, air, and fire), each of which had its special rank in the structure of the universe. According to this theory all the elements were subject to a definite order from top to bottom. The nature and the movement of each element were determined according to its position in relation to the center of the cosmos. Nearest of all to this center is the earth, and any part separated from the earth tends to move back to the center along a straight line; in other words, it falls. Fire moves in the opposite direction; it continually tends upward, therefore away from the center. Water and air lie between earth and fire. The basic principle of all physical phenomena is the transformation of one element into the element nearest it. Thus fire is transformed into air, air into water, water into earth. This transformation is the law of creation and destruction to which all earthly things are subject. But above the earthly world there rises the world of celestial bodies, not ruled by this law. The celestial bodies are composed of a special kind of matter, *quinata essentia*, which is not subject to transformation. Celestial bodies, as the most perfect, are endowed with pure movement only, the circular movement around the center of the earth. Concerning the sky's "substance," that is, "quintessence," there were endless scholastic debates, which found their expression in Rabelais' Fifth Book in the episode of the Queen of Quintessence.

Such was the medieval picture of the cosmos. The characteristic trait of this picture was that all degrees of value correspond strictly to the position in space, from the lowest to the highest. The higher the element on the cosmic scale (that is, the nearer to the "immovable motor") the more nearly perfect was this element's quality. The conceptions and the images of the higher and lower stratum as expressed in space value became the flesh and blood of medieval man.

The Renaissance destroyed this hierarchical picture of the world; its elements were transformed to one single plane, and the higher and lower stratum became relative. The accent was placed on "forward" and "backward." This transfer on the world from the vertical to the horizontal was realized in the human body, which became the relative center of the cosmos. And this cosmos was no longer moving from the bottom to the top but along the horizontal line of time, from the past to the future. In bodily man the hierarchy of the cosmos was reversed and cancelled; he asserted himself outside it.

This reconstruction of the cosmos from vertical to horizontal in man and the human body was strikingly expressed in Pico della Mirandola's famous speech, *Oratio de hominis dignitate* ("Of the Dignity of Man"). This oration was Pico's introduction to the defense of the 900 theses to which Rabelais alludes by having Pantagruel undertake the defense of the 9764 theses. Pico asserted in his speech that man is superior to all beings including the celestial spirits, because he is not only being but also becoming. He is outside all hierarchies, for a hierarchy can determine only that which represents stable, immovable, and unchangeable being, not free becoming. All the other beings remain forever what they were at the time of their creation, for their nature is ready-made and un-changing; it receives one single seed which can and must develop in them. But man receives at his birth the seeds of every form of life. He may choose the seed that will develop and bear fruit. He grows and forms it in himself. Man can become a plant or an animal, but he can also become an angel and a son of God. Pico preserves the language of the hierarchy, he preserves in part the old values (he is cautious), but essentially the hierarchy is suspended. Such concepts as becoming, the existence of many seeds and of many possibilities, the freedom of choice, leads man toward the horizontal line of time and of historic becoming. Let us stress that the body of man reunites in itself all the elements and kingdoms of nature, both the plants and the animals. Man, properly speaking, is not something completed and finished, but open, uncompleted. Such is Pico della Mirandola's basic idea.

In Pico's *Apologia* we find the theme of the microcosm (in connection with the idea of natural magic) and the form of "universal sympathy," thanks to which man can combine in himself the higher and lower, the near and the distant, and can penetrate into all the secrets hidden in the depths of the earth.

Ideas of "natural magic" and of "sympathy" between all phenomena, were widespread during the Renaissance. These ideas, as expressed by

Giambattista Porta, Giordano Bruno, and especially Campanella, played a considerable role in destroying the medieval notion of hierarchical space in which natural phenomena had their own distinct levels. The new ideas brought together that which was divided, effacing false boundaries, contributing to the transfer of all to one horizontal plane of the becoming of the cosmos in time.

We especially stress the extreme popularity of the idea of "universal animatization." This idea was defended by Ficino, who sought to prove that the world is not an aggregate of elements but an animate being in which each part is an organ of the whole. Patrizzi proved in *Panpsychia* that everything in the universe is animate, from the stars to the simplest element. This idea was also shared by Cardano, who considered all natural phenomena as similar in some respect to organic matter. For example, metals are "buried plants" leading their life underground; stones experience youth, growth, and maturity.

All these ideas could exercise some direct influence on Rabelais, since all of them stem from the general tendencies of the Renaissance. All things in the universe, from heavenly bodies to elements, had left their former place in their hierarchy and moved to the single horizontal plane of the world of becoming, where they began to seek a new place and to achieve new formations. The center around which these perturbations took place was precisely the human body, uniting all the varied patterns of the universe.

For all the Renaissance philosophers mentioned previously – Pico della Mirandola, Pomponazzi, Porta, Patrizzi, Bruno, Campanella, Paracelsus, and others – two tendencies appear characteristic. First is the tendency to find in man the entire universe with all its elements and forces, with its higher and lower stratum; second is the tendency to think of the human body as drawing together the most remote phenomena and forces of the cosmos. This philosophy expressed in theoretical terms the new awareness of the cosmos as man's own home, holding no terror for him. It was reflected by Rabelais in the language of images and on the plane of laughter.

In most Renaissance philosophies astrology and "natural magic" play a more or less important role. Rabelais took neither seriously. He brought together the separate, infinitely remote phenomena of the medieval hierarchy, making them collide, uncrowning and renewing them on the material bodily level; but he used for this purpose neither "magic" sympathy nor astrological "concordance." He was consistently materialistic, and moreover approached matter only in its bodily aspect. In his mind the body was the most nearly perfect form of the organization of matter and was therefore the key to all matter. The material components of the universe disclose in the human body their true nature and highest potentialities; they become creative, constructive, and are called to conquer the cosmos, to organize all cosmic matter. They acquire a historic character.

In the eulogy of Pantagruelion, a symbol of man's entire technical culture, we find the following striking passage:

> … those heavenly intelligences we call the gods, both terrestrial and maritime, took fright, when they perceived how, thanks to the blessed herb pantagruelion, the Arctic peoples, under the very eyes of the Antarctic, crossed the Atlantic Ocean, passed the twin tropics, pushed through the torrid zone, spanned the zodiac, frolicked beneath the equinox, and held both poles within sight on the horizon.
>
> Faced with such a situation, the gods, terrified said:
>
> "Pantagruel has, by this mere herb, caused us more worry and labor than ever the Aloides or Giants, Otus and Ephialtes, when they sought to scale Olympus. He will soon marry and beget children by his wife. This is a fate we cannot forestall, for it has been woven by the hands and shuttles of the three fatal sisters, daughters of Necessity. Who knows but Pantagruel's children will discover some herb equally effectual? Who knows but humans may, by its means, visit the source of hail, the springs of the rain, the forge where lightning is produced. Who knows but they will invade the regions of the moon, intrude within the territories of the celestial signs? Some, then, will settle at the sign of the Golden Eagle, others at the Ram, others at the Crown, others at the Harp, others at the Silver Lion. They will sit down at our divine board, take our goddesses to wife, and thereby themselves become divine." (Book 3, Chapter 51)

In spite of the somewhat rhetorical and official style of this excerpt, the idea it expresses is far from having official implication. We find here the divinization and apotheosis of man. Earthly space is defeated; all peoples who were scattered throughout the world are united. Thanks to navigation and the invention of the sail, men have entered into material contact. Mankind has become one. After the invention of aviation (which Rabelais foresees), man will direct the weather, will reach the stars and conquer them. This entire image of the triumph of mankind is built along the horizontal line of time and space, typical of the Renaissance. Nothing remains of the medieval hierarchic vertical.

The movement in time is guaranteed by the birth of generation after generation, a never-ending succession that fills the gods with fear. Pantagruel, too, intends to get married and to have children, and this is the relative immortality of which Gargantua speaks in his letter to his son. The immortality of the ancestral body of mankind is rhetorically proclaimed. As we have seen, this living and deep awareness gives form to all the popular-festive images of the Rabelaisian novel. Not the biological body, which merely repeats itself in the new generations, but precisely the historic, progressing body of mankind stands at the center of this system of images.

Thus, in the grotesque concept of the body a new, concrete, and realistic historic awareness was born and took form: not abstract thought about the future but the living sense that each man belongs to the immortal people who create history.

Notes to Part II

5 V. N. Voloshinov:
'Language, speech, and utterance'

1   For interesting and ingenious distinctions between a signal or combinations of signals (in maritime usage, for instance) and a linguistic form or combinations of linguistic forms in connection with the problem of syntax, see K. Bühler, "Vom Wesen der Syntax," *Festschrift für Karl Vossler*, pp. 61–69.

2   We shall see later that precisely this kind of understanding in the proper sense, an understanding of process, lies at the basis of response, i.e., at the basis of verbal interaction. No sharp dividing line can be drawn between understanding and response. Any act of understanding is a response, i.e., it translates what is being understood into a new context from which a response can be made.

3   The principle advanced here underlies the practice (though proper theoretical awareness may be lacking) of all sensible methods of teaching living foreign languages. What is central to all these methods is that students become acquainted with each linguistic form only in concrete contexts and situations. So, for instance, students are acquainted with some word only through the presentation of a variety of contexts in which that word figures. Thanks to this procedure, the factor of recognition of identical word is dialectically combined with and submerged under the factor of the word's contextual changeability, diversity, and capacity for new meanings. A word extracted from context, written down in an exercise book and then memorized together with its Russian translation undergoes signalization, so to speak. It becomes a particular hard-and-fast thing, and the factor of recognition intensifies in the process of understanding it. To put it briefly, under a sound and sensible method of practical instruction, a form should be assimilated not in its relation to the abstract system of the language, i.e., as a self-identical form, but in the concrete structure of utterance, i.e., as a mutable and pliable sign.

4   On this basis, as we shall see later, one would have to disagree with Vossler in his postulating the existence of a separate and distinct kind of linguistic taste that in each instance would remain apart from some specific kind of ideological "taste" – aesthetic, cognitive, ethical, or other.

5   N. Ja. Marr, *Po ètapam jafetskoj teorii* [Through the stages of the Japhetic Theory] (1926), p. 269.

6   *Ibid.*, pp. 94–95.

7   According to Vedic religion, the sacred word – in that usage to which it is put by the "gnostic" consecrated priest – becomes the sovereign of all Being, including both gods and men. The priest-gnostic is defined here as the one who commands the word – therein lies all his power. The doctrine to this effect is contained already in the

Rig Veda. The ancient Greek philosopheme of Logos and the Alexandrian doctrine of Logos are well known.

8 N. Ja. Marr, *Japhetic theory*, p. 268.

9 *Ibid.*, pp. 315–316.

10 Thus to a significant degree it was the alien word that determined prehistoric man's magical perception of the word. We have in mind in this connection all the relevant phenomena in toto.

11 One should not forget in this connection that abstract objectivism in its new formation is an expression of the condition that the alien word had reached when it had already lost its authoritativeness and productivity to a significant degree. Moreover, specificity of perception of the alien word has declined in abstract objectivism, owing to the fact that the latter's basic categories of thought have been extended to perception of living and native languages. Linguistics studies a living language as if it were a dead language, and native language as if it were an alien tongue. That is why the postulations of abstract objectivism are so different from the ancient philosophemes of alien word.

12 Utterance is merely a neutral medium for change of linguistic form.

13 See Vossler, "Grammatika i istorija jazyka, *Logos*, I (1910), p. 170.

14 For the time being, we disregard the distinction between meaning and theme about which we shall speak below (Chapter 4).

15 We shall further amplify the points made here in the fourth chapter of this section of our study.

16 The process of a child's assimilation of his native language is the process of his gradual immersion into verbal communication. As that process of immersion proceeds, the child's consciousness is formed and filled with content.

'Verbal interaction'

1 "Spoken thought is a lie" (Tjučev); "Oh, if one could speak from the soul without words" (Fet). These statements are extremely typical of idealistic romanticism.

2 On the possibility of a set of human sexual experiences falling out of social context with concomitant loss of verbal cognizance, see our book, *Frejdizm* [Freudianism] (1927), pp. 135–136.

3 Interesting material about expressions of hunger can be found in Leo Spitzer's books, *Italienische Kriegsgefangenenbriefe* and *Die Umschreibungen des Begriffes Hunger*. The basic concern in these studies is the adaptability of word and image to the conditions of an exceptional situation. The author does not, however, operate with a genuine sociological approach.

4 In this respect, the very organization of the book is symptomatic. The book divides into four main chapters. Their titles are as follows: I. *Eröffnungsformen des Gesprächs.* II. *Sprecher und Hörer*; A. *Höflichkeit (Rücksicht auf den Partner)*. B. *Sparsamkeit und Verschwendung im Ausdruck*; C. *In einandergreifen von Rede und Gegenrede.* III. *Sprecher und Situation.* IV. *Der Abschluss des Gesprächs.* Spitzer's predecessor in the study of conversational language under conditions of real-life discourse was Hermann Wunderlich. See his book, *Unsere Umgangssprache* (1894).

5 See *Die Probleme der Sprachpsychologie* (1914).

6 On the topic of disjuncture of a literary work of art with conditions of artistic communication and the resulting inertness of the work, see our study, "Slovo v žizni i slovo v poèzii" [Word in Life and Word in Poetry], *Zvezda*, 6 (1926).

7 R Šor, "Krizis sovremennoj linvistiki" [The Crisis in Contemporary Linguistics], *Jafetičeskij sbornik*, V (1927), p. 71.

6 M. M. Bakhtin and P. N. Medvedev: from 'Material and device as components of the poetic construction'

1 For related elaboration of the difference between sign and signal, see V. N. Voloshinov, *Marxism and the Philosophy of Language*, L. Matejka and I. R. Titunik, trans. (New York and London, 1973), particularly pp. 68–69, 71, and 80. – Trans.
2 Shklovskii, *Rozanov,* p. 4; *O teorii prozy,* "Literatura vne siuzheta," p. 226.
3 Shklovskii, *Rozanov,* p. 5; "Literatura vne siuzheta," p. 226.
4 Even the majority of formalists do not deny this.
5 An instructive example of attempts to do this is Gustav Shpet's *Vnutrenniaia forma slova* [*The Inner Form of the Word*] (Moscow, 1927). Shpet's attempt to bring in dialectics and history does not prevent him from seeking inner form in language and trying to substantiate it there. And, on idealist grounds, it could not be otherwise.
6 Of course, this is only a figurative analogy. The ideal space of the painting should not be equated with meaning in the literary work.
7 Eikhenbaum, "*Shinel*," *Literatura*, p. 163; *Théorie de lat littérature*, pp. 231–32; Maguire, "Gogol's 'Overcoat,'" p. 288.

7 M. M. Bakhtin: 'The hero's monologic discourse and narrational discourse in Dostoevsky's short novels'

1 *Pis'ma* 1, p. 86. [Letter of 1 February 1846, to Mikhail Dostoevsky]
2 A splendid analysis of Makar Devushkin's speech as that of a specific *social character* is given by V. V. Vinogradov in his book *O jazyke khudozhestvennoi literatury* [On the Language of Artistic Literature], (Moscow, Goslitizdat, 1959), pp. 477–92.
3 *Pis'ma* 1, pp. 81–82. [Letter to Mikhail Dostoevsky, 8 October 1845]
4 There were, to be sure, already rudiments of interior dialogue in Devushkin as well.
5 Working on *Netochka Nezvanova*, Dostoevsky writes his brother: "But soon you shall read *Netochka Nezvanova*. It will be a confession, like *Golyadkin*, although of a different tone and sort." [*Pis'ma*, I. p. 108: letter to Mikhail Dostoevsky, Jan-Feb. 1847]
6 Not long before Golyadkin had said that to himself: "That's just like you!... You go plunging straight in, you're delighted! you guileless creature."
7 In *Crime and Punishment*, for example, there is one such literal repetition by Svidrigailov (Raskolnikov's partial double) of Raskolnikov's most intimate words, spoken by him to Sonya, a repetition with a meaningful wink. We quote this passage in its entirety:

> "Ah! you sceptical person!" laughed Svidrigailov, "I told you I had no need of that money. Won't you admit that it's simply done from humanity? She wasn't 'a louse', you know" (he pointed to the corner where the dead woman lay), "was she, like some old pawnbroker woman? Come, you'll agree, is Luzhin to go on living and doing wicked things or is she to die? And if I didn't help them, Polenka would go the same way."
> He said this with an air of a sort of gay winking slyness, keeping his eyes fixed on Raskolnikov, who turned white and cold, hearing his own phrases, spoken to Sonya. (ss V, 455: *Crime and Punishment*, Part V, ch. 5)

8 Other autonomous consciousnesses appear only in the longer novels.

9 In Thomas Mann's novel *Doktor Faustus*, a very great deal was suggested by Dostoevsky and precisely by Dostoevsky's *polyphony.* I quote here an excerpt from a description of one of the composer Adrian Leverkühn's works, very close to Trishatov's "musical idea":

> "Everywhere is Adrian Leverkühn great in *making unlike the like* . . . So here – but nowhere else as here is the effect so profound, mysterious and great. Every word that turns into sound the idea of Beyond, of transformation in the mystical sense, and thus of change, transformation, transfiguration, is here exactly reproduced. The passages of horror just before heard are given, indeed, to the indescribable children's chorus at quite a different pitch, and in changed orchestration and rhythms: but in *the searing, susurrant tones of spheres and angels there is not one note which does not occur, with rigid correspondence, in the hellish laughter."* [Bakhtin cites from a Russian translation of *Doktor Faustus* (Moscow, 1959, pp. 440–41); the passage above is the H. T. Lowe-Porter translation of Thomas Mann, *Doctor Faustus* (Vintage Books, 1948), ch. XXXIV (conclusion), pp. 378–79.]

10 The first to note this characteristic of the narration in *The Double* was Belinsky, but he offered no explanation for it.

11 See *F. M. Dostoevskii, Stat'i i materialy,* 1, ed. A. S. Dolinin (Moscow-Leningrad: "Mysl'," 1922), p. 241–42. [The article is V. V. Vinogradov, "K morfologii natural'nogo stilia" (Toward a Morphology of the Naturalist Style). A portion of this article has been translated by Stephen Rudy in Priscilla Meyer and Stephen Rudy, eds., *Dostoevsky & Gogol: Texts and Criticism* (Ann Arbor: Ardis, 1979), pp. 217–28.

12 Ibid. p. 248

13 This perspective is absent even for the generalizing "authorial" construction of the hero's indirect speech.

14 On the literary parodies and literary polemic in *Poor Folk,* there are some very valuable historico-literary remarks in Vinogradov's article in *Tvorcheskii put' Dostoevskogo* [Dostoevsky's Creative Path] (ed. by N. L. Brodskii, Leningrad, "Seyatel'," 1924).

15 These stylistic peculiarities too are all connected with the tradition of carnival and with reduced ambivalent laughter.

16 "Notes from Underground" was originally announced by Dostoevsky under this title in "Time."

17 This can be explained by the generic similarities between "Notes from Underground" and Menippean satire.

18 According to Dostoevsky, such an admittance would serve to calm down the discourse and purify it.

19 Exceptions will be pointed out below.

20 We recall the characterization that Dostoevsky himself gave to the hero's speech in "A Meek One:"

> "... he either argues with himself or addresses some unseen listener, a judge as it were. However, it is always like that in real life."

8 M. M. Bakhtin: 'Heteroglossia in the novel'

1 For more detail on hybrid constructions and their significance, see ch. 4 of the present essay.

2 Such a device is unthinkable in the epic.

3 Cf. the grotesque pseudo-objective motivations in Gogol.

4 Intellect as embodied in the forms and the methods of verbal and ideological thought (i.e., the linguistic horizon of normal human intellectual activity) becomes in Jean Paul something infinitely petty and ludicrous when seen in the light of "reason." His humor results from play with intellectual activity and its forms.

5 It is of course impossible in the strict sense to include Rabelais himself – either chronologically or in terms of his essential character – among the representatives of comic novelists.

6 Nevertheless sentimentality and "high seriousness" is not completely eliminated (especially in Jean Paul).

7 In neoclassicism, this double-voicing becomes crucial only in the low genres, especially in satire.

8 Within the limits of the world of poetry and a unitary language, everything important in such disagreements and contradictions can and must be laid out in a direct and pure dramatic dialogue.

9 The more consistent and unitary the language, the more acute, dramatic and "finished" such exchanges generally are.

10 In his well-known works on the theory and technique of the novel, Spielhagen focuses on precisely such unnovelistic novels, and ignores precisely the kind of potential specific to the novel as a genre. As a theoretician Spielhagen was deaf to heteroglot language and to that which it specifically generates: double-voiced discourse.

11 Alexei Alexandrovich Karenin had the habit of avoiding certain words, and expressions connected with them. He made up double-voiced constructions outside any context, exclusively on the intonational plane. "Well, yes, as you see, your devoted husband, as devoted as in the first year of marriage, is burning with impatience to see you,' he said in his slow high-pitched voice and in the tone in which he almost always addressed her, a tone of derision for anyone who could really talk like that" (*Anna Karenina* [New York: Signet, 1961] part 1, ch. 30; translation by David Magarshack).

12 We offer an analysis of this example in the essay "From the Prehistory of Novelistic Discourse".

9 M. M. Bakhtin: from 'The grotesque image of the body and its sources'

1 This grotesque logic is also extended to images of nature and of objects in which depths (holes) and convexities are emphasized.

2 Let us recall Goethe's remarks as reported by Eckermann in "Conversations with Goethe" concerning Correggio's painting "The Weaning of a Child." Goethe is attracted by the duality of the image, preserved in an attenuated form.

3 Similar classical concepts of the body form the basis of the new canon of behavior. Good education demands: not to place the elbows on the table, to walk without protruding the shoulder blades or swinging the hips, to hold in the abdomen, to eat without loud chewing, not to snort and pant, to keep the mouth shut, etc; in other words, to close up and limit the body's confines and smooth the bulges. It is interesting to trace the struggle of the grotesque and classical concept in the history of dress and fashion. Even more interesting is this struggle in the history of dance.

4 The images reflecting this struggle are often interwoven with images of a parallel struggle in the individual body against the memories of an agonizing birth and the

fear of the throes of death. Cosmic fear is deeper and more essential. It is hidden in the ancestral body of mankind; this is why it has penetrated to the very basis of language, imagery, and thought. This cosmic terror is more essential and stronger than individual bodily fear of destruction, though both voices often mingle in folklore and especially in literature. Cosmic terror is the heritage of man's ancient impotence in the presence of nature. Folk culture did not know this fear and overcame it through laughter, through lending a bodily substance to nature and the cosmos; for this folk culture was always based on the indestructable confidence in the might and final victory of man. Official culture, on the contrary, often used and even cultivated this fear in order to humiliate and oppress man.

5 Considerable folklore material concerning the broken body of stone and the stoneware of the giant is given by Salomon Reinach, *Cultes, Mythes et Religions,* Vol. 3: *Les monuments de pierre brute dans le langage et les croyances populaires,* pp. 364- 433; see also P. Sébillot, *Le Folklore de France,* Vol. 1, pp. 300—412.

Suggestions for further reading

As the title of this section implies, this is a list of *suggestions*; I have made no effort to provide a full bibliography of Bakhtin, and the list of books under his name is of course a list of translations. *Bakhtin and Cultural Theory*, edited by Ken Hirschkop and David Shepherd, provides a very useful bibliographical essay, though of course only up to 1989. It also provides a convenient glossary of Bakhtin's vocabulary and the different choices that have been made in translating it into English. An ongoing and exhaustive annotated bibliography of Bakhtin is provided in *The Bakhtin Newsletter*; the last issue to hand took entries up to 1991.

Books by Bakhtin and the Bakhtin circle

BAKHTIN, M. M. *Art and Answerability: Early Philosophical Essays by M. M. Bakhtin*, edited by Michael Holquist and Vadim Liapunov (University of Texas Press, 1990).

—— *Problems of Dostoevsky's Poetics*, edited and translated by Caryl Emerson, with an introduction by Wayne C. Booth (Manchester University Press, 1984).

—— *The Dialogic Imagination: Four Essays*, edited by Michael Holquist; translated by Caryl Emerson and Michael Holquist (University of Texas Press, 1981).

—— *Rabelais and his World*, translated by Helene Iswolsky (Indiana University Press, 1984).

—— *Speech Genres and Other Late Essays*, translated by Vern W. McGee (University of Texas Press, 1986).

BAKHTIN, M. M., AND MEDVEDEV, P. N., *The Formal Method in Literary Scholarship: A Critical Introduction to Sociological Poetics*, translated by Albert J. Wehrle (Havard University Press, 1985).

VOLOŠINOV, V. N. *Freudianism: A Marxist Critique*, translated by I. R. Titunik (Academic Press, New York, 1976).

—— *Marxism and the Philosophy of Language*, translated by Ladislav Matejka and I. R. Titunik (Academic Press, New York, 1986).

—— *Bakhtin School Papers*, edited by Ann Shukman (Russian Poetics in Translation, vol. 10, Oxford, 1983).

Books about Bakhtin and the Bakhtin circle

CLARK, KATERINA AND HOLQUIST, MICHAEL, *Mikhail Bakhtin* (Havard University Press, 1984).

DANOW, DAVID K., *The Thought of Mikhail Bakhtin* (Macmillan, London, 1991).

GARDINER, MICHAEL, *The Dialogics of Critique: M. M. Bakhtin and the Theory of Ideology* (Routledge, London, 1992).

HIRSCHKOP, KEN AND SHEPHERD, DAVID (eds), *Bakhtin and Cultural Theory* (Manchester University Press, 1989).

HOLQUIST, MICHAEL, *Dialogism: Bakhtin and His World* (Routledge, London, 1990).

LODGE, DAVID, *After Bakhtin: Essays on Fiction and Criticism* (Routledge, London, 1990).

MORSON, GARY SAUL, (ed.), *Bakhtin: Essays and Dialogues on His Work* (University of Chicago Press, 1986).

MORSON, GARY SAUL AND EMERSON, CARYL, *Rethinking Bakhtin: Extensions and Challenges* (Northwestern University Press, 1989).

—— *Mikhail Bakhtin: Creation of a Prosaics* (Stanford University Press, 1991).

TODOROV, TZVETAN, *Mikhail Bakhtin: The Dialogical Principle*, translated by Wlad Godzich (Manchester University Press 1984).

Books drawing significantly upon Bakhtin

BAUER, DALE M., *Feminist Dialogics: A Theory of Failed Community* (State University of New York Press, 1988).

BAUER, DALE M., AND MCKINSTRY SUSAN JANET (eds), *Feminism, Bakhtin and the Dialogic* (State University of New York Press, 1991).

BRISTOL, MICHAEL D., *Carnival and Theater: Plebeian Culture and the Structure of Authority in Renaissance England* (Routledge, London, 1989).

CASTLE, TERRY *Masquerade and Civilisation: The Carnivalesque in Eighteenth-Century English Culture and Fiction* (Methuen, London, 1986).

STALLYBRASS, PETER, AND WHITE, ALLON, *The Politics of Transgression* (Methuen, London, 1986).

In addition, Bakhtin's ideas have been taken up in a variety of ways by a host of scholars, whose work appears in academic journals. A starting-point in this now massive body of work is to be found in the special 1993 edition of *Critical Studies*, 'Bakhtin, Carnival, and Other Subjects', which is a collection based on the 1991 International Bakhtin Conference.

Index